Transnational Discourses on Class, Gender, and Cultural Identity

Comparative Cultural Studies
Steven Tötösy de Zepetnek, Series Editor

The Purdue University Press monograph series of Books in Comparative Cultural Studies publishes single-authored and thematic collected volumes of new scholarship. Manuscripts are invited for publication in the series in fields of the study of culture, literature, the arts, media studies, communication studies, the history of ideas, etc., and related disciplines of the humanities and social sciences to the series editor via email at <clcweb@purdue.edu>. Comparative cultural studies is a contextual approach in the study of culture in a global and intercultural context and work with a plurality of methods and approaches; the theoretical and methodological framework of comparative cultural studies is built on tenets borrowed from the disciplines of cultural studies and comparative literature and from a range of thought including literary and culture theory, (radical) constructivism, communication theories, and systems theories; in comparative cultural studies focus is on theory and method as well as application. For a detailed description of the aims and scope of the series including the style guide of the series link to <http://docs.lib.purdue.edu/clcweblibrary/seriespurdueccs>. Manuscripts submitted to the series are peer reviewed followed by the usual standards of editing, copy editing, marketing, and distribution. The series is affiliated with *CLCWeb: Comparative Literature and Culture* (ISSN 1481-4374), the peer-reviewed, full-text, and open-access quarterly published by Purdue University Press at <http://docs.lib.purdue.edu/clcweb>.

Volumes in the Purdue series of Books in Comparative Cultural Studies include <http://www.thepress.purdue.edu/comparativeculturalstudies.html>

Irene Marques, *Transnational Discourses on Class, Gender, and Cultural Identity*
Comparative Hungarian Cultural Studies, Ed. Steven Tötösy de Zepetnek and Louise O. Vasvári
Hui Zou, *A Jesuit Garden in Beijing and Early Modern Chinese Culture*
Yi Zheng, *From Burke and Wordsworth to the Modern Sublime in Chinese Literature*
Agata Anna Lisiak, *Urban Cultures in (Post)Colonial Central Europe*
Representing Humanity in an Age of Terror, Ed. Sophia A. McClennen and Henry James Morello
Michael Goddard, *Gombrowicz, Polish Modernism, and the Subversion of Form*
Shakespeare in Hollywood, Asia, and Cyberspace, Ed. Alexander C.Y. Huang and Charles S. Ross
Gustav Shpet's Contribution to Philosophy and Cultural Theory, Ed. Galin Tihanov
Comparative Central European Holocaust Studies, Ed. Louise O. Vasvári and Steven Tötösy de Zepetnek
Marko Juvan, *History and Poetics of Intertextuality*
Thomas O. Beebee, *Nation and Region in Modern American and European Fiction*
Paolo Bartoloni, *On the Cultures of Exile, Translation, and Writing*
Justyna Sempruch, *Fantasies of Gender and the Witch in Feminist Theory and Literature*
Kimberly Chabot Davis, *Postmodern Texts and Emotional Audiences*
Philippe Codde, *The Jewish American Novel*
Deborah Streifford Reisinger, *Crime and Media in Contemporary France*
Imre Kertész and Holocaust Literature, Ed. Louise O. Vasvári and Steven Tötösy de Zepetnek
Camilla Fojas, *Cosmopolitanism in the Americas*
Comparative Cultural Studies and Michael Ondaatje's Writing, Ed. Steven Tötösy de Zepetnek
Jin Feng, *The New Woman in Early Twentieth-Century Chinese Fiction*
Comparative Cultural Studies and Latin America, Ed. Sophia A. McClennen and Earl E. Fitz
Sophia A. McClennen, *The Dialectics of Exile*
Comparative Literature and Comparative Cultural Studies, Ed. Steven Tötösy de Zepetnek

Transnational Discourses on Class, Gender, and Cultural Identity

Irene Marques

Purdue University Press
West Lafayette, Indiana

Copyright 2011 by Purdue University. All rights reserved.

Printed in the United States of America.

Library of Congress Cataloging-in-Publication Data

Marques, Irene, 1969-
  Transnational discourses on class, gender, and cultural identity / Irene Marques.
    p. cm. -- (Comparative cultural studies)
  Includes bibliographical references and index.
  ISBN 978-1-55753-605-1 (pbk.) -- ISBN 978-1-61249-164-6 (epdf) -- ISBN 978-1-61249-165-3 (epub) 1. Political fiction--History and criticism. 2. Couto, Mia, 1955- Contos do nascer da terra. 3. Saramago, José. Ano da morte de Ricardo Reis. 4. Lispector, Clarice. Hora da estrela. 5. Coetzee, J. M., 1940- Life & times of Michael K. 6. Other (Philosophy) in literature. 7. Identity (Psychology) in literature. 8. Postcolonialism in literature. 9. Language and languages in literature. I. Title.
  PN3448.P6M37 2012
  809.3'93581--dc23
                    2011036982

Cover image: Statue of Siddhartha Gautama Buddha. Photo: Nyo.

Dedication

I dedicate this work to my father, Adelino (who already lives on the other side) and my mother, Alzira, who have worked very had all their lives in that place high up on the mountains called Adsamo. I also dedicate it to the wild goats of Serra do Caramulo and to my times with them as a goatherdess.

Contents

Acknowledgments ix

Note on Translations and Use of Abbreviations xi

Introduction to *Transnational Discourses on Class, Gender, and Cultural Identity*
Irene Marques

Part One
The Bolder Politics of Agency

Chapter One
The Politics of Agency in Couto 13

Chapter Two
The Politics of Agency in Saramago 55

Part Two
The Deeper Politics of Agency

Chapter Three
Authenticity of Being as the Politics of Agency in Lispector 105

Chapter Four
Authenticity in Coetzee's *Life and Times of Michael K* 155

Conclusion 182

Works Cited 191

Index 203

Acknowledgments

A deep thank you goes to J.E. Chamberlin, who is a person of immense humanity, kindness, and beautiful ideas, and from whom I have learned a great deal. A special thank you also to Linda Hutcheon for all her feedback and her taming of my sometimes overly unsettling way of writing. To Ricardo Sternberg, Julie Leblanc, and Rosemary Jolly, I also extend my gratitude. I would like to thank Steven Tötösy de Zepetnek, series editor of the Purdue University Press print monograph Series of Books in Comparative Cultural Studies, for his constant support in the publication of this book. Last but not least, I thank the anonymous readers of my manuscript and the helpful comments I received to improve the book.

A section of chapter 1 has been published in *The Journal of African Literature and Culture* 4 (2007): 101-24. under the title "Mia Couto and the Holistic Choric Self: Recreating the Broken Cosmic Order (Or: Relearning the Song that Truly Speaks . . .)" and a section of chapter 2 has been published in *TRANSverse: A Comparative Studies Journal* 2 (2004): 31-43 under the title "The Sterility of the Individual Ontological Search versus the Fecundity of the Relational Ontological Search in Saramago's *The Year of the Death of Ricardo Reis*." Copyright of the above articles is released to the author.

Note on Translations and Use of Abbreviations

All translations pertaining to Couto's short stories are my own. In order to preserve Couto's peculiar language and style and to be faithful to the original text as much as possible, my English translations of his stories often use language in an unfamiliar way (i.e., I mix, change, or create certain words). In the case of Saramago's and Lispector's novels, I use the published translations by Giovanni Pontiero. In cases where I feel the need to alter the original translation, I use braces—{ }—to signal the change (the same applies to Lispector's other works used herein). When using secondary sources that are in Portuguese, the translation provided is my own. When using secondary sources that are in Portuguese, the translation provided is my own. In these instances, no page number is provided after the English translation.

For practical purposes, the works under analysis will often be referred to by abbreviations: *Contos* (*Stories of the Birth of the Land*), *A hora* (*The Hour of the Star*), *O ano* (*The Year of the Death of Ricardo Reis*) and *Michael K* (*Life and Times of Michael K*).

Introduction

This study revolves around three different issues: class, feminist, and cultural identity discourses, the latter more specifically in relation to race, nation, colonialism, postcolonialism, and economic and cultural imperialism. The analysis focuses on works by four world writers: the Mozambican Mia Couto, the Portuguese José Saramago, the Brazilian Clarice Lispector, and the South African J.M. Coetzee. I demonstrate that all these four writers are political in the sense that they bring to the forefront important issues pertaining to the power of literature to represent, misrepresent, and debate issues related to different subaltern subjects: the postcolonial subject, the poor subject (which I often refer to as the "poor other"), and the female subject. I also deal with the "ahuman other" and thus I discuss the subjectivity of the natural world, the dead, and the unborn, and show how these aspects are present in the different societies addressed and point to the mystical dimension that permeates most societies. In Couto's chapter this ahuman other is approached mostly through a discussion of the holistic, animist values and epistemologies that inform and guide Mozambican traditional societies, while in the other chapters this ahuman other is approached via discussions on phenomenology, elementality, and divinity taking mainly after the philosophies of Emmanuel Lévinas and Luce Irigaray and mystical consciousness, taking after Zen Buddhism or sometimes the psychology of Carl Jung.

Part one, "The Bolder Politics of Agency," includes chapter 1 and chapter 2, and addresses the politicality of two works by the following writers: Couto's collection of short stories *Contos do nascer da terra* (Stories of the Birth of the Land) and Saramago's novel *O ano da morte de Ricardo Reis* (*The Year of the Death of Ricardo Reis*). In this section of the study, the analysis concentrates on what I see as being these writers's bold political posture. While acknowledging that these two writers do not necessarily see their art as an exact portrayal of their sociopolitical reality, in this section I argue that Couto and Saramago take a bolder political stand vis-à-vis sociopolitical concerns, compared with Lispector and Coetzee. I suggest that the former are politically more direct in their works than the latter in the sense that they seem generally to see their writings as a medium which can more or less represent and critique the reality of the oppressed person, be it the colonized or postcolonial subject, the woman, or the poor other. I contend that Couto and Saramago take their art as a site where politics ought to be directly discussed and where the voice (and the language) of the artist has the power, ability, and responsibility to unmask certain oppressive structures, give voice to the oppressed, and expose some of the myths guiding the society in question. For these two writers, the novel is indeed the place where sociopolitical matters are addressed openly and where the voice of the artist can often even take a clear (and didactic) position in regards to the issues being addressed—in this case specifically issues of representation of women and the colonial or postcolonial subject.

Part two, "The Bolder Politics of Agency," includes chapters 3 and 4 and discusses works by Clarice Lispector and J.M. Coetzee. Here I analyze two novels by these writers and illustrate how they are also political, but on a different plane. My focus is on the meta-discursive as the main politics of agency of the two novels. I argue that Lispector and Coetzee use their novels as the site to question the limits of the power of narrative representation, that is, as the place that "dramatizes the risks involved in finding a place from which to speak" (Attwell 101), as David Attwell puts it in referring to Coetzee's *Life and Times of Michael K*, or as Marta Peixoto says, when referring to Lispector's *A hora da estrela* (*The Hour of the Star*), a site that "enact[s] a knowing, guilt-ridden struggle with the mastering and violent powers of narrative" (98). The conscious inability or unwillingness of these two authors to narrate the other accurately and responsibly will be discussed on two different levels. On the one hand, due to class and racial differences, the narrator or implied author cannot represent the poor and colored other (the subaltern subjects) accurately, and any attempt to represent that other boldly and directly will amount to the annihilation of that same other. The representation of the other by the narrative voice is limited because it speaks from a privileged class and racial point of view, which is inherently guided by discriminatory dichotomies of good/bad, superior/inferior, white/black, educated/uneducated, same/other, and so forth. On the other hand, because language is a medium that potentially imprisons the individual in artificial, constructed categories linked to power structures—a medium always polluted by sociopolitical ideologies that often discriminate against one group (or quality) in favor of another—the writer has no possibility of telling the truth about the narrated subject through conventional, discursive, narrative strategies. Here my focus is on the relation between history and story and how the representation of the other in narrative is similar to his or her insertion into historical discourses, which are presented as artificial, power based and discriminatory constructions. The only way to get closer to the authenticity of the other and away from the narrative and historic violence that tends to incorporate otherness into sameness is through the use of seemingly paradoxical narrative strategies such as silence, music, poetic language, and ambivalent metaphors. It is in this ambivalence and paradox that the other finds some space to remain different, unreachable, and untouched by power-based structures and by the "I" of the writer: free from all discursive categories of definition and from the oppression inherent in them, free from all violence, even if only theoretically. It is this use of ambivalence in narration that I choose to call "the deeper politics of agency" of Lispector and Coetzee. I call it "deeper" because it goes beyond any discrimination (value judgment) that is inherent in linguistic and symbolic discourses in order to reach the equality that resides outside language and outside all power structures or discourses. I call it "deeper" because it obliges one to reach beyond any politics of oppression in order to reestablish the before-the-law, the before-language, the presymbolic, the true emptiness, as Buddhists would say, where everything is assigned similar value: it obliges one to see that social categories are human constructs that do not necessarily have any inherent value and are often power based. And, that, in itself, might serve to show us humans the futility of our greed, which in turn can make us rethink and question all our actions—and this constitutes probably the very first step towards any fundamental societal change.

In the first chapter I analyze Couto's *Contos* and discuss the issue of cultural identity affecting contemporary Mozambique, concentrating on matters related to language, culture, race, colonialism, economic and cultural imperialism, nationhood, and the formation of the postcolonial subject. Given that Mozambique falls under the umbrella of a postcolonial nation, my discussion will inevitably have to address issues related to the legacy of colonialism and examine not only its devastating economic effects (economic imperialism and exploitation) but also its effects on the local Mozambican cultures (cultural imperialism), and the racialization and "othering" that came with the implantation of a white Western (Portuguese) hegemony and cultural episteme. My exposition examines and links colonial economic exploitation with cultural colonization and investigates how Couto, in a manner similar to other postcolonial writers, is trying to address these issues as they affect contemporary Mozambique in order to engage in a critical conversation with the past for that very past is deeply affecting the present nation and the formation of a national identity. To use Quayson's terminology and definition of postcolonial and postcolonialism, I am thus illustrating how Couto brings up "the experience of colonialism and its past and present effects, both at the local level of ex-colonial societies as well as at the level of more general global developments thought to be the after-effect of Empire" (Quayson 2). I argue that Couto is profoundly concerned with the multiculturality of Mozambique and wants to see a nation that reflects the many cultures of Mozambique and not only the culture of the colonizing country, or more generally, the western culture—a nation that is truly culturally syncretic by giving voice and allowing the Mozambican epistemologies to shine through so that a truly multicultural Mozambique can emerge. My examination of economic and cultural imperialism also focuses on the economic and cultural exploitation that continues to take place in contemporary Mozambique, for not only is the postcolonial government in many ways following the western hegemonies in a manner similar to the colonial power, but the country has also seen an invasion of foreign institutions that further reinforce the dominance of exogenic values at the expense of cultural Afrocentric values, thus making it difficult for Mozambique to come forth as a truly multicultural country; or at least this seems to indicate that there is no real effort to rediscover or embrace the precolonial epistemes. I am thus, in some respects, grounding my arguments in Jameson's reasoning when he contends that "all third world texts are necessarily. . .

and in a very specific way . . . *to be read* as national allegories" and that "the story of the private individual destiny is always an allegory of the embattled situation of public third-world culture and society" (Jameson 69), even though my intention is not to reinforce dichotomies of first world and third world, for as we will see, Couto is in fact attacking those very categorizing presuppositions and refusing to be defined in terms of western paradigms of thought and qualifying systems.

My analysis of the above issues makes use of several postcolonial and language theories that are well suited to discuss issues of othering, white hegemony, western versus Afrocentric epistemologies, nation building, and economic and cultural imperialism. Furthermore, I make use of psychoanalytical and Zen concepts to enhance my arguments, particularly when analyzing the last two stories to show the commonality that sometimes exists between seemingly different epistemologies. My arguments take into account the overall nature of the stories of the entire collection. Yet, since it would be impossible to analyze all the stories in this work in detail, my study is specific to three stories: "Governados pelos mortos: fala com um descamponês" ("Governed by the Dead: Talk with a Dis-peasant"), "A luavezinha: Primeira estória para a Rita" ("The Little-Moon Bird: First Story for Rita"), and "A menina sem palavra: segunda estória para a Rita" ("The Little Girl without Words: Second Story for Rita"). Although it was difficult to opt for these and not other stories in the collection, the stories chosen are appropriate to argue my case. The analysis of the stories revolves around three main points. First, how the notion of nation-state imposed by the postindependence Mozambican state has in fact encountered resistance on the part of many Mozambicans, proving (as pointed out by Gregório Firmino) that the construction of nationalism involves "the imposition of social and cultural hegemony" and "encode[s] social inequalities" (24), thus making contemporary Mozambique closer to being a state-nation than a nation-state, as suggested by Lee Skjon (3-8). Second, the imposition of Portuguese as the official language has created cultural conflicts in the sense that it has robbed, altered, and impoverished Mozambican epistemologies. Third, by altering and adulterating standard Portuguese and using specific narrative techniques, Couto is able to recreate a genuine "Mozambicanness" and thus recapture a culture that has been endangered by colonial and postcolonial states. Since my argument revolves around the issue of language use in a postcolonial state, and in order to prepare the terrain for the analysis of the stories, the first part of the chapter addresses current linguistic trends in Mozambique and discusses issues related to language use in postcolonial societies.

The second chapter is a study of Saramago's novel, *O ano*. Saramago presents a negative critique of the type of art that contributes to the fabrication and perpetuation of myths regarding the feminine subject and how that serves to keep both sexes unfulfilled and alienated from one another. I discuss the "ideality" of Reis's Lídia versus the "reality" of Saramago's Lídia—showing how the former is absent, bodiless, spiritual, and unengaged and how the latter is bodily, present, engaged, yet also spiritual, and how these latter qualities are praised by the narrator. Saramago's positive depiction of Lídia points to another relevant sociopolitical and ontological issue: the issue of what I designate as relational and phenomenological ethics. This expression is used loosely here and is rooted in some of the theories of Edmund Husserl, Maurice Merleau-Ponty, and Emmanuel Lévinas, and to a certain extent the philosophy of Zen Buddhism that encourages what can be termed as a "clean stare." I use it to denote the idea that the ontological and epistemological search of the subject departs from the phenomenological realm and "tries to get out of the mind" (outside of the psychological realm) as much as possible, concentrating on the relationship of the subject with the outside world, be it other human subjects or the physical world. This permits the subject to "start clean" and exit, or at least reconsider, his or her beliefs and vision of the world, thus contributing to the demolition of values that might be contributing to oppressions of all sorts and to human unfulfillment.

Relying primarily on Lévinas's ethics of relationality and otherness and Irigaray's reading and critique of Lévinas's "The Phenomenology of Eros," I address the following questions: How does Saramago offer a negative critique of the individual ontological search in the persona of its main character, the Pessoan heteronym Reis? How are Reis's aloofness, intellectualism, solitude, and social disengagement portrayed? And how does such a portrayal serve to demonstrate that humans ought to be inserted in what I loosely call the "phenomenology of life" ("in-the-element," as Lévinas puts it) so that they can find real existential fulfillment and also directly engage themselves in the fight against the structures that might be oppressing them? How is Reis's individual ontological search counterposed with Lídia's relational ontological search? As the female protagonist of the novel, Lídia is depicted as being quite the opposite of Reis: engaged, physical, and relational and even happier and surer of herself. Saramago opposes the sterility of Reis's existence to the fecundity of Lídia's life and shows how such fecundity is achieved through Lídia's insertion in the "phenomenology of life": in physical or sexual love, in the simple activity of domestic housecleaning and in the caring for others. Lídia's fecundity is linked to the grounding of the body in the spatio-temporal present and realities that require the use of the physical capacities or intelligences and of the senses and emotions. This grounding is even depicted as being conducive to the experiencing of a "real" spiritual ecstasy. The opposition between the fecundity of Saramago's Lídia and the sterility of the other women of the novel will also be discussed in order to demonstrate how Saramago offers a negative critique of women who would rather ally themselves with a patriarchal system that oppresses them than fight against it: women who live under the shadow of men's lives and do not fight for dignity and authenticity in their own lives, women who live as the other of the male subject and do not seem to mind, or even be aware of it. My overall intention is therefore threefold: to show how, through the rewriting of Lídia as a subject, Saramago brings to the forefront the importance of accuracy in artistic representation; to show how the writer offers a negative critique of the men and women who have bought into ready-made concepts about gender and sexual roles, no longer questioning them, and how they have thus become alienated from themselves and one another; and to demonstrate Saramago's emphasis on the importance of relational and phenomenological ethics and how such an ethics is portrayed as being the one that brings about positive sociopolitical change (in the sense that it allows one to exit, or at least reconsider, ready-made, abstract concepts and ideologies and start anew by reconnecting with and absorbing phenomenological realities). As I demonstrate, the paralleling of the two Lídias in the novel, also allows Saramago to tackle another crucial issue within Portuguese society: the sharp class and social distinctions that have tended to permeate the country's social fabric and the almost impossibility of interclass marriage.

Chapter 3 is devoted to Lispector's novella, *A hora*, concentrating on the meta-discursive aspects of the work and on its questioning of the limits and powers of narrative representation. Although my discussion is centered on this novella, I bring other of Lispector's works into the discussion to elucidate my points. In this chapter I demonstrate how Lispector sees literature as a medium incapable of portraying the reality of the poor, Brazilian, feminine other and how she in fact mocks those writers who see themselves as politically engaged individuals whose writing activity is indispensable for the betterment of society and for the resolution of its problems. My discussion revolves around four main arguments. First, the class incompatibility between author and protagonist impedes the novelist's accurate representation of the other and the novel, in fact, becomes a site that creates and recreates clichés and stereotypes about that other and thus commits narrative violence. Second, Lispector's general mistrust of language also points to the impossibility of writing the other or even the self accurately. Third, writing does, in fact, function as a search for the writer's authentic or whole self and as a remedy for the malaises of her soul, and it also becomes very autobiographical, thus pointing to the fact that literary writing is often a selfish, self-indulgent, and self-fulfilling act, having less to do with social commitment than with individual commitment and realization. Fourth, Lispector uses ambivalent narrative strategies such as silence, music, poetic language, and ambivalent metaphors to get closer to the reality of the other and that becomes the very politics of agency of the novel. The otherness that is the reality of the other, whom the writers tries to write about, is captured only partially through the use of ambiguous narrative strategies. The writer knows that the reality of the other is inaccessible to her in its fullness. She also knows that she needs to write ambivalently about the other and that very knowledge and awareness makes her ethical and respectful towards the different other—a political stand in itself. If it is true that in this novel, Lispector is asking the reader to not believe blindly in the authorial voice and in the power of literary language (or any language) to portray the other and her or his reality, it is also true that she is pointing to other literary and linguistic means which might be closer to reality. Thus, on one hand, *A hora* deconstructs old views on language and literature such as those held by the writers of the regionalist novel ("romance regionalista"), who saw their literary writings and their language as exact reflections of Brazilian social reality and the Brazilian poor. On the other hand, this work offers the reader another way of describing the reality of the other—perhaps the best way of all, for it allows us to get closer to the presocial or presymbolic reality, the before-the-law, and thus, closer to the authenticity of beings. It is this that I call going from linguistic negation to linguistic regeneration.

Given the fact that Lispector seems to have been influenced by a wide number of ideas and theories, and given the complexity of her work and the broad range of my arguments, I resort to different theories to illustrate my points: Marxist theories, theories of language, and theories of otherness such as those put forward by Hélène Cixous, Emmanuel Lévinas, and Luce Irigaray. Moreover, I also use abundantly certain Zen (or Buddhist in general) and psychoanalytical concepts I believe suited to describe the presymbolic and prelinguistic world that I believe the author is pointing to in her text and link those with the ambivalent metaphors and narrative strategies being discussed.

In chapter 4 I discuss Coetzee's novel, *Michael K*. Similar to *A hora*, Coetzee's novel can be seen as a critique of the powers of narrative representation. Using as the backdrop the idea that language is intrinsically affiliated with all kinds of social discourses and ideologies, I demonstrate how the novel's main character, Michael K, tries to escape the highly politicized, racialized and classed South African context by refusing to speak and by physically removing himself from life in society. The refusal to speak and be understood through conventional storytelling is presented in the novel as the only way to escape oppression and find some dignity—even though that also means losing one's place in society. The otherness of the novel's protagonist is retained by the narrating voice mostly through the use of silence and ambivalent metaphors, which I refer to as "capsules," borrowing from Coetzee's description of himself in *Doubling the Point: Essays and Interviews* (393). These capsules allow for K's identity to remain undisclosed and unframed by the Coetzeean narrative and also by the discriminatory sociopolitical discourses of South Africa at the end of the novel, and that constitutes the main politics of agency of Coetzee's work and demonstrates the author's ethical concerns—concerns which lead him to avoid incorporation of otherness into sameness. As in chapter 2 and 3, I use Lévinasian theories of otherness, elementality, and divinity, and Zen (or Buddhist in general) concepts I believe appropriate to describe the ambivalent metaphors of the novel, as well as Coetzee's own definition of "white writing."

The theoretical approach used for the analysis is multifaceted relying on postcolonial, feminist, Marxist, psychoanalytical, Buddhist, and various language theories, as well some notions of Western philosophy. This multifaceted theoretical approach is used partly to point to the fact that different theoretical traditions (from West, East, North, and South) do have several commonalities, even though they may use what I choose to designate here as disparate metaphors of framing and telling, proving thus that we have much more common ground than we might think, as Edward Chamberlin has put it in his book *If This Is Your Land Where Are Your Stories—Finding Common Ground*. Specifically, I point to some of the commonalities between Western psychoanalysis, Jungian psychology, *écriture féminine*, Lévinasian, Irigaraian, and Heideggerian philosophy, Buddhism, and African epistemologies. These commonalities are particularly visible in my discussion of the "ahuman other," or as I also demonstrate, in the need that human subjects from different parts of the world seem to have to connect with the spiritual, the uncanny, and the mystical and exit rational paradigms that are too reductive in order to find a more fulfilling and holistic identity (ontology). There is a shared need to exit the individual ego in order to experience a vaster and grander self and that movement from the individual self towards the distended ego is, as I demonstrate, a welcoming and fulfilling exercise for many of the subjects of the novels addressed, even if sometimes they resist it and go back to the isolated self, as is the case of Ricardo Reis in Saramago's novel. One of my main objectives is to illustrate how the relationship of the human subject, who may live in different sociocultural contexts, with the subjectivity of the natural world, the dead, the unborn, the uncanny, and the mystical is in some ways similar, even if the metaphors or allegories used to explain such binding connection vary. This is specifically important in terms of offering a framework of comparative cultural analysis and demonstrating how different cultures deal with the subjectivity of this otherness in a different or similar manner, and how multiple cultures access (or interact with) the uncanny and the mystical, despite the fact that they may resort to different paradigms to do so. This is partly why I make use of seemingly disparate theories: I want to argue that the differences between cultures and peoples are frequently more related to the ways we "say" ourselves, and frame our living paradigms, than to what we are actually saying, and thus, that there is a certain universality "of being and in being." This aspect of my argument is crucial to my discussion of transnational cultural identity discourses and is especially innovative as it shows that what we often have seen as very different paradigms are after all similar in many ways. By resorting to a multitude of Western and non-Western theoretical approaches and showing the similarity between those epistemological paradigms, which traditionally have been viewed as very contrary to one another, I hope to reveal a fresh insight and show that humans from different parts of the world have more common ground than they may think.

The fact that I discuss authors from very different sociocultural contexts and show that they often address issues in a similar manner (along with the fact that these authors have never been studied in a single volume together and seem at first glance quite different) is, I expect, another innovative aspect of this work. My goal is to demonstrate how different authors, coming from different sociohistorical contexts, deal with the political and face the various brands of oppression that most, if not all societies, are necessarily bound to experience: How do they differ in denouncing the oppressions of their respective societies? How similar are they? Are some deeper and others bolder, and how effective are these two strategies in calling attention to the problem at hand, the problem of oppression, exploitation, and dehumanization, which may be related to class, gender, or cultural identity within a colonial or postcolonial context? By discussing writers from four different countries and three continents I am able to expose the particularities of different societies and discuss a wide variety of voices, voices which despite their diverging sociocultural contexts, do end up by facing similar problems: gender, class, and racial oppression as well ontological problems related to what seems to be a universal intrinsic human yearning for deeper fulfillment, a fulfillment which often is at odds with the walls of civilization that continuously imprison humans in multiple ways, thus cutting (or restraining) their truer and whole self. By discussing the particulars of the sociocultural, religious, and political local nexus I am able to show differences and similarities between human beings in relation to their existential conditions: I am able to move between worlds and living codes. This angle of the study aims again at revealing transcultural paradigms.

Coetzee and Lispector are examples of writers who describe different societies and yet use similar methods to do so: they both try to be ethical writers in the sense that they do not think that they can ever completely, accurately, and ethically represent the other in their writing. Saramago and Couto, on the other hand, are writers who seem to be more directly political and yet have very different styles of writing. While the former uses a conventional type of language and rhetoric—in some ways very linked to Western traditions—the latter uses what can be described as a new language, a language that aspires to "get out of the old one" not only in the literal sense, but also in all the rhetorical and epistemological aspects that speaking a language entails. These differences allow me to compare Western with non-Western discourses and illustrate how they speak to one another, and in so doing, deconstruct or question certain status quos of knowledge. This is not to suggest that Saramago is not addressing issues of oppression himself in his writing, but he does so more from an intranational viewpoint, whereas Couto, being a postcolonial writer, is enviably engaged in discussing and navigating through international boundaries and raising issues of colonialism and postcolonialism.

The division of this work in two sections—the bolder and the deeper—allows me to compare different strategies of being political, thus addressing some of the issues related to the old debate of art for art's sake and art for politic's sake. However, my intention is not necessarily to claim the superiority of one strategy over the other or offer a final word on this controversial issue, but rather show that both strategies constitute different ways of being political. I do believe, though, that despite the fact that the deeper political might entail being apolitical in the usual or immediate term, it does present more profound solutions for the problems of human oppression in its many facets. It does so because it tries to go beyond any human-made laws, laws that are the cause of much exploitation of humans by humans and of alienation from our most complete or real self. It must be noted that despite the fact that Couto and Saramago are bolder in their political assertions, at times they too, doubt the power of language and rhetoric and see language as a medium that has the capacity to construct reality. In this sense, they too become in some ways deep in the manner of Lispector and Coetzee. But they seem to be surer of their own convictions; they are more overtly political, less metadiscursive, and less worried about the accuracy of their narrative representation and how it might incarcerate the other in its rhetorical tentacles. By discussing the issue of bolder politics and deeper politics I hope to bring a new perceptiveness into the old debate of art and politics and show how politicality in literature can attain multifaceted versions, each of them having its very own powerful effects.

Part One

The Bolder Politics of Agency

Chapter One

The Politics of Agency in Couto

The language issue in Mozambique

As in many other postcolonial African societies, the so-called language question in Mozambique continues to be much debated, and is perhaps the very question whose real solution is dependent on the finding of a model that would be able to accommodate the various multicultural and multilingual aspects of the country. The 2004 edition of *The Ethnologue* indicates that there are 38 Bantoid living languages in Mozambique today—apart from the official language, which is Portuguese. The 1997 census indicates that Portuguese is only spoken by 39.6% of the total Mozambican population, and out of that percentage only 6.5% have it as their mother tongue (Governo de Moçambique, *II Recenseamento Geral*). The 2007 census shows an increase of the population speaking Portuguese, putting it at 55.2% (Governo de Moçambique, *Quadros do 3° Censo*). This demonstrates a significant change from the 1980 census which, as observed by Firmino, indicated that Portuguese was spoken by only 24.4% of Mozambicans and among those only 1.2% had it as mother tongue (Firmino 120). One can therefore conclude that the official language has become increasingly accessible to a larger number of people. In fact, there has been a considerable number of primary, high school, and postsecondary institution openings in Mozambique in the last few years, again suggesting that the state is making an effort to reach (and Europeanize) a wider number of Mozambicans. The illiteracy rate for 2011 was at 48.1% ("Mozambique")—a dramatic change when compared to 93% at the time of independence in 1975. All Bantu languages are considered national or Mozambican languages ("línguas nacionais, línguas moçambicanas") but not official languages and thus all formal education is conducted in Portuguese. There has been, however, a certain willingness on the part of the current government to change, or at least discuss, the education and language policy in Mozambique. For example, a pilot project was conducted between 1993 and 1997 using Bantu languages as mediums of instruction at the primary level in the provinces of Gaza and Tete. As argued by Armando Lopes in "The Language Situation in Mozambique," such a project was formulated mainly to address the high failure rates of elementary school children who speak Bantu languages at home and only come into contact with Portuguese upon entering the school system—a system using Portuguese as the only medium of instruction. Due to the success of this pilot project and the perception by a large number of Mozambicans of the importance of Bantu languages for the development, maintenance, and promotion of the Mozambican identity, Bantu languages are currently being used in several provinces as teaching media in the primary school system (see "Proposal for Mozambique" and Benson, "Bridging the Experimentation-Implementation in Bilingual Schooling"). Yet this move towards the use bilingualism in elementary school has also been received with some resistance by parents who want their children to be taught in Portuguese, for that is the official language and thus the one seen as the key to open the "right" doors: the way to access good jobs and a higher standard of living. This reaction on the part of the parents only seems to support what Firmino had already argued in his 1995 study of the language question in Mozambique, where he indicated that Portuguese (and in fact a particular type of Portuguese, in many respects close to European Portuguese) is still one of the greatest marks of social status and the tool that allows prospective workers to obtain prestigious and better paid jobs.

The making official of a language that is spoken only by a minority of citizens can cause numerous problems, as several Africanists have already pointed out, Ngũgĩ being one of the most passionate exponents of an Africanist solution to such problems in his well-known book, *Decolonizing the Mind: The Politics of Language in African Literature*. Poor access to national resources, such as education and well-paid jobs by the majority of Africans, pronounced social stratification, and an inability to express genuine "Africanness" in a colonially imposed language, which in many respects does not have the capacity to understand African ways of life, are some of the reasons against the officialization of excolonial languages. Of course, one can also assert all kinds of reasons why these languages are the best suited to become official languages. In the case of the adoption of Portuguese as the official language for independent Mozambique, Gregório Firmino writes:

> In independent Mozambique, the Portuguese language has been granted the status of official language, which means that, just like during the colonial period, Portuguese continues to be the only language used in official functions. Besides, Portuguese has also been promoted by official discourse as *língua de unidade nacional* (language of national unity). The choice of Portuguese as official language and symbol of unity was a predictable outcome given its history of use in Mozambique, the type of linguistic diversity prevailing in the country, the ideological premises related to the type of society conceived for the country, as well as the need to co-opt the elites in the power structure and the bureaucratic institutions of the new state. . . . No indigenous languages could claim an overwhelming majority of speakers evenly distributed over the national territory. . . . However, the most important rationalization behind the officialization of Portuguese . . . is connected with the development of an ideological framework that associated Portuguese with the promotion of national identity and the creation of a national

consciousness. . . . This politically strategic decision signalled the first appropriation of Portuguese and consequent expurgation of its colonial connotations. Portuguese, which had been known by Mozambicans as a colonial language, was now serving anti-colonial purposes. (225-26)

Benedict Anderson has claimed that the modern notion of a nation-state does not require that a group of people share the same cultural traits and beliefs and that it suffices for a group of people living in a given territory to identify themselves with the same national language, even in cases where there are several languages being spoken in the same territory, as is most often the case with postcolonial societies. Anderson's assumption is rightly based on the fact that the notion of nation-state is an ideological and constructed notion molded by sociohistorical contexts. Furthermore, Anderson claims that the notion of modern statehood is highly dependent on the development of capitalism and print technology, which enable people to think about themselves and relate to each other in new ways, a process that then allows people to see or imagine themselves as a unified group of people, as a sort of community. If we take the case of Mozambique, it would then seem that Anderson's notion of nation-state can fit perfectly. In fact, Anderson even addresses the Mozambican situation: "If radical Mozambique speaks Portuguese, the significance of this is that Portuguese is the medium through which Mozambique is imagined (and at the same time limits its stretch into Tanzania and Zambia). Seen from this perspective, the use of Portuguese in Mozambique (or English in India) is basically no different that the use of English in Australia or Portuguese in Brazil" (134).

In his comprehensive study of the language question in Mozambique, and using Richard Fox's notion of national ideologies and the production of national cultures, Firmino has argued that Anderson's notion of nationhood neglects or at least underplays an important point, namely the fact that "a national culture is generated and maintained by agents and agencies, which is to say that the production of nationalism and national cultures is a process rooted in power relationships. So, in the same way that nationalist ideologies and national cultures are practiced, they are not neutral: they are linked to the imposition of social and cultural hegemony, and they encode social inequalities" (24). This point is, of course, of great importance for postcolonial African countries such as Mozambique. Since the rate of illiteracy is still very high in Mozambique, the spread of the so-called notion of nationhood and "imagined community" as identified by Anderson has not yet occurred at the scale desired and needed to make Mozambique a nation-state in the Andersonian sense. In other words, the technological conditions viewed as necessary to modern nation-state formation—such as literacy, mass communication, and industrialization—are not yet in place, and thus the notion of a Mozambican nationhood remains only in the "imagination" of a minority of Mozambicans, while the rest seem to be living in their own communities, speaking their own (many) languages and thus being Makua, Makonde, Shona, Shangaan, and so forth, which can be positive in the sense that it entails at least cultural freedom. For as Firmino argues, meeting the Andersonian conditions for statehood formation in Mozambique also involves entering a notion of nationhood that has been and continues to be controlled, generated, and maintained by Mozambican state agencies and agents and by the small governing bourgeois elite. In fact, since its independence—and particularly until 1985—the Mozambican state acted in very aggressive ways precisely to implement, construct, and impose the notion of a Mozambican nationhood on Mozambicans. As Lee Skjon has argued in his insightful paper, "The Vanguardist Imperative, Statement of Nation, and the Language Question in Mozambique's *Sociedade Nova*, 1975-1985,"

> At the national level of social organization, Frelimo [Liberation Front of Mozambique] sought to produce a surplus of specific forms of modernist social(ist) values . . . for circulation—namely, rationality, discipline, and moral will. The vanguard's control of the state and attempt to organize productive forces more "rationally" through socialist modernization was not primarily for the purpose of realizing collective benefit, nor even bureaucratic power or private gain, but rather to realize and circulate ample evidence of the vanguard's superiority in these values relative to the mass citizen. Validation of this superiority—i.e., realization of surplus—necessitated production of a citizenry assimilated to these values. Schooling provided the means *par excellence* for this production, and Portuguese, adopted as the official language of national identity and scholastic instruction, served as a ready-made, standardized semiotic medium through which the social(ist) values would circulate. Accordingly, the vanguard embodied the forms and conditions—school programming, literacy campaigns, organization of collective production, villagization, etc.—of the production of the relations of production constituting the national citizen. . . . But since this nationalist form of consciousness remained culturally distinct and alienated from the majority of the state's citizens, its expression was synecdochic: the identity and values of the *assimilado* minority stood for national identity, but had not been internalized by the nation's unassimilated majority. . . . In this sense it is more appropriate to think in terms of postcolonial state-nations [term borrowed from Abrahamsson and Nilsson], rather than nation-states. (Skjon 3-8)

Thus, the Mozambican nation is literally a "statement" put forward by the elite governing the country, a statement that has often little to do with the values and interests of the many Mozambican groups and furthermore, a statement stated in a language that the majority of Mozambique's people still cannot—or have great difficulty—understanding. As Hubert Devonish would say, the ideal for Mozambique (and other countries in similar circumstances) would be to arrive "at a situation in which the language of specific local communities, regardless of their size, is employed for the whole range of official language functions within these communities" (40). This has been achieved in countries where bilingualism or multilingualism is implemented, for example, Canada and Switzerland, proving that the notion of nation (nationalism) does not necessarily have to be linked to one specific language and culture but that it can include several.

The language that creates, recreates, and rescues

Along with the Angolan Luandino Vieira and the Brazilian Guimarães Rosa—writers he claims to have been influenced by—Mia Couto is one of the most inventive contemporary Lusophone writers and poets and, many would agree, one of the most innovative and refreshing crafters of the Portuguese language. His style is full of linguistic novelties, including the frequent invention of words often resulting from the mixture of verbs and nouns, the reinvention or recreation of Portuguese proverbs, the use of Mozambican proverbs, sayings, and maxims, and even structural changes, where the language patterns of Bantu languages may be detected. It should be noted, however, that Couto's language does not necessarily reflect the way people speak in contemporary Mozambique and does not resort to the use of Bantu words very often, contrary to that of Luandino Vieira, who frequently uses words of African origin in his writings. As Couto has put it, "I am of Portuguese origin, I am someone who departs from his own mother tongue and I want to prove that that is not an operation of façade, but that within my own language—which is already also a Mozambican language—such operations can be done profoundly, without having recourse to terms of Bantu languages" ("eu sou de origem portuguesa, sou alguém que parte da sua própria língua materna e quero provar que essa não é uma operação de simples fachada, mas que, dentro da minha própria língua—que também já é uma língua moçambicana—estas operações se podem fazer profundamente, sem fazer recurso a termos que são das línguas bantos" [qtd. in Labin 1019]).

Couto's use of Portuguese language and the manipulation of discourse that goes along with it constitutes a political act—an act that contests, revises, and refutes not only the Portuguese colonial cultural legacy, but also the political regime imposed by the postindependence Mozambican state, and as Phillip Rothwell points out, "the political models of Europe in general" and the "International Community that tries to set the agenda for the country it seeks to render independent" (172):

> Couto has always demonstrated an awareness of Portuguese and, more generally, Western influence on his work. Rather than recusing such influence, he understands and then distorts it. He disrupts the paradigms of Western orthodoxy as he fashions identity by turning European epistemology into a raw, repackageable material. Couto's propensity to dissolve boundaries [is] apparent, particularly those frontiers that enforce the demarcations of Western tradition. The resultant identity he writes is premised on fluidity, and challenges the rigidity of the systems, both colonial and Marxist, imported from Europe that have dominated Mozambique for most of its history. In the latter phase of his writing, his disavowal of the postmodern project, through an attack on the International Community's invasion of Mozambican sovereignty, logically completes the postmodern and the nationalist strands in his work. He can justifiably be termed a postmodern nationalist. (28)

Couto is able to recreate (to write) a more balanced Mozambican identity, where the values of the different Mozambican ethnic groups are recognized as being important and given a place to flourish. Given the fact that proverbs, maxims, and sayings are deeply rooted in the oral culture from which they issue, and since they are in fact considered axiomatic truths, Couto's challenge of Portuguese proverbs and the insertion of Mozambican proverbs in his writing constitute further indication of his deep desire to rescue Mozambican cultural identities and epistemologies, which have been endangered by the long colonial presence and, in many respects, also by the postcolonial regime that followed independence, a regime which valued scientific knowledge and perceived reality utilizing a rather strict, Marxist materialist model. Such a rescuing is undoubtedly very important for a country like Mozambique, where orality has always played (and continues to play) a central role in defining and understanding the general cultural framework. Moreover, Couto's stylistic innovations can in fact serve to illustrate how the Portuguese language in Mozambique is going through a process which Gregório Firmino has termed as "nativization" (10), "Mozambicanization" (308), or even "endogenization" (198), a process similar to what has happened in many other postcolonial societies with the emergence of the now familiar new Englishes.

In an introductory note to *Contos* we are told that the stories included in the collection were published in 1996 and 1997 in various newspapers and magazines and then were altered in some ways to be published (with other additional new stories) in the current collection. The note also indicates that the stories are based on the Mozambican quotidian. This supports the idea that the stories do indeed display the current cultural dilemmas affecting Mozambique, a nation struggling to forge a postcolonial identity that is respectful towards the many Mozambican ethnic groups and their epistemologies and ways of life. Couto's stories are generally characterized by a great emphasis on the traditional precolonial African ways of life and epistemologies mentioned earlier: myth, orature, different cosmogonies, conceptions of time, the interrelation between the world of the living and the world of the dead, and animistic and holistic perceptions of life, where humans, nature, and the universe at large are connected in deep ways and often not perceived as separate entities. For similar and detailed arguments about the multifaceted poetics and narrativistic strategies used by Mia Couto to recover the old Mozambican ways, see also Selina Martins, *O Entrelaçar das Vozes Mestiças*, Anita Martins Rodrigues de Moraes, *O Inconsciente Teórico,* and Maria N. Soares Fonseca and Maria Zilda Ferreira Cury, *Mia Couto: Espaços Ficcionais*). The characters of the stories are often people who live in rural areas—these constitute the vast majority of Mozambique's citizens—or people who do not adhere completely to and show resistance towards the assimilation of Western cultural values brought about by both the colonization and postcolonization processes. This suggests that indeed Couto wants to show (display) the rural side of Mozambique, the side less touched by Western cultural values, less touched by the colonization and postcolonization processes: the endogenic or internal side of Mozambican cultures (see also Luís Madureira 175-205).

Although we get the sense that the characters of Couto's stories live in the colonial or postcolonial present, since there are many references to those historical time frames, be they implicit or explicit, we often sense a strong resistance to those historical realities on the part of the characters. That resistance is frequently accompanied by a sense of loss, a feeling of nostalgia or a confusion (an existential nausea of sorts), which suggest that the characters live in a time of deep cultural crisis, in a society that is robbing them of what they value most and what their ancestors have believed for thousands of years. This feeling might be similar to what the anthropologist W.E.H. Stanner calls "a kind of vertigo in living" (qtd. in Chamberlin 80) felt by the Aborigines of New Guinea as a result of land displacement and cultural impositions brought about by the colonization process. There is in *Contos* and in much of Couto's other fictional writing a feeling that the revolution that brought about colonial independence for Mozambique has failed to create a country where all voices can be heard—and thus we often encounter characters that want to recover an "old time" ("um antigamente") that gives them the identity and fulfillment they crave, or at least its promise. There is in the current postcolonial condition a painful apathy, a death of spirit, and thus one yearns for the force of a dream to awaken us, like in the times of the anticolonial struggle when Mozambicans were fighting— their hearts and soul in pure expectation—the colonialist masters, having as their ultimate vision a better nation, free of the shackles of oppression which could fulfill their soul and make them feel at home. As Madureira explains,

> In Couto's novels, which (in Patrick Chabal's apt definition) are "much more explicitly about the history of independent Mozambique, and in this way touch more directly. . . . on the calamity of its postcolonial condition" . . . this promise of a new Mozambique has become a memory. It has reverted to a nostalgic desire for precisely the "ancient dreams"—"the rebellious dreams [sonhos de revolta] which [as Jorge Rebelo proclaims at the time of the armed struggle] you, your parents and your forefathers nourished in silence"—the very aspirations to which the war of liberation itself ("dreams turned into war") was to give expression, and "awaken like birds." (217-18)

Couto places the following message in his introduction to *Contos*:

> It is not the light of the sun that we lack. For millions of years the big star has been illuminating the earth and despite that we have not really learned how to see. The world needs to be seen under another light: the moonlight, that clarity that falls with respect and tenderness. Only the moonlight reveals the feminine side of beings. Only the moon reveals the intimacy of our terrestrial dwelling place. It is not the rising of the sun that we need. We lack the birth of the land.

> Não é da luz do sol que carecemos. Milenarmente a grande estrela iluminou a terra e, afinal, nós pouco aprendemos a ver. O mundo necessita ser visto sob outra luz: a luz do luar; essa claridade que cai com respeito e delicadeza. Só o luar revela o lado feminino dos seres. Só a lua revela intimidade da nossa morada terrestre. Necessitamos não do nascer do Sol. Carecemos do nascer da Terra. (7)

This quotation is illustrative of the overall nature of the stories included in the collection and of the didactic (and thus political nature) of Couto's stories: it suggests that Mozambique needs to rebuild its identity by looking at (and rediscovering) the land and its old ways. It suggests that Mozambican identity must come from within that land and not from the outside, or at least not merely from the outside. What Mozambique needs is not necessarily (or certainly not only) the knowledge and the development traditionally associated with the modern world and the West, which has tended to value reason, technology, objectivity, compartmentalization, intellect, and masculinity over the unconscious, emotion, nature, imagination, femininity, and an epistemology of holism. The above excerpt associates the sun with the masculine, the rational, the compartmentalized and violent forces; and the moon with the feminine, the earth, the tender, and the holistic. What Couto asserts is that Mozambique needs to reawaken its nonmasculine, nonrational, nonconscious, sacralized, mystical, and mythical side so that the old Mozambican epistemologies can be rescued and reinvented and a truer Mozambique can then emerge—a more complete and authentic nation where all Mozambicans will be able to see, place, cherish, and express themselves. Otherwise stated, what is needed is for the many Mozambicans to feel that their voices, needs, and desires—cultural, political, and economical—are being met by the state representing them. That is why Couto's stories are important: they are an attempt to rescue and value those multiple Mozambican cultures, which until recently have not been given much attention by the postcolonial state and which have also been put down over and over again by the colonialists.

Couto often calls himself a storyteller and he feels that storytelling is the medium that best suits his style and best expresses the Africanness he is trying to put forward in his stories. Indeed he is a very good storyteller in the sense that he knows how to get closer to the African ways of life and being. Through his stories, the history, or better yet, histories and cultures of many different Mozambican peoples are expressed. Since storytelling seems to be the best medium to transmit the oral knowledge inherent to Mozambican consciousness and ways of being in the world, then Couto is the man we want to hear telling it. His language does indeed represent the Mozambican cultures at a much deeper level than does the standard Portuguese language. As I will demonstrate in my analysis of Couto's three stories, by breaking up the colonial language and using it in unfamiliar ways, Couto is able to get closer to the soul of Mozambique, to its philosophy of life and epistemology: he is able to bring the word closer to the thing it describes so that we are able to regain some of what might have been lost in the process of transposing African values and realities onto European languages. In the following quotation, we find the origins of Couto's own introduction to written storytelling and how his storytelling is rooted into Mozambican cultures and epistemologies:

> I was in Inhambane and there I was told a legend related to the whales. It would be very interesting to tell that story, to fictionalize that legend. I was with a group of friends who encouraged me: "Write a story!" And I wrote a story. And, as I was writing it, I realized that I could not use the classical Portuguese, the standard Portuguese in order to tell the story with all the poetic charge it had. It was necessary to recreate a language that would bring forward that ambiance of magic in which the story had been told to me. And

so I started that experience, and, interestingly, I was suddenly transported to my childhood, transported to the moments I told you about, when the elders were telling me stories. At that moment when they were telling me the story there was something religious, a feeling of fascination, of magic, and suddenly the world ceased to exist and those individuals were transformed into gods. It was impossible for you not to believe, for you not to be completely present and imprisoned in that fantasy that they were creating. It is important to understand how these storytellers functioned. Now they barely exist, there are very few of them, they are old. But they tell stories in the complete sense, they do all the theatre: they sing, dance . . . And I thought: it would be necessary to transport this magical ambiance created by these storytellers to the writing domain, to the domain of paper. And that is only possible through, one, the use of poetry, and two, the use of a language that utilizes this game of dance and theatre that they were making. So it was there that I started, in fact, to experiment the limits of language itself and to transgress with the intent of creating a space of magic.

estive em Inhambane e lá me contaram uma lenda ligada às baleias. Era muito interessante contar esta história, ficcionar esta lenda. Eu estava com um grupo de amigos que me entusiasmaram: "Faz uma história!" E eu fiz uma história. E, há medida que eu ia fazendo, eu me apercebi que não podia usar o português clássico, a norma portuguesa, para contar a história com toda a carga poética que ela tinha. Era preciso recriar uma linguagem que trouxesse aquele ambiente de magia em que a história me foi contada. E aí comecei essa experiência, e, interessantemente, eu fui de repente projectado para a infância, para os tais momentos de que te falei, em que os tais velhos me contavam as histórias. Naquele momento em que eles me contavam a história havia uma coisa religiosa, um sentimento de fascínio, de magia, em que de repente o mundo deixava de existir e aqueles sujeitos se transformavam em deuses. Era impossível tu não acreditares, tu tão estares completamente presente e preso naquela fantasia que eles criavam. É preciso ver como é que funcionavam estes contadores de histórias. Agora já quase que não existem, há muito poucos, são velhos. Mas eles contam as histórias no sentido completo, eles fazem o teatro todo: cantam, dançam . . . E eu pensei: seria necessário transportar para o domínio da escrita, do papel, este ambiente mágico que esses contadores de histórias criam. E isso só é possível através de, número um, a poesia, e número dois, uma linguagem que utilize este jogo de dança e de teatro que eles faziam. Então foi aí que eu comecei, de facto, a experimentar os limites da própria língua e a transgredir no sentido de criar um espaço de magia. (qtd. in Labin 1015-16)

The unveiling of histories and stories in "Governados pelos mortos: fala com um descamponês" ("Governed by the Dead: Talk with a Dis-peasant")

The story "Governed by the Dead: Talk with a Dis-peasant" involves two characters: an old man who lives in a rural, desolate, and poor area and what seems to be a younger person, someone who is from another region (most likely the city) and is only passing through. The old man is the addressee and the younger man is the interlocutor. The questions asked are brief and fairly specific and the answers given are longer, subjective in character, and have a didactic, even preaching tone. The listener is inquisitive, attentive to the answers, does not argue with (or interrupt) the addressee and seems to show respect for what is being said (even though it may be said that there are instances when one can see that he is doubting and questioning the reasoning of the old man).

In this story we can find illustrated several aspects of Couto's politico-cultural and linguistic agenda. The story uses several words that are "Mozambicanized," as Firmino would put it. The title of the story is followed by a subtitle which reads as follows: "Talk with a Dis-peasant" ("fala com um descamponês" equals a mixture of the prefix "dis" ["des"] plus the noun "peasant" ["camponês"]). What might be some of the implications of the word dis-peasant (descamponês) here? Taking into account what Skjon says about the Frelimo policy, we can arrive at a few conclusions. We can infer that the dis-peasant of this story is a man who lost his land as a result of the land reform that took place after Mozambique's independence in 1975. Such reform resulted in the collectivization of land and the forming of collective villages where people were forced to work for the collective rather than their own (familial) benefit. And this was something that went against the traditional rights of private property ownership and disrupted traditional forms of land administration. As Malyn Newitt points out in *A History of Mozambique*, "Communal Villages . . . were treated with great suspicion by the peasants involved who found that they fitted ill with the continued pattern of family farming. . . . The Communal Villages met with opposition above all because they involved the forcible movement of peasants from land they had traditionally farmed, and which was controlled by their own lineage, into large semi-urban settlements where they depended on the village commune for access to land" (549).

It has been argued by several theorists (Skjon, "The Pragmatics of Language"; Vines; Stroud) that the collectivization of the land by Frelimo following colonial independence might in fact have been one of the major factors fueling the anger and extreme terrorism undertaken by RENAMO (Resistência Nacional Moçambicana, Mozambican National Resistance) during Mozambique's bloody civil war, which took place from 1975 to 1992. Thus, the old man is calling himself a dis-peasant because he no longer has the land that he previously had: he has been dispossessed of it, as the prefix *dis* indicates. The man was forced off his own land and put into a collective village and by extension forced to enter a new system of production, which alienated and disrespected his cultural values. It is precisely because he was forced to do so that he calls himself a dis-peasant. In other words, he is still a peasant at heart even though he has lost the right to own his land. Rather than calling himself an agrarian worker ("trabalhador agrário"), for example, which would probably best qualify his new status as a man working the land under the collective system, he calls himself a dis-peasant, therefore implying that he has not accepted the new system and even refuses the language associated with it. By refusing to enter the linguistic classification of the new agrarian system, the old man is thus refusing the system itself. It is important to note here that postindependence Mozambique speech had in many ways incorporated words, expressions, and tones associated with the idiom and the spirit of Marxist, materialist revolutionary theory. Frelimo also exerted much pressure on Mozambicans to speak and learn the Portuguese language and even considered Portuguese a more suited, rational language for the advancement and modernization of the country. This is why it placed high importance on literacy campaigns and often forced people to speak Portuguese in public places by posting signs in the youth courts for example, such as: "It is expressly mandatory to speak the official language" ("É expressamente mandatório falar a língua oficial") (qtd. in Stroud 365).

The old man could also be seen as a victim of colonial land displacement. Like many other Africans in other colonial countries (e.g., South Africa and Rhodesia), Mozambicans were often either forced to leave their fertile lands by the colonialist powers and go work as laborers for the colonialists or put on poor lands that were not good for agricultural exploitation. Thus, the dis-peasant of this story could very well be a victim of colonialism and the land displacement that came with it. In this story, the interlocutor asks the old man: "And these fields, traditionally yours, were taken away from you?" ("E estes campos tradicionalmente vossos, foram-vos retirados?" [116]). The old man answers: "Yes they were taken away from us. We only kept the desert. . . . Now we are dis-peasants" ("Foram. Nós só ficámos com o descampado. . . . Agora somos descamponeses"). The old man's answer again suggests that he and his people are peasants at heart but peasants without good land to cultivate. The use of the word *dis-peasants* can therefore be indicative of the resistance Mozambicans have shown towards the processes both of colonization and of state collectivization of the land imposed by Frelimo. Both states (colonial and postcolonial) have forced on the old man (and his people) a system that he does not willingly accept: he refuses to become a subject of the colonial master and his subsequent replacement—the Frelimo government. In sum, he refuses to accept their notions of nationhood (or better yet, statehood as Abrahamsson and Nilsson, followed by Skjon, would rather call it).

It is clear from the conversation between the two people in the story that the interlocutor is not from the same social milieu as his addressee. The interlocutor is trying to learn and find out information about the life and the physical environment of the old man: how he sees the world, his relationship with the natural environment such as trees and animals, the land, the birds, and animals of that region. The interlocutor could very well be Couto having a conversation with a Mozambican during one of his several trips throughout the country as a biologist, his primary profession. Couto has indeed indicated that his profession allows him to travel throughout Mozambique and further learn about the different people inhabiting this country, about their close relation with nature and their environment, as well as the hidden dimensions that all things in life have. He tells us for example, he has learned how to see a tree as a live being, as a "house of spirits" ("casa de espíritos"), a "place of legends" ("lugar de lendas") (Labin 1033) and to understand that by preserving a tree he is in fact helping to preserve the cultural framework of Mozambique—a world often guided by animistic values and epistemologies whereby plants and animals tend to be seen as other selves and not as separate and inferior entities. Couto also says these values were not really taught to him at university, since the university tended to follow a Western, modern epistemological paradigm which valued science, reason, compartmentalization, and so forth. In his work as a biologist, Couto might thus experience some degree of alienation, since he was trained according to Western epistemologies and is most likely applying such methods to study the Mozambican land: he is Europeanizing the land, so to speak. In that sense, he becomes much like the European scientists of the eighteenth and nineteenth centuries who went to Africa to study and understand Africa and Africans using, for the purpose, a Eurocentric model, which they arrogantly (or perhaps just ignorantly) took to be a model of universal validity—as well argued by Coetzee in "Idleness in South Africa" (*White Writing* 12-35) and by Mary Louise Pratt in *Imperial Eyes* (15-86). The model of dialogue of the conversation between the old man and the interlocutor suggests that the latter had at least some control over the conversation, for he gets to ask the questions, questions which are already based on a certain theoretical conception of the world—in this case Eurocentric.

When the interlocutor asks the old man the name of the family's sacred tree under which they are sitting, the latter answers: "Why do you want to know? . . . What you should know sir is the name that the tree gives you" ("Porquê? . . . O senhor devia saber era o nome que a árvore lhe dá a si" [115]). Such an answer only serves to point out that the old man has a very different thought system and obeys different thought systems: he sees trees as sacred entities, as beings who are not inanimate but rather have their own thought system and do in fact exert power over humans by giving them names, and not the other way around, as more modern cultures tend to think. During their discussion about birds, the addressee goes so far as to contest the Portuguese names given to birds: "Before we had the desert, the ostrich used to land on trees, it used to fly from branch to flower. Its name was tree-strich. Today, there are names which I believe are distanced" ("Antes de haver deserto, a avestruz pousava em árvore, voava de galho em flor. Se chamava de arvorestruz. Agora, há nomes que eu acho que estão desencostados" [116]). Such an answer is very telling at different levels. By saying that in the old days the ostrich was not called "avestruz" but rather "arvorestruz" (árvores ["trees"] plus "truz"), the old man is suggesting that in precolonial times Africans had their own names for their birds, names which have now been changed by a different language and, by extension, a different system of classification and organization of animals and the world in general. The incorporation of the word "árvore" ("tree") in the old name of the ostrich also suggests that in precolonial times there were many trees, flowers, plants, and forests where birds existed in abundance—all of which were decimated with the arrival of the colonialists and their exploitation of African natural resources. The old name further suggests that in precolonial times the trees and the birds were inseparable entities, thus attesting to the African holistic view of the world, according to which animals and trees are part of one another: they depend on one another to achieve their fullest potential as creatures or entities and to maintain the natural (holistic) order of the world. The world is an entity with a distended ego, and the human self is a part of that enlarged self, and so are the trees, the birds and any other entities. The new name, "avestruz" only includes "aves" ("birds") leaving out the "árvores" ("trees") and thus compartmentalizing and breaking the original holistic world order.

As many language relativists have already argued (e.g., Humboldt, Boas, Whorf, Fanon, Ngũgĩ), language shapes the way we perceive, conceive, see, and understand the world—especially if we change language groups—from Portuguese to Bantu, as is the case in Mozambique. By imposing a new language on a people, the colonizers were also changing their views about life in general—an act that constitutes a form of cultural violation and alienation. In addition, European languages were often not equipped to describe the plants and animals of the African habitat (for languages are often related to and dependent on physical environments) and thus the imposed names often did not capture the essence of the thing being described. No wonder Ngũgĩ is so passionate about the preservation of African languages. It is not merely that language is a cultural mark of a people that shapes and informs the way that they see themselves, their community, and the world; it is also true that different language groups are born out of different physical realities and thus are best suited to describe such realities. By transposing certain languages out of their initial habitat, we are in some ways killing the language and the reality it was intended to describe in the first place. In this case, then, the arbitrariness of language does indeed matter, and calling the ostrich an "avestruz" rather than an "arvorestruz" ("tree-strich") would be the same as killing if not the entire bird, at least some part of it. As the old man says, the new names are "distanced" ("desencostados") (116). The new names are distanced because they are not close enough to the trees, the birds, or the stones or whatever else that they are intending to describe, for they belong to another physical world, a world in which the African reality cannot quite fit.

The old man gives other examples of names that he considers distanced. He says, for example, that the name of the "Beija-flor" ("hummingbird"—literally meaning "kissing flower") should in fact be "repaired" ("consertado") (116). He is implying that it is not the hummingbird that kisses the flower but the other way around, and so the flower should be the one to receive the name "Beija-pássaros" ("Kissing-birds"): "The flower is the one that should have the title of kissing-birds" ("A flor é que levaria o título de beija-pássaros" [116]). This justification for the name change points to another, very important fact: the old man's classification and view of nature are different from the common Western perception, which tends to view flowers as being inferior to animals, which is why birds are the ones kissing flowers and not the other way around. As we know, within the Western hierarchical classification of nature, flowers are inserted in the general category of plants and are perceived as having less life than animals; in other words, as inanimate entities which cannot move and take any action. As Couto has put it, "[People] are dealing with a language that belongs to another world, with another logic, and they have to break it up so that the language can be theirs." ("[As pessoas] estão lidando com uma língua que é de outro mundo, com outra lógica, e elas têm que despedaçá-la para que a língua possa ser sua.") (qtd. in Thomaz and Chaves 7). This "breaking up" of the colonial language serves as cultural agency in the sense that it restores and reawakens the old Mozambican epistemologies. Moreover, by suggesting that it is the flower that kisses the birds and not the other way around, the old man is also hinting at something else: the fact that the feminine force (flower as woman) occupies a central place within the African society and epistemology. In other words, the flower-woman is not just a passive receiving entity: it actually takes charge of her life and sexual desires by becoming the one who kisses the bird (man) who is often perceived as the more sexually aggressive entity, the one who tends to initiate sexual contact. In addition, the flower-woman in fact kisses more than one bird (man) since the old man says it should be called "beija-pássaros" ("kissing-birds") and not just "beija-pássaro" ("kissing-bird"). From this, three points can be deduced: 1) the feminine can be a very powerful force within traditional Africa, 2) women can have access to more than one man (they are not bound to monogamy or virginity), and 3) women are active beings who will take charge of and act on their sexual desires. And I should also note that when the old man is discussing the name of the "avestruz" ("ostrich"), he identifies it as being a feminine entity, for he calls it "a avestruz" and not "o avestruz," which is the correct form in standard Portuguese. This again could suggest that the feminine force or entity holds a central role within African traditional epistemologies. In traditional African societies, women are often powerful entities, entities who, because of their reproductive capacities, are seen as the creators and bearers of life—in other words, as symbols of wealth; and they are compared to the earth, which is what feeds and gives life to all life through the food that it provides. This is of course also a view generally shared by many other societies around the world—Western and otherwise.

Further evidence of the power of the feminine can be found in the name the old man gives to his wife: ("But your wife, doesn't she keep you company?—She is my lady boss. Once in a while we strike up a conversation. She is company, like a raining season. But tradition warns us: we must not do intimacies with women. Otherwise we end up charmed" ("Mas a sua mulher não lhe faz companhia?—Ela é a minha patrã. De vez em quando a gente dedilha uma conversa. É uma companhia, faz conta uma estação das chuvas. Mas a tradição nos manda: com mulher a gente não pode intimizar. Caso senão acabamos enfeitiçados" [117]). The old man calls his wife his "patrã" ("lady boss")—an altered form of the standard feminine "patroa" ("lady boss")—suggesting that she does have quite a bit of power over him and around the house. In addition, by calling his wife "patrã" rather than "patroa," he might also be pointing to the fact that women in traditional Mozambique are the ones who gave birth to the male and not the other way around, as the biblical story of Adam and Eve suggests, for example. By taking the "o" (general mark of the masculine in Portuguese) out of the word "patroa," the old man seems to be restoring the procreative or life giving power of the woman and admitting that men came from women—which ultimately ties into all kinds of other symbolic associations of earth with woman and life. In his book, *Aspects de la civilisation africaine (personne, culture, religion)*, Amadou Hampâté Bâ offers a discussion of the importance of the feminine element in traditional African societies and its association with woman-mother-earth (128-32).

The latter part of the old man's answer further suggests that women in traditional Mozambique (as in much of the rest of world) are also often perceived as seductresses, as beings who must not be trusted, as they are endowed with powerful capacities; they are sorceresses (enchantresses) and can therefore control and use their powers to do evil to men. Thus, my intention here is not to suggest that patriarchy did not exist in precolonial societies or that the sexuality of African women was not repressed. The existence (to date) of the practice of various forms of female genital mutilation and other traditions such as polygamy constitute in my view an aggressive and oppressive form of controlling and suppressing women's sexuality and, therefore, a powerful form of patriarchy. Moreover, patriarchy in precolonial Africa and Mozambique was widespread, and was, for the most part, the norm even in matrilianeal socities (see Walker 29; Hay and Stichter 11; Chiziane 41). As I demonstrate, in "Confused 'Slaves' of Many Traditions: The Search for the Freedom Dance in Chiziane's Niketche, A Tale of Polygamy," women's oppression in contemporary Mozambique is a result of the convergence of Western and Afrocentric traditions—for it is important to acknowledge that colonialism also contributed to the deterioration of the power African women held in their traditional communities and it increased their workload. As indicated by Sally Baden in relation to Mozambique,

> Economic options for the majority of women in pre-independence Mozambique were mainly concentrated in subsistence agriculture. With a well-established system of forced labour (*chibalo*) and labour migration of men to plantations (in the north) and South Africa (in the south), women's agricultural workload intensified as they struggled to maintain family plots alone, during men's long absences. Women supplemented declining subsistence production by working as casual hired labour, through making and selling beer, small-scale trading or by prostitution. Some women were forced to forge independent existences and raise children alone, due to lack of support from absent partners. Lack of education and biases in employment and commercial activity against both Africans in general and women specifically meant that few African women had access to formal employment. (34)

In Couto's story, the name given to the "flamingos" is also contested and corrected by the old man. He calls them "inflamingos," a mix of the verb "inflamar" ("to inflame") with the suffix "ingos," rather than flamingos. On what it is perhaps a more obvious level, we could say that because the word "inflamingo" is composed of the prefix "in," which denotes a negative or contrary characteristic, plus the substantive "flamingo," the bird is actually the contrary of what it is called in standard Portuguese: that is, it is a "nonflamingo." This points again to the incapacity of the Portuguese language to describe African reality. Moreover, and leaving out the possibility of the narrator's humor, what might such name reveal in terms of the old man's ways of thinking and understanding the bird in question and by extension, the reality of his or its own universe? It can be suggested that the name is not "flamingo" but "inflamingo," because the bird is usually pink-red, which is the color of the fire or the color of the sky during sunset and sunrise. When asked about the flamingos the old man says, "Those become inflamed in the crepuscule: they are the in-flamingos" ("Esses se inflamam no crepúsculo: são os inflamingos" [116]). What the man seems to be saying, then, is that the color of the bird is pink-red because he gets it from the sky, from the power of the sun—and by extension, one could say, from the power of God, since God is seen as the creator of all things that exist in the universe which are all reflections and manifestations of his power. As John Mbiti notes: "We have many peoples whose names for God mean sky, heaven or the above. . . . Among many societies, the sun is considered to be a manifestation of God Himself, and the same word, or its cognate, is used for both. Examples of this may be cited from among the Chagga (*Ruwa* for both God and the sun), peoples of the Ashanti hinterland (*We* for both). . . . Among others . . . the sun is personified as a divinity or spirit, and thought by some to be one of God's sons" (52). Thus, the flamingo becomes "inflamingo" because he gets "inflamado" ("inflamed") by the power of the sun, the power of the sky and the power of God. Although the word "flamingo" also connotes fire, that which has the color of fire or flame, it is important to note that it does not carry the same connotation as the word "inflamingo," for the latter implies that the bird literally becomes inflamed by the power of the skies, and by extension the power of the sun and God. Such a name implies a much stronger power from above, a power responsible for the color (and ultimately for the life) of the bird. Were there no God (sun, sky), the bird would not become inflamed with its dazzling color of fire, it would not even exist. The "inflamingo" becomes itself the symbol of God's creations and the link between the earth and the sky: it is the symbol of the holism that characterizes the African traditional epistemology, which sees all the elements as being interlinked to from a complete "whole." If we take into account the symbolic power of fire in most traditional societies (Western and otherwise) and its strong associations with life, wealth, as well as intellectual and spiritual enlightenment, we can further see the importance of the color of the bird and its relation to divine creation, power, enlightenment (see Chevalier and Gheerbrant 379-82, 391).

The bird is given the name of "inflamingo" because its creator is God himself: such a name takes into account the power of the skies, the power of the sun, all of which ultimately symbolize God and his power over the universe of humans and animals. Ultimately then, what the old man is suggesting with the renaming of the bird is that his ancestral African language was more in sync with his African universe and holistic conception of the world, contrary to the new language (Portuguese) which came from another reality and is not equipped with the proper linguistic tools to accurately represent the African reality: language is, after all, a highly complex web that is intrinsically bound to its local environment (physical, cultural, political, religious, etc.). Otherwise stated, the colonial language is not able to capture the sacred and holistic dimensions of the African traditional epistemology, the reason why the old man must change the name from "flamingo" to "inflamingo": the name change is an attempt to restore some of what has been lost with the imposition of the colonial language onto the African reality. The name "inflamingo" is best suited to describe the African epistemology precisely because it takes into account the deeply religious and spiritual African cultural contexts according to which all things are not only interdependent, but also dependent on the ultimate creator: the God of the skies above. In other words, things are whole and fundamentally holy (divine and sacralized). It is precisely this wholeness and holiness, which was in some ways annihilated by the colonial language that the name "inflamingo" tries to regain.

In *Imperial Eyes*, Pratt discusses the global nature classification system developed by the European scientific minds in the eighteenth century, a system that was then applied to the African and American ecological systems and which in many ways served to aid the colonial and imperial enterprise. In this instance, the European discourse is used to appropriate a world that is totally different from itself: the European languages and thought systems become the organizing and oppressing paradigm guiding the colonial mind. In order to explore and conquer the African continent, the Europeans needed to understand it, and they could only do so through their own cultural framework. The Europeans constructed and invented a world order based on a European model—a highly ethnocentric and self-serving maneuver. And thus the colonies ended up with a reality that had little to do with them. As Pratt explains,

> One by one the planet's life forms were to be drawn out of the tangled threads of their life surroundings and rewoven into European-based patterns of global unity and order. The (lettered, male, European) eye that held the system could familiarize ("naturalize") new sites/sights immediately upon contact, by incorporating them into the language of the system. The differences of distance factored themselves out of the picture: with respect to mimosas, Greece could be the same as Venezuela, West Africa or Japan; the label "granitic peaks" can apply identically to Eastern Europe, the Andes, or the US-American West. Barbara Stafford mentions probably one of the most extreme instances of this globalizing resemanticizing, a 1789 treatise by German Samuel Witte claiming that all the pyramids of the world, from Egypt to the Americas, are really "basalt eruptions." The example is a telling one, for it suggests the system's potential to subsume culture and history into nature. Natural history extracted specimens from their organic or ecological relations with each other, but also from their places in other people's economies, histories, and social and symbolic systems. (31)

Couto's language tries to break away from the European model of classification pointed out by Pratt and in some ways becomes similar to "dread talk" as used by Rastafarians in the West Indies (i.e., Jamaica). In the same way that dread talk symbolized the forging of a new identity (or better, yet, an identity for the very first time) and the refusal or contesting of the colonial cultural legacy for the Caribbean people, so does Couto's language function as the agent that permits the reinvention or building of a new Mozambican identity—an agent that takes history in its own hands, by appropriating the language of the colonizer and changing it to accommodate present cultural Mozambican needs, to affirm its own and unique way of life. In addition, like dread talk, Couto's language seems to put into practice the concept of "overstanding," that is, is seems to be an attempt to restore the wonder of language, its power to connect us with the mystical forces, the unknown, the spiritual, giving us a strength that helps us bear the difficulties of life. As J. Edward Chamberlin tells us, "One of the strategies of the Rastafari has been to rename things. It's an old trick, as colonizers have realized for centuries. I have seen maps of Canada where as many as a dozen different names are layered onto one place, reflecting the different traditions of people who live there . . . and sometimes driven others out. The Rastafarian renaming, too, has involved turning language around so that it reflects their own imaginings and recovers their realities. 'Dread talk,' it is sometimes called; with the word 'dread' signifying that fearful and fragile wonder. . . . The signature of 'dreadlocks' of Rastafari are a way of catching the mysterious power, or of not losing it" (187-88).

When asked about the existence and presence of other animals in the area where he lives, the old man responds: "The wild creatures are disappearing. The *mabeco* (the so-called wild dog) continues to suffer human barbarities. Before the lesson is finished, he will already have learned how not to exist" ("A bichagem vai acabando. O mabeco, dito o cão-selvagem, vai sofrendo as humanas selvajarias. Antes de acabar a lição, ele já terá aprendido a não existir" [116]). Here the old man is again contesting the name given to the mabeco. By calling the mabeco a "cão-selvagem" ("wild dog") the Portuguese are again attributing foreign characteristics to the African animal, characteristics which the animal did not have in his natural African physical habitat. The animal was not "wild" before the Portuguese arrived. Likely the Portuguese decided to call it "wild-dog" because they did not recognize it, and since it looked like a dog to them, they decided the best name to give it would "naturally" be wild-dog. Who is committing "barbarities" then? As the old man says, it is certainly not the mabeco but rather the humans, for they are inventing a "wild" animal which never really existed. Because of their invention, misunderstanding, and assumptions about the mabeco, the colonialists go after the animal and kill it: they seem to assume that the animal will be aggressive towards them, that it will automatically attack them and so they kill it. Yet, the animal does not even seem to sense that it is because of its supposed wildness that the Portuguese colonialist is attacking it and so it does not really run away from humans (proving thus that, in fact, it is not wild, for it seeks human contact). This is why the old man says: "Before the lesson is finished, he will already have learned how not to exist" ("antes de acabar a lição, ele já terá aprendido a não existir" [116]). In other words, before the animal can understand the human malicious and distrusting ways and the erroneous assumptions of the colonial intruder which are based on a Eurocentric model (and more specifically, the Eurocentric physical and biological habitat), it will be killed by him and thus cease to exist.

It has been argued by many and for quite some time, as Montaigne's *Des Cannibales* can in some ways attest, that the barbarians were mostly an invention of the European colonial mind which needed to find a justification for its control of the colonies and use of extreme force against the colonized peoples. Coetzee's novel *Waiting for the Barbarians* is also a good and more recent example of a literary work that further explores the idea that the barbarians do not in fact exist; they are merely a fabrication of the empire which often uses its civilizational flag (excuse) in order to gain access to a wide range of economic wealth. The barbarian is often that which does not have the same culture, religion, and belief system as oneself: for the Greeks, the term *barbarian* referred to anyone who did not speak the Greek language (specifically the Persians). The mabeco becomes the "almost the same, but not quite" (86) as Homi Bhabha's would say—except that in this case one would need to rename his article "Of Mimicry and Man" to "Of Mimicry and Dog" instead. However, in the end the message would be, if not quite the same, at least very close to it. What I am arguing here is that, although the story in question deals with a so-called wild dog and its tragic relationship with the colonizer, the connotations embedded in it can also be extended to the power dynamics and perceptions regulating the relationships between colonizer and colonized. In *The Location of Culture* Bhabha writes:

> colonial mimicry is the desire for a reformed, recognizable Other, *as a subject of a difference that is almost the same, but not quite.* Which is to say, that the discourse of mimicry is constructed around an ambivalence; in order to be effective, mimicry must continually produce its slippage, its excess, its difference. The authority of that mode of colonial discourse that I have called mimicry is therefore stricken by an indeterminacy: mimicry emerges as the representation of a difference that is itself a process of disavowal. Mimicry is, thus the sign of a double articulation; a complex strategy of reform, regulation and discipline, which "appropriates" the Other as it visualizes power. Mimicry is also the sign of the inappropriate, however, a difference or recalcitrance which coheres the dominant strategic function of colonial power, intensifies surveillance, and poses an immanent threat to both "normalized" knowledges and disciplinary powers. (86)

What Bhabha is saying above, much as Pratt does in *Imperial Eyes*, and others before him like Césaire, Fanon, Walcott, Naipaul, and Brathwaite is that the colonizers needed to understand and control the unknown; they needed to "reform" and make "recognizable" the different other in order to have access to his or her power and land and so they allowed and forced (through education) others to become like them; in other words, to act, think, and speak like them. However, in the colonial gaze, the colonized other could never become like the colonizer, for the latter was in fact the only same or the complete subject—the original copy who could not be totally imitated by the colonized who continued to possess the mark of otherness (usually in the form of physical characteristics or speech). Despite all this, the fact that the "mimic man" (the colonized) lives between the two worlds (has access to both cultural codes) poses a danger to the colonialist, for the former can use the knowledge of the latter to work against him and achieve colonial independence (as indeed have many "assimilados" ("assimilated persons") in Lusophone Africa—e.g., Agostinho Neto in Angola, Amílcar Cabral in Guiné Bissau, and Eduardo Mondlane in Mozambique).

If we transpose this rationale to the situation of the Mozambican colonized subject, we can then say that the subject was destroyed by the colonialist because the latter did not consider the former a full human being or a complete same: he or she always remained "almost the same but not quite." The colonizer destroys psychologically the colonial subject because he takes away his or her full personhood and makes him or her the incomplete double, the split, the mimic man—that which is between the two (the African and the European) but can never be either one entirely. Thus, the killing of the mabeco symbolizes the destroying of the "completeness" of the Mozambican subject—the wholeness, integrity, and value he or she held in his or her African precolonial context. Of course, in the instances where the colonizer cannot domesticate the local subject (that is, produce the mimic man), he often feels the need to kill physically that subject before he or she turns against himself. This is also why the old man says that before the mabeco can learn the lesson, he will be killed. In other words, without being domesticated, the local subject cannot be trusted by the colonist and so the former's death is often the only way for the colonialist to achieve his goals in the "new" land. Here we only need to think about the many genocides that took place in various colonial states (Africa, the Americas, and so forth) where the colonial subject was literally killed, for he or she did not accept the colonial impositions and demands and, in fact, fought against the colonial intruder. In sum, the colonial subject refused to become a mimic person; he or she refused to become the "Black skin split under the racist gaze" (92), to use yet again Bhabha's notion. Were they killed because they failed to understand that in order to survive, they (like the mabeco) needed to become a mimic person (and a "mimic dog")? Were they killed because they consciously chose to remain truthful to themselves—refused to become mimic and subdued to white power? Whatever the answer to these questions may be, the end result is almost the same: if one does not die from physical death, one will die from psychological death, since one's culture is, if not totally annihilated by the colonialist, at the very least put in the realm of the uncivilized.

Couto goes on to describe how the old man believes in the power, intelligence, and wisdom of the animal and even the inanimate world. The old man says that he is happy to be living among animals and plants: happy to be called "creature of the woods" ("bicho-do-mato") by some, because that gives him "distinction" ("distinção" 117). Such response demonstrates that the old man does not live by the same values and standards as those who call him "creature of the woods," those who have assimilated the western mores which have tended to value urbanization and modern over rural ways of life; he is happy to live life according to traditional African animistic principles which value and favor a close interaction with all the various elements of nature (animate and inanimate), and according to which nature is seen as having high spiritual, sacred powers and as being a fundamental part of oneself, and not as a separate and inferior entity. The African philosopher Mbiti has described well the African traditional way of life, its epistemologies, cosmogonies, spiritual, sacred, religious and holistic dimension:

> According to [traditional] African peoples, man lives in a religious universe, so that natural phenomena and objects are intimately associated with God. They not only originate from Him but also bear witness to Him. Man's understanding of God is strongly colored by the universe of which man is himself a part. Man sees in the universe not only the imprint but the reflection of God; and whether that image is marred or clearly focused and defined, it is nevertheless an image of God, the only image known in traditional African societies. . . . There are myths which tell how domestic animals originated at the same time or in the same way as man himself. . . . The Akamba hold that cattle, sheep and goats accompanied the first human beings whom God lowered from the sky. The Maasai firmly believe that since God gave them cattle from the very beginning, nobody else has the right to own cattle. As such, it is their duty to raid cattle from neighbouring peoples, without feeling that they are committing theft or robbery. . . . Cattle, sheep and goats are used for sacrificial and other religious purposes, and examples of this are found in all over the continent. Many people have a sacred attitude towards their animals. For example, the Herero regard all cattle as sacred, and as having originated from their mythical "tree of life," from where human and other life comes. (48-50)

And in the words of Bâ, "It must be borne in mind that in a general way all African traditions postulate a *religious vision of the world.* The visible universe is thought of and felt as the sign, the concretization or the outer shell of an invisible, living universe, consisting of forces in perpetual motion. Within this vast cosmic unity everything is connected, everything is bound solidly together; and man's behaviour both as regards himself and as regards the world around him (the mineral, vegetable, animal world and human society) is subject to a very precise ritual regulation—which may vary in form from the various ethnicities and regions" (Unesco, *A General History of Africa* 171; see also Okolo and Malherbe).

The addressee of Couto's story is certain that the animals do possess their own intelligence (and a very important one) and that we should learn from their ways, rather than associate them with low intelligence and backwardness. He believes in the power of the hidden things, in the power of the irrational, the unconscious, the mystical, and the mythical: in the power of what the modern, secular, scientific order has often associated with the low kind of knowledge, the low perception and understanding of the world:

> *You seem disillusioned with men.*
> The prophecy of the mole is right: one day, the other existing wild creatures will keep it company in its undergrounds. I believe in the knowledge of that which does not exist. After all, not all that shines is a may-bug. Such is the case of the glow-worm. Does the glow-worm die? Or does it melt? Its dead remains augment the dark.
>
> *You hold so much certainty in the wild creatures.*
> You have not looked carefully at the world of this side. Have you ever seen a left-handed bird? A squint-eyed chameleon? A stuttering parrot?

You believe in the teachings of the wild creatures?
Every crab is an engineer of burrows. He knows everything of nothing. There are others, many others. The oldest one is the little beetle. But, of all of them, the fresh water tortoise is the one who is always at the window.

Don't you suffer from a certain isolation?
I am a man supplied with solitudes. Some call me a creature of the woods. Instead of becoming diminished, I become swollen with such distinction. As I before-said: from the wild creature, we learn how not to waste. Just like the wasp, who makes her house from spit....

A last message...
I don't know. Happy is the cow that does not foresee that one day it will become a shoe. Happier even is the shoe which does its job lying on the ground. So close to the ground that it doesn't even notice when it dies.

Parece desiludido com os homens...
O vaticínio da toupeira é que tem razão: um dia, os restantes bichos lhe farão companhia em suas subterraneidades. Eu acredito é na sabedoria do que não existe. Afinal, nem tudo que luz é besouro. É o caso do pirilampo. Pirilampo morre? Ou funde? Suas réstias mortais aumentam o escuro.

Tanta certeza na bicharada...
Você não olhou bem esse mundo de cá. Já viu pássaro canhoto? Camaleão vesgo? Papagaio gago?

Acredita no ensinamento dos bichos?
Todo o caranguejo é um engenheiro de buracos. Ele sabe tudo de nada. Há outros, demais. O mais idoso é o escaravelhinho. Mas, de todos, quem anda sempre de janela é o cágado.

Você não sofre de um certo isolamento?
Sou um homem abastecido de solidões. Uns me chamam bicho-do-mato. Em vez de me diminuir eu me incho com tal distinção. Como antedisse: agente aprende do bicho a não desperdiçar. Como a vespa que do cuspe faz a casa....

Uma última mensagem...
Não sei. Feliz é a vaca que não pressente que, um dia, vai ser sapato. Mais feliz é ainda o sapato que trabalha deitado na terra. Tão rasteiro que nem dá conta quando morre. (115-16)

    The old man is disillusioned with the world of humans, the new world order that overvalues the so-called higher intelligences (i.e., rationality, scientific knowledge) and discards the old and more traditional ways of knowing which utilize alternative sources of knowledge such as the unconscious, the spiritual, the body, and the abstract. As he puts it, "The prophecy of the mole is right: one day, the other existing wild creatures will keep it company in its undergrounds. I believe in the knowledge of that which does not exist" ("O vaticínio da toupeira é que tem razão: um dia, os restantes bichos lhe farão companhia em suas subterraneidades. Eu acredito é na sabedoria do que não existe. Afinal, nem tudo que luz é besouro" [116]). Why is the mole the animal whose prophecies are wisest? Because this animal lives underground: it is in constant contact with the hidden, the abstract, the spirit (and the spiritual), the unconscious and the irrational—the forces which are fundamental to the understanding of oneself and the world, and the understanding of self through otherness too, since his self is part of that larger otherness: the material world and the invisible, spiritual world. It is the "undergrounds" ("subterraneidades") (the hidden, the old, the archaic) that the old man wants to see reawakened and revalued by the new world orders (the colonial and postcolonial states). By saying that one day all the other animals will join the mole in its "undergrounds," the old man is also suggesting that after death both humans and animals will become the same, for they will all become part of the underground, the "other" world, the invisible, the world of the spirits and gods. In other words, life does not really end but it only becomes something else. According to traditional African religious beliefs, physical death allows one to enter the realm of the "collective immortality," as Mbiti calls it (26). Death merely means that one is becoming part of another type of life, another type of world, another type of existence. The dead are not really dead. Rather, they depart one world, one state of being to enter another: they join the world of the spirits, of the ancestors, of the gods. Again, in the words of Mbiti: "Human life has another rhythm of nature which nothing can destroy. On the level of the individual, this rhythm includes birth, puberty, initiation, marriage, procreation, old age, death, entry into the community of the departed and finally entry into the company of the spirits. It is an ontological rhythm, and these are the key moments in the life of the individual" (Mbiti 24).

The values defended by the old man are not exclusive to African traditional societies. They have (approximate) longstanding traditions in Christianity, in some contemporary Western philosophies, Eastern Zen philosophy, and the psychology of Carl Jung, for example. Eastern Zen philosophers tend to see life as a cycle, a cycle according to which all living things do not really die but are only transformed into something else. They also see all things as being interrelated and conceive God as an entity present in all living things (see Roy; Iisuka). Lispector too shares similar views, for as she says, "God is the world," (*The Hour* 11) ("Deus é o mundo" [*A hora* 13]). God is what exists and in order to experience true existence one must let go of intellectual concepts and enter the realm of experience where one "tastes" and "savors" existence, as it were. Just like the old man of Couto's story says that he believes in the knowledge of that which does not exist, as noted above, the Lispectorian narrator also says that he is "aware of many things [he] cannot see" (*The Hour* 8). Like African traditional societies, Zen philosophy follows a holistic perspective which defends that in order for humans to be happy and find balance, they need to be in touch with all their sides: spiritual, emotional, communal, individual, environmental, intellectual, unconscious, conscious, and so forth. This is also similar to what in

Jungnanian terms might be termed as "the integration of personality": the argument that humans must listen to and feed all their many sides so that they can then "integrate" their split self and find equilibrium (Jung, *The Integration* 139-62, 456-79). The collective unconscious—understood loosely—represents the place where the spirits of the elders can be found, the place of communication between the living and the dead, the reservoir of collective memory and culture. The various similarities between Lispector's and Couto's epistemologies and between Eastern, Western, and African epistemologies will become more apparent throughout this study as I delve into my analysis of the other authors.

If it is true that many similarities exist between traditional African epistemologies and Eastern and Western epistemologies, it is also true that the interrelation between the world of the living and the world of the dead or the spirits is stronger in African traditional societies. Like Africans, many Christians believe that the dead will enter the spiritual realm, and, some even believe they can have contact with the living through medium apparitions. Yet, in the case of African traditional peoples, the presence of the dead or spirits and their power over the life of the living seem to assume a much more cogent role. Such presence and power is imbedded in (and affects) every aspect of the lives of the living and the living are always aware of the death conducting themselves in ways that will not create animosity between the two world orders (Mbiti 25-27, 75-83, 149-62; Teffo and Roux 161-74). Wole Soyinka's well known play, *Death and the King's Horseman,* explores the dynamics between the world of the living and the world of the death quite well and shows the consequences of not respecting the traditions of death (and of the dead) and the entrance into the spirit world. Within the traditional Africa world order, not only do the spirits enter into frequent contact with the living, but they also dictate many aspects of the lives of the living: they are highly respected and venerated by the living. Furthermore, after they are dead, humans cease to be humans and become gods themselves. This crucial relationship between the world of the death and the world of the living is addressed by the old man in Couto's story:

> *After so much war: how did your hope survive?*
> We chewed it. Because of the hunger. Like the birds: they were eaten by the scenery.
>
> *What happened to the houses?*
> The houses were smoked by the earth. Lack of tobacco, lack of *suruma* [marijuana]. Now all I do is become sad from premature memory. The memory of the cashew-tree makes scents abound in my eyes.
>
> *How do you explain so much suffering?*
> It's a curse. A very big and bad curse. The only thing left is for the snake to become left-handed.
>
> *And why?*
> We don't accept the ruling of the dead. But they are the ones who govern us.

And they became angry?
The dead have lost access to God. Because they themselves became gods. And they are afraid of admitting so. They want to become alive again. Only so that they can ask someone.

Depois de tanta guerra: como vos sobreviveu a esperança?
Mastigámo-la. Foi da fome. Veja os pássaros: foram comidos pela paisagem.

E o que aconteceu com as casas?
As casas foram fumadas pela terra. Falta de tabaco, falta de suruma [marijuana]. Agora só me entristonho de lembrança prematura. A memória do cajueiro me faz crescer cheiros nos olhos.

Como interpreta tanta sofrência?
Maldição. Muita e muita má maldição. Faltava só a cobra ser canhota.

E porquê?
Não aceitamos a mandança dos mortos. Mas são eles que nos governam.

E eles se zangaram?
Os mortos perderam acesso a Deus. Porque eles mesmos se tornaram deuses. E têm medo de admitir isso. Querem voltar a ser vivos. Só para poderem pedir a alguém. (116)

As this passage indicates, the old man believes the reason why there is so much suffering in the nation is because the new world order regulating Mozambique neither respects nor believes in the power of the dead, the power of the spirits and the ancestors. People are deaf to the old and only direct their ears to the "new," which in this case might mean the rational, the logical, the visible, and so forth. The lack of respect for traditions has made the ancestors mad, and that is why they have cursed the country by bringing about war and destruction of all sorts. As Bâ puts it, "Violation of the sacred [African traditional] laws [is supposed] to cause an upset in the balance of forces which would take expression in disturbances of different kinds" (Unesco, *A General History of Africa* 171). What is needed, then, is for the living to reestablish communication with the world of the dead: to listen to their messages, their advice and their predicaments so that a new and truer "order" can be reestablished in Mozambique—an order that includes the old values of the land. Then the living will "see" into and communicate with the nonvisible and be literally "governed by the dead," as the title of the story suggests. There is no doubt that the old man is offering resistance to the cultural values imposed by both the colonial and the postcolonial states, which tend to view rationality, technology, urbanization, compartmentalization, secularization, and the control and exploitation of nature as progressive and civilized aspects of life and according to which human beings are placed at the top of the hierarchy of life. The very title of the story, "Governed by the Dead," functions thus as an overall metaphor for the old man's way of life: he is literally governed by the dead because he is still guided by his ancestral African principles and philosophy of life, even if those values are being (and have been) discarded and undervalued by colonial and postcolonial Western epistemologies and power structures. At the figurative level, the title also speaks to the fact that the governors of Mozambique (the state) are dead because they do not acknowledge the power of the dead over the living and do not respect the old Mozambican traditions: in this sense too, the old man ends up by being governed by the dead. Thus, the old man has a strong message: to rediscover one's ancestors and past. The story then achieves a highly didactic character. The fact that the old man answers all the questions and the interlocutor (the outsider, the modern, urban man) merely asks them and listens to the answers in a seemingly nonjudgmental way is also suggestive of Couto's cultural-political agenda: the importance of giving voice to and rediscovering the past, the importance of literally traveling throughout the Mozambican land to learn from (and listen to) the people and their ways (see Rothwell).

Rather than being the "new" (the modern, secular, urban, external) that teaches the "old," it is the "old" (the archaic, sacralized, rural, internal) that teaches the "new." Rather than being the young and formally educated person who teaches the old and formally uneducated man, it is the old man who is put in a position of teacher or preacher, who must be listened to with respect, for his voice is important and contains the cultural "seed" of the Mozambican land. Can this old man and his ways be kept alive for much longer? Can he and many like him find the proper support to nourish this old and wise way of life? In order for that to happen, in order for those old epistemologies to be revalued or reawakened, the state power governing will need to embrace them so that a more equalitarian nation can emerge, a nation which will not be defined solely by modern principles and the values of the Westernized minority in power, but also by African needs, concerns, views and ontology. To use Abrahamsson and Nilsson's terms, that would mean the passage of Mozambique from a state-nation to a nation-state, a country whose socioeconomic and cultural policies would reflect not only the values of a small elite but more generally, the values of the many different ethnic groups living within Mozambique.

"A menina sem palavra: segunda estória para a Rita" ("The Little Girl Without Words: Second Story for Rita")

This story is about a little girl who does not speak at all—much to her father's and mother's dismay and worry, as well as everyone else's in her community. In an attempt to make the little girl speak and in order to be able to communicate and connect with her, the father tries all kinds of methods: holds her hands tightly, addresses to her tenderly and patiently, implores her to speak, cries out of frustration, takes her to the beach, and finally decides to tell her what seems to be a very unrealistic story. In the end, the story proves to be the very medium that allows for the beginning of communication between father and daughter. The story opens like this:

> The little girl did not possess any words. No vowel would come out of her. Her lips were occupied only with sounds that did not add up to two or four.

Did she have a language that belonged only to her, her own personal and intransmissible dialect? Despite her parents' efforts, they were not able to achieve perception of the little girl. When she remembered the words she would forget the thought. When she constructed her reasoning she would lose her idiom. It wasn't that she was mute. She spoke in a language not available to the current humanity. There were people who thought she was singing. And it must be said, her voice was so beautiful as to enchant. Even if people could not understand anything, they would get imprisoned in the intonation. And it was so touching that there were always some who would cry.

A menina não palavreava. Nenhuma vogal lhe saía, seus lábios se ocupavam só em sons que não somavam dois nem quatro. Era uma língua só dela, um dialecto pessoal e instrasmixível? Por muito que se aplicassem, os pais não conseguiam percepção da menina. Quando lembrava as palavras ela esquecia o pensamento. Quando construía o raciocínio perdia o idioma. Não é que fosse muda. Falava em língua que nem há nesta actual humanidade. Havia quem pensasse que ela cantasse. Que se diga, sua voz era bela de encantar. Mesmo sem entender nada as pessoas ficavam presas na entonação. E era tão tocante que havia sempre quem chorasse. (87)

This story occupies a place of great importance in Couto's collection and, I suggest, even in Couto's overall writings. The story—a series of mise en abymes, a story within a story, within a story, within a story—can also be seen as the mise en abyme par excellence (the big Russian doll, as it were), for it brings to the forefront many of the cultural identity problems affecting contemporary Mozambique, and it even offers a solution for them. One of the main characteristics of stories which employ the mise en abyme as a medium, is that they aim at teaching the reader something. In the case of Couto's story, the teaching is in fact multidimensional—and the existence of the mise en abyme can be detected at many levels: structural, semantic, morphological, and symbolical. All these levels work together to give the story an even more unified and coherent character, which in itself is yet another mise en abyme and serves to further reinforce Couto's cultural agenda: the illustration (display) of the metaphysical, holistic conception of the world, as shared by traditional Mozambicans. Couto's use of language (and his storytelling techniques) also shows us how language assumes the character of a trickster and how such a quality serves different and very important purposes; it brings wonder to storytelling, it creates suspense, and it keeps our soul alive by connecting us with that which is beyond our reach, the uncanny. But the uncanny always remains uncanny: just like Couto's language, which is constantly playing tricks and evading our understanding (overstanding, that is). Couto's constant use of the mise en abyme, in all its different manifestations, ends up creating a very special effect. When reading the stories, some of us might have the impression that we are entering a circling or whirling dance, a cascade of sorts, a musical realm even, a place where we might feel detached from ourselves and experience the universe with all its powerful energy—as if we were in a state of trance or spiritual ecstasy. And so, Couto's writing teaches at least two things: that traditional (old) epistemologies have something wonderful to offer, and also that, when used well and "strangely," language can become the very medium that allows one to experience the beauty and power of what lies beyond our grasp and to reach spiritual fulfillment.

The subtitle of the story is "Second Story for Rita" ("Segunda estória para a Rita"). The title occupies a central importance in the story for it suggests that the "true" meaning of the story is not what might at first appear to be. Put differently, the true meaning is not, or at least not only, the first meaning, but the second meaning, or even the third or the fourth meaning. The true meaning is to be found in the metaphoric, the poetic, the unobvious, the hidden, the untold or unwritten even. Not only does the second (sub)title tell us literally that the story has a second story imbedded in itself, but it also appears within brackets, as if reinforcing once again (visually in the text) the idea of the importance of going beyond what we see and literally read throughout the story: the idea of looking beyond the material or real possibility, and ultimately, beyond language and its meaning—and this will become more clear as I develop my analysis of the story. Thus, the subtitle of the story is the very first mise en abyme of the many others that are displayed throughout the rest of story: it is the first Russian doll, enveloping the many other little ones that are to come out after our careful reading of the Great Mother, enveloping multiple twins in her womb. However, this argument only holds if we read the first title superficially. A more careful reading of the title will tell us that it already contains the second story of the story, for the title does not say that the little girl is mute, but rather that she possesses no words—which is not the same thing. In fact, being able to speak without words might be a better way of speaking, if we take into account the idea that words are only an arbitrary (and thus incomplete) system, invented by humans to name and comprehend that which is ultimately unnamable and incomprehensible to us in its true dimension. This reading of the first title makes sense, for in the story we do discover that the little girl speaks through musiclike sounds and thus, possesses a language, a system of communication. In that case then, the first title is already a big Russian doll with many little dolls inside, ready to be played with (or play "the player"). Or to use another metaphor, the fist title is the Great Mother, who wants all her babies to be born and yet, she also wants to keep them inside for protection just in case the child snatchers are around the corner (a mother always playing tricks with our minds or teasing us to disclose her various meanings while at the same time evading our understanding, in other words, overstanding us). Couto has stated the following: "The secret, in my case, is to transport the childhood. . . . We have all preserved in ourselves that childhood, which people have taught us how to tame, how to forget, how to look at as an unproductive place. Children do not fit well into our present concept of what it means to be productive, responsible. [Yet] that childhood has survived in all of us" ("O segredo, no meu caso, é transportar a meninice. . . . Todos nós temos essa infância guardada, que mais ou menos nos ensinam a domesticar, a esquecer, a olhar como lugar improdutivo. As crianças não se encaixam bem na ideia que é pedida hoje de ser rentável, responsável. [Mas] todos temos essa sobrevivência da infância" [qtd. in Jeremias, "O meu segredo" 2]). As the story tells us, the little girl does indeed possess a language, but one that no one understands. Why does no one understand it? Little girls (and little boys) often have a language of their own, one that is highly poetic, musical, and fluid and which does not obey the rules of adult language. As Julia Kristeva (see *Pouvoirs de l'horreur: essai sur l'abjection*) and Hélène Cixous (see *Three Steps on the Ladder of Writing*) (and now Couto) would put it, children speak a presymbolic language, a language which is detached from social connotations and where gender roles and other assigned social roles and classifications of the world, things, and people in general do not yet exist or are not yet formed. Children are close to what Kristeva (following Plato) calls the chora, that sacred or sacralized (and whole, in the sense of being unfragmented, undichotomized) side which allows them to listen to all their unconscious or subjective intelligence—imagination, instinct, emotion, body, and so on. That chora is broken, or at least suppressed and disrupted, when children enter the symbolic world of the adults which imposes roles, regulations, and classification on the world and people based on the so-called higher intelligence—reason, science, objectivity, culture, and so forth. This is why the adults do not quite understand children and the world they live in, and also the reason why one can suggest that the father of this little girl does not understand her. In this story, the father has entered the rational adult world and thus broken (or suppressed) his contact with the world of the little girl (the world of his "little boy," as it were)—a world which obeys different linguistic and cognition patterns. But his chora still exists inside of him: it is "preserved" (kept) somewhere, as Couto suggests and it only needs to be brought to the surface. In psychoanalytical terms, this loosely means that the chora of the little boy (father) has been pushed to the very back of his unconscious; it has been repressed because adult life and society do not value or favor it, and in fact consider it immature and inferior to the so-called higher intelligences associated with adult life.

The father loves his little girl (and his little boy) dearly and so he wants to "find" them, to understand them, to reconnect with them. He suffers immensely from the fact that he cannot speak to and reach them. The father knows (senses, feels) that the language spoken by them is beautiful: "so beautiful as to enchant," so beautiful as to "imprison [him and other people] in the intonation," and so "touching" that it has the power to make one cry (87). It is a language that sounds more like a song, a song of yearning for something beautiful and powerful and good—something that one has lost and wants back madly—but does not really know how to bring or call back to us. The song-language sung by the little girl awakens in the father a powerful urge, an almost visceral need; it is like a demand, seemingly as strong as the one expressed in Derek Walcott's poem "Sainte Lucie": "come back to me, my language, come back cacao, grigri, solitaire, ciseau the scissor-bird" (*Collected Poems* 309). "Speak to me daughter!" ("Fala comigo filha!" [87]), says the father to the girl. It is the magnitude of the father's urge that makes him search for ways to communicate with his daughter (just like Walcott makes use of all kinds of words [i.e., French,

English, Spanish, Creole] in an attempt to create a language that will "tell him" as accurately as any language can allow):

> Her father would dedicate a lot of attention to her, afflicted by her inability to speak. One night he held her hands tightly and implored, certain that he was speaking to himself:—*Speak to me daughter!* His eyes gave in. The little girl kissed the tear. She tasted and enjoyed that salty water and said:—*Sea*. . . . The father was surprised from mouth to hear. Had she spoken? He jumped and shook his daughter's elbows. *See, you can speak, she speaks, she speaks*! He would scream so that people could hear him. *She said sea, she said sea*, the father would repeat throughout the house. The relatives came running and leaned over her. But no other intelligible sound was announced. The father could not accept this situation. He thought and rethought and he came up with a plan. He took his daughter to where there was sea and more sea beyond the sea. If that had been the only word that she had articulated in all her life, then it would be in the sea that one would unveil the reason behind her inability.

> Seu pai lhe dedicava muita afeição e aflição. Uma noite lhe apertou as mãozinhas e implorou, certo que falava sozinho:—*Fala comigo filha!* Os olhos dele deslizaram. A menina beijou a lágrima. Gostoseou aquela água salgada e disse:—*Mar*. . . . O pai espantou-se de boca e orelha. Ela falara? Deu um pulo e sacudiu os ombros da filha. *Vês, tu falas, ela fala, ela fala!* Gritava para que se ouvisse. *Disse mar, ela disse mar,* repetia o pai pelos aposentos. Acorreram os familiares e se debruçaram sobre ela. Mas mais nenhum som entendível se anunciou. O pai não se conformou. Pensou e repensou e elaborou um plano. Levou a filha para onde havia mar e mar depois do mar. Se havia sido a única palavra que ela articulara em toda a sua vida seria, então, no mar que se descortinaria a razão da inabilidade. (87-88)

The communication between father and daughter is hard to achieve. Yet, the need for that communication to happen is of such profound and demanding that it forces the father to keep searching deeper and deeper inside himself, in order to find the language, the "magic" word that will "speak" to his daughter. Finally, he does come to a brilliant idea: to tell his daughter a story. This idea works. The idea of the story comes to the father because it had in fact never left him; it was in some part of his unconscious self and just needed to be called back to conscious life (awareness): it was there, underneath, like a latent, soft lullaby, just waiting and wanting to be brought to the surface, so that the father could feel the wonder again—the wonder of feeling whole, connected, unbroken, the wonder of entering the choric realm. The reason why the song-language of the little girl is able to reach the subconscious of the father is because music (like poetry) functions as the presymbolic language or way of communicating, which has the power to liberate us from societal (conscious) constraints and allows us to go deeper inwards. In fact, the language of the little girl is both music and poetry since it is a sound that resembles music and it also has a metaphorical meaning which the listeners cannot understand, but a meaning that exists nonetheless, and which needs to be understood through the unconscious intelligences that cannot truly be captured via conventional language:

It was then that it came to him: his daughter could only be saved by a story! And right there he invented one, like this: Once upon a time a little girl asked her father to catch the moon for her. The father took a boat and sailed far away. When he arrived at the place where the horizon meets the sea, he put himself at the tip of his dreams so that he could reach the heights. He held the celestial body with his two hands and a thousand cares. The planet was light as a female-balloon. When he pulled, to tear away that fruit of the sky, a bursting-world could be heard. The moon was shattered in a thousand star-like particles. The sea foamed, the boat sunk, swollen up in an abyss. The beach became covered with silver, flakes of moonlight covering the sands. The little girl started walking contrary to all directions, there and beyond, collecting the lunar pieces. She looked at the horizon and called:—*Father!* Then, a deep crack opened on the ground, the scar of the earth's own birth. From the lips of that scar blood was shedding. Was the water bleeding? Was the blood watering? And so it was. That was once. When he arrived at that point the father lost voice and became quiet. The story had lost its string and thread inside his head. Or perhaps it was the cold from the water which was already covering his feet, and the legs of his daughter? And in a desperate state, he said:—*Now, it will never be.* Right away and very quickly, the little girl got up and walked through the waves. The father followed her, scared. He saw his daughter pointing at the sea. It was then that he could vislumbrate it: in the entire extension of the ocean, a deep crack. The father was surprised with that unexpected fracture, fantastic mirror of the story he had just invented. A deep strange fear invaded his entrails. Would it be in that abyss that they would both disappear?—*Daughter please, come back. Slow down, daughter, please* . . . Rather than stepping back, the little girl penetrated further into the sea. Then, she stopped and passed her hand through the water. The liquid scar closed itself, instantaneously. And the sea restored itself, it became one. The little girl walked back, took her father's hand and guided him back home. Above, the moon recomposed itself.—*See father? I finished your story.* And both of them, illuminated, vanished from the room, which they had never left.

Foi quando lhe ocorreu: sua filha só podia ser salva por uma história! E logo ali lhe inventou uma, assim: Era uma vez uma menina que pediu ao pai que fosse apanhar a lua para ela. O pai meteu-se num barco e remou para longe. Quando chegou à dobra do horizonte pôs-se em bicos de sonhos para alcançar as alturas. Segurou o astro com as duas mãos, com mil cuidados. O planeta era leve como uma baloa. Quando ele puxou para arrancar aquele fruto do céu se escutou um rebentamundo. A lua se cintilhaçou em mil estrelinhações. O mar se encrespou, o barco se afundou, engolido num abismo. A praia se cobriu de prata, flocos de luar cobriam o areal. A menina se pôs a andar ao contrário de todas as direções, para lá e para além, recolhendo os pedaços lunares. Olhou o horizonte e chamou:—*Pai!* Então, se abriu uma fenda profunda, a ferida da nascença da própria terra. Dos lábios dessa cicatriz se derramava sangue. A água sangrava? O sangue se aguava? E foi assim. Essa foi uma vez. Chegando a este ponto, o pai perdeu voz e se calou. A história tinha perdido fio e meada dentro da sua cabeça. Ou seria o frio da água já cobrindo os pés dele, as pernas da sua filha? E ele, em desespero:—*Agora é que nunca.* A menina, nesse repente, se ergueu e avançou por dentro das ondas. O pai a seguiu temedroso. Viu a filha apontar o mar.

> Então ele vislumbrou, em toda a extensão do oceano, uma fenda profunda. O pai se espantou com aquela fractura, espelho fantástico da história que ele acabava de inventar. Um medo fundo lhe estranhou as entranhas. Seria naquele abismo que eles ambos se escoariam?—*Filha, venha para trás. Se atrase, filha, por favor* . . . Ao invés de recuar a menina se adentrou mais no mar. Depois, parou e passou a mão pela água. A ferida líquida se fechou, instantânea. E o mar se refez, um. A menina voltou atrás, pegou na mão do pai e o conduziu de rumo a casa. No cimo, a lua se recompunha.—*Viu, pai? Eu acabei a sua história!* E os dois, iluminados, se extinguiram no quarto de onde nunca haviam saído. (89)

The story told to the little girl is a story where doubt is suspended: a story that in fact makes and gives sense to the world, without concerning itself with truth boundaries. It is a story (seemingly) very unrealistic which merges the real and the imaginary, reason and unreason, possible and impossible; it is a story full of trickery, as if we were in fact dealing with a real trickster who is constantly tricking us into believing things that are unreal or seemingly opposite. As Lewis Hyde puts it, "The trickster is a boundary-crosser" (7), the one who blurs distinctions and connections between "right and wrong, sacred and profane, clean and dirty, male and female, young and old, living and dead" (7). The bridge between such opposites can, of course, be questioned, if we argue that the stories or histories or theories that explain the world and ourselves to ourselves are in fact all human makings—made out of an arbitrary language system—and so we end up with all kinds of "fabulous" stories about who we are, what we must do, feel, eat, dress and how it is that the world or universe "really" functions. As well reasoned by Chamberlin in *If This Is Your Land, Where Are Your Stories?*, many (if not all) of the stories (and thus histories) informing and giving sense to our lives, are make-up or made-up fables, which serve to ease our existential nausea, hide our ignorance, fragility, and fears of the unknown—and yet, also fables that make us feel at home and give sense and purpose to our lives.

Couto's first lesson then is that we must all try to reconnect with the world of our childhood, the world of wonder, the world of the chora—it is a lesson for all the adults of the world. But the story aims at much more than that. The story can (and should) be read as a direct exponent of the sociocultural context of contemporary Mozambique, its dilemmas, epistemological and ontological splits. The use of the little girl and father metaphor in this story can be taken as another trick used by Couto to point to the multiple meanings of his stories. Before further exploring the direct relationship of this story with the Mozambican sociocultural context, I must bring up another story also included in the collection.

"A luavezinha: primeira estória para a Rita" ("The Little-moon Bird: First Story for Rita")

This story precedes "The Little Girl Without Words" and bears the title of "The Little Moon-bird: First Story for Rita" ("A luavezinha: primeira estória para a Rita"). This means, of course, that "The Little Girl Without Words" can be taken as a continuation of the first story—a reasoning reinforced by the fact that it has the subtitle of "Second Story for Rita." This does not invalidate my previous argument pertaining to the subtitle of the second story and its function as the first mise en abyme of the second story. It actually reinforces it by suggesting that each single story in Couto's collection always contains multiple messages or stories in it, and that what each story says is always incomplete: its meaning always surpasses what it openly says, what the eye can directly catch. Furthermore, the first story ends with the question "And then what happens father?" ("E depois pai?"), further indication that the story has not been completed (at least not according to the little girl, who was receiving it from the father). In fact, in the first story the father is frustrated with the little girl, for every night she demands a story from him and when he tells her one, she never seems satisfied with its ending and always asks the same (stubborn) question: "And then father what happens?" At the structural level, the first story also contains two stories: the one about the girl and the one about the bird.

After telling the little girl several stories, and not being able to satisfy her constant thirst for knowledge or wonder, the father decides to tell her the story of a bird whose dream is to fly to the moon. It is a very unrealistic dream and the bird is constantly mocked by other birds for having such a grand and absurd desire. Yet, on a bright night of full moon, and against all the odds, the adventurous bird decides to take off and fly to the moon. After flying for what seems to be a long time and having lost all sense of time, space and distance, the bird finally lands on the moon. The bird soon discovers that there is no night on the moon and so it cannot sleep, which is why the bird is forced to be in a state of constant vigil—a tiring state that prevents it from sleeping, dreaming, and entering the world of the imagination and wonder. And so the bird yearns to return to the earth. But when it tries to fly, it discovers that it can no longer do that; it cannot sing or move either—it has become part of the moon (petrified by it) and is thus condemned to live there forever in sad solitude:

> My daughter has a painful time falling asleep. No one knows the fears that sleep brings to her. Every night I am called to my duty as a father and I invent her a lullaby. I always perform that duty poorly. When I am about to put end to the story she asks me for more:—*And then what happens?* What Rita wants is for the entire world to fall asleep. And she always argues a dream that might happen in her sleep: she wants to become the moon. The little girl wants to travel to the moon, and, she tells the two of us, so that I become the land, and she the moon. The Mozambican traditions are still inflating her lunar courtship. . . . Once upon a time a little bird was dreaming in its little roost. It would look at the moonlight and it would make fantasies go up in the sky. Its dream would become more immense:—*I will land there, on the moon.* The others would call it to the earthy reality. But the little bird, would rave, foolishly insisting: I am going to go up there, above and further than the firmaments. Its branch colleagues would laugh: that was no more than child-play. Everyone knew: no flight would be sufficient to win that distance. But the dreaming little bird did not take pity. It wanted to reach the moon. So it all amounted to nothing. On a given night, of full moon, it launched itself to the skies, full of dream. And it flew, and flew and flew. It

lost count of time. At a given moment it did not know whether if was going up, or falling down. Its senses became all twisted. Had it fainted? Or did it dream that it was dreaming? But the truth is that its body was shaken by a clash against another body. And it landed on that land of the moon, immense petrified savannah. . . . That's why today we still see, there, in the silver of the moon, the starry pupil of the dreaming little bird. And no creature, except the night, can hear the song of the moony little bird. In the first leaves of the morning, the drops of dew fall. They are little tears of the bird that dreamed of landing on the moon.—*And then father?*

Minha filha tem um adormecer custoso. Ninguém sabe os medos que o sono acorda nela. Cada noite sou chamado a pai e invento-lhe um embalo. Desse encargo me saio sempre mal. Já vou pontuando fim na história quando ela me pede mais—*E depois?* O que Rita quer é que o mundo inteiro seja adormecido. E ela sempre argumenta um sonho de encontro ao sono: quer ser lua. A menina quer luarejar e, os dois, faz contarmo-nos assim, eu terra, ela lua. As tradições moçambicanas ainda lhe aumentam o namoro lunar. . . . Era uma avezita que sonhava em seu poleirinho. Olhava o luar e fazia subir fantasias pelo céu. Seu sonho se imensidava:—*Hei-de pousar lá, na lua.* Os outros lhe chamavam à térrea realidade. Mas o passarinho devaneava, insistonto: vou subir lá, mais acima que os firmamentos. Seus colegas de galho se riam: não havia voo que bastasse para vencer aquela distância. Mas o passarinho sonhador não se compadecia. Ele queria luarar-se. Pelo que o tudo ficava nada. Certa noite, de lua inteira, se lançou nos céus, cheio de sonho. E voou, voou, voou. Perdeu conta do tempo. Em certo momento ele não sabia se subia, se tombava. Seus sentidos se enrolavam uns nos outros. Desmaiou? Ou sonhou que sonhava? Certo é que seu corpo foi sacudido pelo embate de um outro corpo. E pousou naquela terra da lua, imensa savana pétrea. . . . É assim que ainda hoje se vê, lá na prata da lua, a pupila estrelinhada do passarinho sonhador. E nenhuma criatura, a não ser a noite, escuta o canto da avezinha enluarada. Sobre as primeiras folhas da madrugada, tombam gotas de cacimbo. São lagriminhas do pássaro que sonhou pousar na lua.—*E depois, pai?* (67-69).

The story about the bird is of course also the story about the little girl and her constant craving for stories of wonder: like the bird, the little girl seems to have dreams, needs and wishes that are far too big for her minute human capacity. What the father wants to teach the little girl is that she cannot be both human and nonhuman, both a girl and the moon: she can only be one or the other, and her greedy wish to become both can in fact lead her to lose the abilities she has as a human being, which allow her to speak, move, and sing. The father's story seems to suggest that only people (and to a certain extent animals) have life: the other bodies, such as the moon are petrified, lifeless entities. It is the "moony" ("enluarado") character of the bird (and little girl) that makes it lose its quality as a bird and become petrified and lifeless. The adjective "enluarado," used to describe the bird here, has a second meaning; it is yet another Russian doll, for it implies that the bird suffered from mad ideas, reason why it wanted to fly to the moon. In Portuguese, when someone is angry or reacts in an unpredictable way, we often say that the person "está de lua," literally meaning "is with moon" or "está enluarado" ("is moony") or "está com a lua" ("is with the moon"). All of these expressions imply that that the person is mad and has lost the ability to reason properly: he or she is a lunatic.

Thus, the first story has many messages, many mises en abyme. At first glance, it points to the idea that when one has a dream, a need or a wish, one should try to fulfill it, and if one cannot realistically fulfill it, one must resort to the power of the imagination in order to get it, for the imagination can have the power to satisfy our most grand desires. If it happens in the realm of the imagination, it becomes as real and as fulfilling as if it were to happen in actual reality, as Derek Walcott would say. Yet a more careful reading of the story reveals that too much dreaming and unreasonable desires leads us to madness and the loss of humanness. An analysis of the morphology of the words forming the first title of the story will also show us that the story has at least two meanings (two more little Russian dolls ready to play), again reinforcing the idea that stories and words possess secondary hidden meanings— meanings which we must aim at understanding (or connect with) so that we can have access to the wonder of the infinite, the mystical, the wonder of "overstanding," as the Rastafarian might put it. First, "A luavezinha" ("the little moon-bird") can be read as "luavizinha" ("moon-neighbor"), a reading that will point to the cosmic holistic conception of the universe shared by many Mozambican groups: it implies that all the planets are deeply connected and close to each other, and that the earth is in fact near the moon, like a sister of sorts. By extension, this also implies that birds and humans are part of the greater order and that is why they feel the urge to go beyond their human and animal limits and connect with the rest of the universe, a universe that corresponds to their larger self, their distended ego. Moreover, given the closeness between the words "luavezinha" ("little moon-bird") and "levezinha" ("very light"), we can suggest that the story also wants to point to the fact that the human mind (our spirit and imagination) is very light—so light in fact, that it can fly away, travel and enter other world orders, other realities, and thus experience the wonder of what lies beyond our physical reach. The story did not satisfy the little girl precisely because the imagination of the father was not light (flexible) enough to travel beyond the moon and liberate the bird, not light enough to be able to allow the bird to be both bird and moon, that is. So, in the end the story is telling us that the bird was not the prisoner of the moon but rather the prisoner of the father's imagination. For, even though the imagination of the father was flexible enough to allow the bird to fly to the moon, it was not flexible enough to allow the bird to roam freely wherever it wanted. It is an inflexible imagination that only allows the bird to either be a bird or the moon, but never both: it compartimentalizes reality, it separates that which yearns to be together, to be whole. It is precisely because of the inflexibility of the father's imagination that the little girl remains unsatisfied with the story and demands more with the question "and then father?" Ultimately, the little girl is the metaphor for the Mozambican land, its people, and their holistic or sacralized conception of the universe. The little girl is the nation of Mozambique and the father represents the governing elite of colonial and postcolonial states. But the constantly repeated question of the little girl, "and then father?" also has multiple meanings and functions: it is another trickster. On the one hand, it alludes to the dissatisfaction (and loss of wonder) experienced by Mozambicans who have had their culture and way of thinking dismissed and shattered by the new, modern, secularized, compartmentalized, Western order. And on the other hand, and because of its constant repetition, the question actually reestablishes that same Mozambican world order: the repetition causes us to feel that whirling effect mentioned previously—the effect of something that has no end, like a cascade where all parts are interrelated and work to produce a holistic and sacralized conception of life and the universe. Again, Couto is killing at least two birds with one stone (or two rabbits with a single stroke, as we say in Portuguese).

Yet the father feels the dissatisfaction of the little girl, for ultimately that dissatisfaction refers to himself and his lack of communication with his nation and his people, his realization as a full person who can embrace that which is African and internal and not just what comes from the exterior. It is precisely because of the dissatisfaction of both father and daughter that the father comes back with another story, a second story, which as it turns out, proves to be much more effective. The little girl's muteness is related to the fact that the new order governing the country does not value or really understand the old Mozambican epistemologies. It is not purely a matter of the semantics of the language: the fact that Mozambicans speak Bantu languages and the elite Portuguese—although that also plays a role of course, as already demonstrated in the analysis of the story, "Governed by the Dead." The colonial and postcolonial powers follow a more European line of thought, which gives primacy to reason, objectivity, culture, and conscious forces and tends to see emotion, subjectivity, nature, and unconscious forces as inferior cognitive and epistemological mechanisms associated with backwardness and underdevelopment. If the European line of thought is not subdued by the Mozambican African line of thought, and if the elite governing the country continues to impose and promote foreign languages and foreign values and disregard African ones, Mozambique will not really be able to emerge; it will not be able to be born as a truer and more authentic postcolonial nation, which values the endogenic and is not merely following the exogenic.

In the story, Couto actually goes so as far as to solve the issue of separation between the world of the father and that of the little girl, the world of the Mozambican colonial or postcolonial state and its citizens and thus the culturally and linguistically alienated situation of most Mozambicans. The Kristevan choric self now becomes symbol of the Mozambican land: its people and its traditions, a self that must be reawakened to feed and teach the new order—a choric self that had been relegated to the periphery of the states's interests in the name of modernization and civilization. If we remember back to the story, "Governed by the Dead," we will notice that that story already gives us a sneak preview of that Mozambican choric self. There, we have the urban man travelling inwards to meet and learn from the old man. The physical voyage of the urban person symbolizes his willingness to reconnect and rediscover his land and its traditions: he is literally going into the hinterlands where most people live to listen to what they have to say. Thus the urban man is also travelling to (descending into) his unconscious where all the old knowledge has been stored, for he has been obliged to repress it, due to the fact that it has been undervalued by the new colonial and postcolonial orders. Moreover, the urban man's voyage to the hinterlands also possesses a grander symbolic meaning: in its raw physicality, force, mystery, and danger, the land he is now entering symbolizes his immersion in the greater order of the universe—in the holistic and sacred realm, where man and land become part of one unbroken order; he is thus entering the precolonial African conception of life and the universe. This is further reinforced by what the old man tells the urban one about the flamingo, for example, which is presented as the creature that unites earth and sky, and ultimately God, and all its uncanny signifiers. The choric self then, becomes the universe at large, where all the elements are joined and where the human self becomes decentered, only to experience what can be termed as the force of the universe, or God. This choric self is what in astronomy would correspond to the time before the big bang, or in Zen terms would equate to the "all in one." In its original Platonic sense, the chora refers to that place that merges all the elements: air, water, earth, fire, a place of high power and energy that will give origin to everything—this is why Plato calls it the "nurse of all becoming and change" (*Timaeus and Critias* 67). In Christian terms, these would loosely equate to the "De Profundis" of Psalm 129. All these senses of the choric self are similar to each other, which only serves to show that different traditions (Western and otherwise) do in fact share many of the same underlying beliefs.

Thus, from the child's choric self, Couto moves us to the adult (repressed) choric self, to the Mozambican (repressed) choric self, and then he shows us (discloses) all the choras and the wonder that lies there awaiting to be embraced: he is the teacher, teaching us how to dance in the whirls of the greater or larger life. The language sung by the little girl made people cry because it reminded them of Mozambican choric self, the self that they had forgotten how to connect with and buried deep inside themselves. Their cry symbolizes their loss and profound yearning and desire to reconnect with the grand order of the universe their ancestors once had. That is why the father goes to great extent to (re)learn the language of the little girl. It is important to note that it is the emotion of the father that first speaks to the little girl. Despite the fact that the father had tried all kinds of words and ways to communicate with the little girl, she had remained mute, seemingly deaf and apathetic to his efforts. Yet when the father cries, "she tastes and enjoys" (87) the salty water of his tear and mumbles what seems to be her very first intelligible word: "sea." What this means is that we must allow ourselves to connect with our emotions, for emotions are often ways to express and fulfill our deepest (unconscious) needs and desires: emotions have their own, and very smart "reason." The tear can thus symbolize the priority of the "overstanding" versus the "understanding." Put differently, words will always be pointing to something else and are not capable of capturing the true meaning of things, thus pointing to the hidden power of all that exists. The tear, on he other hand, which is something we can see, functions as a real language—it is a visible thing that speaks through itself, without needing to use conventional language to say (express) what it means, thus becoming a universal way of expressing sorrow, a way of "overstanding" language barriers between cultures, therefore bringing people closer and reducing difference.

On a larger symbolical level, the tear shed by the father has many other meanings. Being a fluid substance, the tear can symbolize the letting go of the individual self and the entering in the choric or cosmic self. This is further supported by the fact that it is by the sea that the girl will finally find a way to speak and be understood by the father. The house (the father) represented the individualized human self which tends to dichotomize and separate things, whereas the sea represents the decentered or choric self. The sea is the place that can "liquidize" (dissolve) both the father and the girl so that they can finally enter the larger cosmic realm. In his book, *A Postcolonial Nationalist*, Rothwell discusses the importance and constant presence of water in Couto's writings and its frequent association with the unconscious realm, that place that allows one to access dream and imagination, to "encounter" all possibilities, to "sea" into the unconscious, as he puts it (91-132). It is in the sea that we witness the disintegration of the entire world. It is in the sea that all becomes shattered and the order of the universe is lost but also reestablished: it is there that we witness the "all becoming one" or the "one becoming all" (as the Buddhists might put it), and thus the restoration of the holistic African conception of the universe. The moon breaks down, the sea opens up and the earth bleeds. Blood becomes indistinguishable from water and water indistinguishable from blood. Sand becomes silver and silver becomes sand. It is the end of the world. Or so the father thought. But then the little girl takes charge of the story and literally jumps inside it to help the father reconstruct the cosmic order, to literally give birth to the land:

> The little girl started walking contrary to all directions, there and beyond, collecting the lunar pieces. She looked at the horizon and called:—*Father!* Then, a deep crack opened on the ground, the scar of the earth's own birth. From the lips of that scar blood was shedding. Was the water bleeding? Was the blood watering? And so it was. That was once. When he arrived at that point the father lost voice and became quiet. The story had lost its string and thread inside his head. Or perhaps it was the cold from the water which was already covering his feet, and the legs of his daughter? And in a desperate state, he said:—*Now, it will never be.*
>
> A menina se pôs a andar ao contrário de todas as direções, para lá e para além, recolhendo os pedaços lunares. Olhou o horizonte e chamou:—*Pai!* Então, se abriu uma fenda profunda, a ferida da nascença da própria terra. Dos lábios dessa cicatriz se derramava sangue. A água sangrava? O sangue se aguava? E foi assim. Essa foi uma vez. Chegando a este ponto, o pai perdeu voz e se calou. A história tinha perdido fio e meada dentro da sua cabeça. Ou seria o frio da água já cobrindo os pés dele, as pernas da sua filha? E ele, em desespero:—*Agora é que nunca.* (89)

Once again, and as in the first story, the father's imagination has not been flexible enough to continue the story he is telling. His rational and compartmentalized self, not used to intricate exercises of the mind, becomes numb: it loses the story's "string" and "thread." He is flexible enough to disrupt the order of the world, but not ingenious enough to reestablish it again. He becomes afraid of the unknown, of that which cannot be measured in rational terms: he becomes afraid of his unconscious, of the dark places of the world, of the universe at large which he cannot measure in human (and Western) quantities, for it escapes his smallness. The little girl is the one who saves both of them and the world from finally disappearing:

> Right away and very quickly, the little girl got up and walked through the waves. The father followed her, scared. He saw his daughter pointing at the sea. It was then that he could vislumbrate it: in the entire extension of the ocean, a deep crack. The father was surprised with that unexpected fracture, fantastic mirror of the story he had just invented. A deep strange fear invaded his entrails. Would it be in that abyss that they would both disappear?—*Daughter please, come back. Delay yourself, daughter, please.*

> A menina, nesse repente, se ergueu e avançou por dentro das ondas. O pai a seguiu temedroso. Viu a filha apontar o mar. Então ele vislumbrou, em toda a extensão do oceano, uma fenda profunda. O pai se espantou com aquela fractura, espelho fantástico da história que ele acabava de inventar. Um medo fundo lhe estranhou as entranhas. Seria naquele abismo que eles ambos se escoariam?—*Filha, venha para trás. Se atrase, filha, por favor.* (89)

At the structural level, this story (like the first one) contains more than one story. It has at least three: the one told being told to Rita about the little girl who did not speak, the one about Rita (or is it the little girl of the story being told?) literally taking over and finishing the father's story, and the one told in the last line, indicating that father and daughter had never left the room, even though we might have thought they did—further proof that it is the imagination that "makes" things happen, it makes them visible through the eye of the mind or spirit, thus giving sense to the world, and it does so through a certain usage of language and storytelling that relay a certain thought system. This story, like the first one, further reinforces the idea that imagination is indeed very powerful, and that words give meaning and sense to that which is meaningless and disorganized: words weave the world, literally inventing it for us, giving sense to the senseless, and they ultimately have the power to make us feel safe at home:

> Rather than stepping back, the little girl penetrated further into the sea. Then, she stopped and passed her hand through the water. The liquid scar closed itself, instantaneously. And the sea restored itself, it became one. The little girl walked back, took her father's hand and guided him back home. Above, the moon recomposed itself.—*See father? I finished your story.* And both of them, illuminated, vanished from the room which they had never left.

> Ao invés de recuar a menina se adentrou mais no mar. Depois, parou e passou a mão pela água. A ferida líquida se fechou, instantânea. E o mar se refez, um. A menina voltou atrás, pegou na mão do pai e o conduziu de rumo a casa. No cimo, a lua se recompunha.—*Viu, pai? Eu acabei a sua história!* E os dois, iluminados, se extinguiram no quarto de onde nunca haviam saído. (89)

The story also serves to show the central importance of orally transmitted knowledge in traditional African cultures; it shows that the mere act of telling a story makes the events being told real; in other words, it demonstrates the magical power of storytelling and language. This magical power can also apply to written stories for, as already mentioned, language is capable of creating an entire world system, of giving meaning to that which has none a priori. On the other hand, we can say that oral stories, as told in the African tradition, carry a more profound effect in the sense that they are accompanied by an entire performance which often physically reenacts the event being told, making it more real, present, and complete. As Bâ puts it, "One peculiarity of the African memory is its restoring the recorded event in its entirety, like a film that unreels from beginning to end, and restoring it in the present. It is a matter not of remembering, but of bringing up into the present a past event in which everyone participates—the person who is reciting and his audience. The whole art of the storyteller lies in that. No one is a storyteller unless he can report a thing as it happened 'live' in such a way that his hearers, like himself, become new living, active witnesses of it" (Unesco, *A General History of Africa* 109). It is precisely this "entirety," the restoring of the past event "in the present" and the "bringing up into the present a past event" pointed out by Bâ that Couto's tries to reconstruct in the story of the little girl, proving thus that he is really engaged in recreating the reality of the orality of African tradition into his written storytelling. The father and the girl do indeed "literately" participate in the story in different ways: he enters the story to try and tell it as it should be told but he fails to do so because he cannot remember or use the eye of the imagination, the eye of the spirit sufficiently, thus breaking the order of the universe, at which point his daughter enters the story to reestablish the cosmic balance that had been at risk because of her father's "inability" or "forgetfulness." Since the order of the universe had been disrupted because the living did not remember the language of the ancestors (and consequently their values and conception of the world), as the father's incapacity to finish the story he started literally illustrates, some "magic action" needed to take place. To quote Bâ yet again:

> Magic action, that is, the manipulation of forces, [is] generally aimed at restoring the troubled balance, reestablishing the harmony . . . man had been set up as guardian by his creator. . . . Good magic, the magic of initiates and "masters of knowledge," aims at purifying men, animals and objects so as to put forces back into order. This is where the force of speech is decisive. For just as Maa Ngala's [God, the Creator] divine speech animated the cosmic forces that lay static in Maa, so man's speech animates, sets into motion and rouses the forces that are static in things. But for the spoken words to produce their full effect they must be chanted rhythmically, because movement needs rhythm, which is itself based on the secret of numbers. Speech must reproduce the to-and-fro that is the essence of rhythm. In ritual songs and incantatory formulae, therefore, speech is the materialization of cadence. And it is considered as having the power to act on spirits, that is because the harmony creates movements, movements which generate forces, those forces are then acting on spirits which themselves are powers for action. In African tradition, speech, deriving its creative operative power from the

sacred, is in direct relation with the maintenance or the rupture of harmony in man and the world about him. (Unesco, *A General History of Africa* 171-72)

The little girl is the one who possesses the magic speech, the formulae capable of restoring the order of the universe. She is the one who can teach the father and make him relearn the sacred language of the ancestors, the one who like the Creator, is capable of "animating the cosmic forces that lay static in [the father, the land]," to use Bâ's own words. The very fact that she speaks in a songlike language, and that she moves inside the story, signals her adherence to, and awareness of, the importance of rhythm and movement. She knows that rhythm and movement must accompany speech in order to produce the right animation of the forces that lay asleep: music, with its intonations, cadences, and movements, becomes intertwined with words producing more of a sound than a distinguishable language—and constitutes precisely the magic formulae that will make the miracle of creation "happen." The following poem, entitled "Awakening of Words" ("Despertar de palavras"), by the contemporary Mozambican poet and academic, Raul Calane da Silva, illustrates the importance of magic speech, its relation to music, poetry, rhythm, and movement, and how all of that is intrinsically tied to a holistic and divine (or highly transcendental) perception of the world:

> The awakened word has awakened me. Suddenly I rediscover that it was divine. I become conscious that it was born sound and free. All the light belonging to it, all the infinite making it creative. The awakened word has rediscovered me in a body, in a mind. Body and mind understand: both are at the service of the practice of the Truth, of the Indivisible and of the Absolute. The word awakened and rediscovered itself reconfirming to me that it is Creating Energy, Fecund and Unifying, Energy of Love.
>
> A palavra despertada, despertou-me. De repente redescobri que era divina. Tomo consciência de que nasceu sã e livre. Toda a luz lhe pertencia, todo o infinito a tornava criativa. A palavra despertada redescobriu-me num corpo, numa mente. Corpo e mente compreendem: ambos estão ao serviço da prática da Verdade, do Indivisível e do Absoluto. A palavra despertou e redescobriu-se redescobrindo-me que é a Energia Criadora, Fecundante e Unficadora, Energia do Amor (91).

The magic formulae referred to by Bâ and used by the little girl to establish the order of the universe is comparable to the Buddhist mantra, "Om ah Hum" for instance, often used in meditation to reach enlightenment or contemplation of the ultimate reality, the state when one moves beyond words and sees the reality through the spirit, a reality that is whole and undivided. Furthermore, the story does in fact literally illustrate the African holistic conception of the universe: the re-integration of the universe we witness at the beach, speaks to the interrelation of all life. We see how the father, who had deviated from the African holistic conception of the universe through the internalization of Western values, proves incapable of finishing the story and thus of reestablishing the order of the African universe. The girl, on the other hand, is closer to the African choric self; she is able to "see" the interrelation of all things and is thus capable of restoring the order of the universe—an order that her father had disrupted. This is why we are told that the girl "took her father's hand and guided him back home" (89). She guides him home because she shows him the power of words, the power of imagination, the power of the whole undivided self, and also the power (and fulfillment) that can be attained when one returns to, or is reconnected with the values of our land, our country and our culture.

In her detailed study of Mia Couto and the Antillean Édouard Glissant, titled *O Entrelaçar das Vozes Mestiças,* Celina Martins discusses what she calls "The Sherazade Effect: The Braid-Stories" ("O efeito Xerazade: os contos-trança") to demonstrate how Couto's writing is characterized by a poetics of hybridity—the existence of a plurality of meanings, stories and messages that can be detected on several planes of the structural, semantic, and linguistic nexus. Such poetics entails the frequent use of neologisms, the constant recourse to the metaphorical which gives primacy to the poetic, the paradoxal, the allegoric, the dream, the subjective, the efabulative, and the language of hyperbolism, all of which serve to create a poetics of delayed revelation. Martins adds that Couto's writing creates a narrative in which the reworking of Portuguese or Bantu proverbs becomes possible in order to inscribe new meanings that frequently have didactic ends serving to attack colonialism or put forward an Afrocentric episteme—and a narrative that also permits the inscription of oral modes into writing as well as the mixing of journalistic modes with fictional ones. This "braiding" ("entrelaçar") of linguistic and narrative techniques allows for the existence of numerous micro narratives to coexist transforming Couto's writing in an infinite series of mise en abymes: "The writing of Mia Couto is characterized by an exploration of the potentialities of the interweaving technique. It is this metaphor of the braid, the incessant braiding of thematic threads that best expresses the mise en abyme of the code ('[A] escrita de Mia Couto distingue-se por explorar as potencialidades do entrelaçamento. É a metáfora da trança, isto é, o entrelaçar incessante de fios temáticos, que melhor exprime a mise en abyme do código [Martins 306]). This technique is indeed a fundamental trait of Couto's narratives, as my analysis of the three stories of *Contos* has demonstrated, and aims at creating or supporting the idea of a multicultural Mozambique where the language and culture of the former master is no longer speaking from one single viewpoint but is imbedded with multiple voicing that reflects the pluri-ethnic reality of contemporary Mozambique. Moreover, this multiplicity of voicing, which is very heteroglossic and dialogical in the Bakhtinian sense (see *The Dialogical Imagination*), also alludes to the idea that Mozambique is a country that is not yet—a country in the process of becoming, of finding itself, and thus Couto's writing is also only an exploration of the identity of the country but not the final one. As Couto states, "Mozambique is a seed that is constantly wrapping itself around a new fruit. When we think we have figured out its identity an unexpected dimension reveals itself." ('Moçambique é um caroço que está sempre inventando um fruto ao seu redor. Quando acreditamos ter adivinhado a sua identidade surge uma dimensão inesperada (qtd. in Martins 369).

Chapter Two

The Politics of Agency in Saramago

Reviving the Female and Building Relational and Phenomenological Ethics in Saramago's *O ano da morte de Ricardo Reis* (*The Year of the Death of Ricardo Reis*)

Saramago's *O ano da morte de Ricardo Reis* revolves around the life, love life, ontological and epistemological search of Ricardo Reis, a doctor by profession and also a poet. Ricardo Reis is not a real person: he is merely one of the several heteronyms of the famous Portuguese poet, Fernando Pessoa. Thus, in this sense, the novel is metafictional; it is fiction about fiction and it has a subtext that refers to Pessoa's own poetry, life style and poetic multiple personas, even though it concerns itself more directly with Ricardo Reis. Pessoa's own subtext runs parallel to Saramago's own narrative. In the novel, Ricardo Reis is much alike the original Pessoan Reis: he is the detached, aloof, fatalistic, neoclassical poet, the politically unengaged figure who lives mostly recoiled within himself and makes little or no real effort to participate actively in life or to connect with people. Although a general medical practitioner by profession, Reis is for the most part unemployed while living in Lisbon, working only part-time for a few months as a cardiologist—a very ironic situation—considering the fact that he is a man who does not know very much about matters of the heart and tends to minimize the importance of the senses.

The novel starts with Reis's return to Lisbon, after a long exile of sixteen years in Brazil. Being a lover of tradition and conservative political forms (i.e., the monarchy), Reis had left Portugal around 1910, when the Portuguese monarchy was abolished and the first Republic installed, and exiled himself in Brazil. It is now 1936 and Pessoa has just died. Having heard about the death of his creator (whom he considers a friend), Saramago's Reis decides to return to Lisbon, even though he is not quite sure why and if such a move is a good one. The Portugal that Reis encounters is not a very pleasant one, for Salazar is now in power, and the country is living under a very oppressive fascist regime. The general mood of the novel is dark, gloomy, and pessimist. Due to the highly internalized nature of the novel, where the voice of the author often becomes indistinguishable from that of the protagonist, we often feel enmeshed in Reis's internal thoughts and way of being and seeing the world: his extreme (almost desperate) loneliness, his lack of personal initiative, his egocentric personality, his doubtful and schizoidlike identity and existential nihilist view. The city of Lisbon appears to us as a phantomlike place, silenced and closed off from the rest of the world. It is a city where is rains a lot and which is often enveloped in fog, a city where the sky is often cloudy and grey, as if pointing to the intellectual inebriation (cloudy vision) of the Portuguese people who are now controlled by the highly repressive, fascist political machinery of Salazar's regime—a regime constantly at work to control people's thoughts, needs, wants, and ideas (see de Oliveira 7-8). As I will demonstrate later, the constant reference to the cloudy sky, the fog, and the rain can also be seen as a narrative technique to point to the fact that the Portuguese people are believers of a God that does not exist, a God that is blind, as Saramago would say in *Ensaio sobre a cegueira* (*Blindness*).

Apart from the oppressive negative climate in Portugal, the world is also at this moment experiencing the most dramatic political events and oppressive regimes of the twentieth century: the rise of Nazism in Germany, the success of fascism in Italy and its war with Ethiopia, and the Civil War in neighbouring Spain. Thus, if Reis was looking for peace of mind and ways of escaping historical reality, he chose the wrong country and century to live in. It is precisely because of the tumultuous political situation of this time that we can suggest that Saramago brings such Pessoan heteronym back to life. Placing Reis in the midst of a society afflicted with so many sociopolitical concerns and evils allows Saramago to raise some questions regarding Reis's life philosophy, his extreme intellectualism, and his aloofness and disengagement. How can Reis escape material reality and social responsibility without feeling guilty, when all he reads about in the newspapers is pointing to the many disasters that go on every day, not only in Portugal but also throughout the world? How can he justify his inaction and apathy when the world is literally killing itself? Is it fair and ethical just to wait and stare at the violence, misery, and atrocities that go on in the world? Is it logical to keep on believing that all that happens is pure fate and the wishes of the Olympian gods? Should art reflect reality or depart from it completely, and furthermore, can it in fact reflect reality as it is, or does it always alter (and idealize) it? These questions are, in one way or another, all raised throughout the novel.

In the novel, the dead Fernando Pessoa often pays visits to Reis's residences or appears to him on the streets of Lisbon when Reis is on his frequent walks throughout the city. Their conversations generally revolve around poetry, the power and limits of language, the nature of life and knowledge, love, women, happiness, the human condition, and sociopolitical engagement. Given the fact the novel is highly intertextual and the idiosyncrasy of Saramago's punctuation and sui generis writing style (generally characterized by extremely long sentences and paragraphs, where the change of voice is mostly marked by the use of commas and capital letters), it is often difficult to discern among the voices of the original Reis, Saramago's Reis, Pessoa, and Saramago. This is further complicated by the fact that in the novel, Reis often composes poems, some of which are a mixture of verses of old Pessoan and Reian poems, while others seem to be new creations (or at least recreations of old poems). Once again, we have a fiction inside a fiction, or fictions inside fictions: a novelist rewriting (correcting as it were) a poet's poems and inserting his own voice in them. Given the multitude of voices displayed in *O Ano* (and in Saramago's novels in general) we might get the impression that we are dealing with a very polyphonic work, where there is no strong authoriarl position. And yet, Saramago's narrating voice is often unmistakably present and he uses it to clearly identify his position on the subject matter, thus demonstrating that his authorial voice is a bold and political one. Here is it is important to note that Saramago does not espouse the common view that there is a difference between narrator and author, at least in his own fiction. In fact he has openly conveyed that he is the one controlling his narration and his views as a person are always in his writing: "I do not hide behind the narrator. Saramago is the author and it is he that narrates what he narrates." ("Eu não me escondo por detrás do narrador. Saramago é o autor e é ele que conta o que conta" [qtd. in Gómez Aguilera 237]).

O Ano depicts Reis as the antihero, although he is in many ways a much more sympathetic and conscientious figure than the original Pessoan Reis, as I demonstrate later. The Pessoan Reis had an idealist conception of women—one which follows a long-standing tradition in history and art. Throughout the centuries, and in different societies around the world, women have often acquired the reputation of being bodily, passive, and incomplete figures; beings who are less intellectual, less rational, and less spiritual than men, and whose main job (and duty) is to please men and make their lives easier—to live for and through them, that is. Many statements have been made by historically influential figures about the "true" nature of women. Aristotle, St. Thomas of Aquinas, and Michelet are examples of Western figures who have voiced their opinions about what it means to be a woman. As pointed out by de Beauvoir in her introduction to *The Second Sex*:

> "The female is a female by virtue of a certain *lack* of qualities," said Aristotle; "we should regard the female nature as afflicted with a natural defectiveness." And St. Thomas for his part pronounced woman to be an "imperfect man," an "incidental" being. . . . Thus humanity is male and man defines woman not in herself but as relative to him; she is not regarded as an autonomous being. Michelet writes: "Woman, the relative being . . ." And Benda is most positive in his *Rapport d'Uriel*: "The body of man makes sense in itself quite apart of that of woman, whereas the latter seems wanting in significance by itself. . . . Man can think of himself without woman. She cannot think of herself without man." And she is simply what man decrees; thus she is called "the sex," by which is meant that she appears essentially to the male as a sexual being. For him she is sex—absolute sex, no less. She is defined and differentiated with reference to man and not he with reference to her; she is the incidental, the inessential as opposed to the essential. He is the subject, he is the Absolute—she is the Other. ("Introduction" 13)

Even Lévinas—the man known for putting ethics before philosophy and for having a special concern for the nonviolation of the other (the different)—has been accused of making false statements about women, reducing them to passive subjects and denigrating the sexual (see Irigaray, "The Fecundity" 119-43; *The Irigaray Reader* 178-85). On the other hand, in literature, poetry, and visual art, women have also been often described as beings who posses a spirituality close to that of a goddess. They frequently appear as angelical, unworldly, and unreachable beings whose bodies are only to be admired but not touched. Late Middle Age and Renaissance lyrical poets, who are in some ways following the European courtly love tradition with its origins in twelfth-century France, such as Petrarca (see *Francis Petrarch: Songs and Sonnets from Laura's Lifetime*) and the Luís Vaz de Camões (see *Os Melhores Poemas de Luís de Camões*), are just some examples of poets who have represented their women as unreachable, altruistic beings who are beautiful on the inside and on the outside and who even seem to possess the capacity to open men's hearts to higher spiritual love. When reading these two poets, one almost has the impression that they are able to reach orgasm through platonic adoration only, and in fact, performing the sexual act often appears as a corruption of that pure, altruistic love the poets are able to feel solely through ideation or idealization. This platonic adoration or ideation is also very much a part of the Western Christian collective conscious (or is it unconscious?) archetype, which has tended to associate women with the Virgin Mary, who apparently became pregnant without making physical love, thus making physical and spiritual love seem incompatible with each other, creating the saint/whore dichotomy—and provoking quite a bit of psychological trauma for many men and women. Yet we can also also find a large Christian tradition pointing to the indivisibility of physical and spiritual love. For example, the Ecstasy of Saint Teresa of Avila, the Spanish mystic who lived during the sixteenth century, would attest to the inseparability of both types of love (see *Lira mística, Santa Teresa de Jesús, San Juan de la Cruz* 25-28).

Charles Boxer's book, *Mary and Misogyny,* offers a good a discussion of the Virgin Mary archetype in the Iberian Peninsula and the prevalent dichotomy between the virgin and the whore (97-112). And in Bram Dijkstra's book *Idols of Perversity: Fantasies of the Feminine Evil in Fin-de-Siècle Culture* we find an excellent discussion on how the notion of woman and the dichotomy of whore/Virgin in the Western world was heavily influenced (and manufactured) by the rise of the capitalist market economy taking place in England since the industrial revolution and how it achieved a climax during the late nineteenth century, as can be detected through a study of visual and written art as well as "scientific" theories produced during that period. The urge to produce and become rich as the capitalist enterprise demanded, and the dishonesty that that entailed, went against the need to keep spiritual integrity as the Puritan theology preached. This dilemma gave rise to the concept of virtuous woman, or as Dijkstra puts it, "The Shopkeeper's Soul Keeper" or the "Cult of the Household Nun": "In a world of this sort, in which it was a virtual everyday necessity for the ambitious middle-class male to risk his soul, the notion that the family was, as it were, a 'soul unit,' that man and his wife shared one soul, rapidly gained appeal. A man's wife, it was thought, could, by staying at home—a place unblemished by sin and unsullied by labor—protect her husband's soul from permanent damage; the very intensity of her purity and devotion would regenerate, as it were, its war-scared tissue and thus keep his personal virtue protected from the moral pitfalls inherent in the world of commerce" (7-8). Contrary to the upper-class women who were seen as asexual and pure beings, women of lower classes who could not afford to become "household nuns" were seen as seductresses, considered inherently bad and lascivious: they were responsible for men's "fall" into the world of carnal love (Dijkstra 362). This separation between the virgin and the whore and class-based sexuality are very present in Saramago's novel and will be addressed later on in this chapter.

In a fashion somewhat similar to Petrarca and Camões, the original Pessoan Reis is a poet who often describes his women in an immaterial, idealized fashion, someone who controls his carnal desires and avoids the sexual act with women—seemingly finding a certain spiritual fulfillment in such a detached relationship. Reis comes across as being stern, fatalistic, sad, and self-controlled. In some ways, he reminds us of a sad stoic. Like the stoic, Reis seeks peace of mind, absence of pain, intellectual pleasures, and wisdom rather than bodily gratifications, and avoids public life and emotional commitments in order to escape the pains (and turmoil) likely to be caused by them (see Zeller 297-39, 341-80). Reis's poetry is generally characterized by the use of a highly classical Portuguese and the careful choosing of each word, stanza, and verse as if to create a rigid and artificial ensemble of meaning. Like his Roman counterpart, Horace, Reis relies heavily on the Hellenic and Latin poetic traditions. The thematic elements of this type of poetry tend to revolve around Attic scenes and are marked by a pronounced belief in paganism, fatalism, and Platonic ideals of perfection. Richard Zenith gives us a good description of the Pessoan Ricardo Reis in *Fernando Pessoa & Co*:

> It is fitting that Reis should be so hard to pin down, for he was not of this world.... [He] celebrated the *spirit* of things. The atmosphere of his poetry is bucolic, but in the Greek manner, nature being appreciated as an ideal—for the spirit it embodies—rather than for its sensorial qualities. Reis was educated by the Jesuits, who no doubt taught him his Latin and perhaps fostered his religious attitude, but he was a pagan and fundamentally hostile to Christianity. He recognized Christ just as one of the many gods, all of whom were subject—like humans—to the indiscernible workings of an impersonal Fate. Far from being a means to an afterlife, the gods were a way for him to elevate this present life, spiritually and aesthetically, in answer to primordial human need.... Ricardo's "brother" (or cousin?), Frederico Reis, summoned up the neoclassical poet's philosophy in this way: "Avoiding pain whenever possible, man should seek tranquility and calm above all else, abstaining from effort and useful activity." The best we can do, since we cannot change Fate, is to accept things as they are.... [Reis] frequently invoked the solace of "clear seeing" in his poetry. In verses dating from 1915 he wrote that the gods could take everything from him as long as they left him his "lucid and solemn consciousness/Of being and of things," his "clear and useless vision of the universe" ... Criticizing the free-verse form of his heteronymic peers, saying they had "no other artistic purpose than to display their sensations," Reis composed terse Horatian odes on

themes reminiscent especially of the Augustan poet's second book of odes: the brevity of live, the vanity of wealth and struggle, the joy of simple pleasures, patience in time of trouble, and avoidance of extremes. (96-97)

Contrary to the other Pessoan heteronyms which Frederico Reis describes as having "no other artistic purpose than to display their sensations," Reis "tell[s] with severity" for he "think[s] what [he] feel[s]" (Pessoa, *Fernando Pessoa & Co* 135). In Reis's poetry it is the intellect that rules the emotions and not the other way around, for each word is chosen carefully to enclose (and even discard or change) the feeling or emotion it is attempting to describe. The intellect, with its capacity for abstractions, rationalizations, and idealizations, not only rules Reis's poetry (and life), but it in fact appears as the highest type of intelligence, the way to achieve true wisdom: it allows him to experience the "clear seeing" referred above. It is as if Reis can experience a spiritual (and superior) ecstasy through his poetry, an ecstasy that can only be achieved once he exits his body, his senses, and the immediacy of the experience being described and enters the abstract world of language. Feelings, emotions, and instinctual reactions tend to be seen as inferior types of intelligence, and in fact, constitute an impediment to the achievement of the proper (and pure) knowledge and happiness. Poetry becomes a way to achieve spirituality and nobleness, a way to enter the world of the mind—that place where the disturbances associated with the human passions are controlled and overcome, so that Reis can see the world and himself in a clear and complete manner. These verses are in some ways reminiscent of Platonic ideals of perfection. Reis becomes close to the image of the Greek philosopher, the person who is free from all passions, enlightened, and thus able to see the real world and the real nature of his self: the world beyond the shadows projected onto the wall of the cave. He assumes an arrogance close to that of the Greek philosopher, who sees himself as the only suited person to be the philosopher-king: the only suited entity to successfully govern the ideal, just and perfect Republic (Plato, *Plato's Republic* 96-108) (the irony, of course, is that Reis is not interested in public and political life at all). Like the philosopher-king, Reis seems to see himself as the right guide for the alienated beings living in the shadow realm—Lídia being, as I will demonstrate, an example of a being who needs his guidance.

The Reian reflective, nonphysical, unemotional, and intellectual poetry does have its drawbacks. For one, it tends to create dichotomies of body/mind, body/soul, and emotion/reason, giving primacy to intellectual, spiritual, and rational epistemological sources, while discarding (or at least putting in a subaltern position) the knowledge achieved through what could be termed, for lack of a better word, "irrational" epistemologies (i.e., body, instinct, emotion). These types of dichotomies have been used in Western epistemological and philosophical traditions at least since the ancient Greek philosophers, and experienced a reinvigoration during the Renaissance. Such discriminatory dichotomies have produced very negative results for the life, dignity, and identity of women in general, for women have often been perceived in this tradition as beings closer to nature, emotion, and instinct and thus inferior to men. These discriminatory dualities have negatively affected the lives of human beings in general, in the sense that they are responsible for the fragmentation of the human self, giving primacy only to certain ways of knowing and understanding oneself and the world. To assume that the right knowledge can be achieved only through intellectual ways is to fall into reductionism and alienation. To write poetry that is ruled solely by the intellect and discards other sources of knowledge, as Reis seems to be doing, is to fall into a grave misunderstanding: it is, in fact, to fall into baseless knowledge, knowledge that disregards what Lévinas calls "the element" (*Totality* 135) and what other philosophers (i.e., Husserl, Merleau-Ponty) might call phenomenology (see Makaryk 363-65, 423-25). Reis's poetry becomes the direct opposite of what Cixous has called *écriture féminine* or what Québécois Canadian feminists (i.e., France Théoret, Louise Dupré) have designated as *écriture au féminin*, a type of writing characterized by an openness to all sources of knowledge available to humans and giving particular emphasis to emotions, body, instinct, and unconscious forces. This type of writing had been previously discarded by patriarchal discourse ruling and defining the construction of knowledge and human identity (in chapter 3 I discuss in more detail what this concept of writing entails).

Another significant drawback of the intellectual poetry practiced by Reis is tied to language. Many people, from writers to literary critics (e.g., Lispector, Wilde) (see Lispector, *The Stream of Life* 20; Wilde "The Critic as Artist" 5-7), have argued that language is only a translation of our thoughts, feelings, and emotions, and a medium which does in fact create an artificial reality. The Pessoan Reis, on the other hand, seems to think that when chosen carefully, language is an exact translation of the truest (ideal) reality regarding himself and the world around him. It seems then that Reis becomes imprisoned in the "house of language" in a negative way. In other words, because he fails to realize that language is an imperfect medium that only allows humans to capture a thin segment of reality, he is fooled by that same language and by his own thought system which is directly tied to that language and thus is artificial also. In order for Reis to be a freer agent in language, rather than a mere agent of it, and closer to his presymbolic self (the self not yet contaminated by the linguistic or rational thought system), he would have to allow himself to write freely and not pay too much attention to the logic of language and its overall form. Or, to borrow from Lispector, he would need "to write absentmindedly" (*The Stream* 14) for that is what saves us from living in a purely speculative, abstract, and intellectual world, putting us in closer touch with the immediacy and reality of our feelings, which she perceives as being the purest forms of being, feeling, knowing, and existing. By writing absentmindedly, Lispector is able to enter what she calls the "thinking-feeling" (*The Stream* 81) stage, the stage where thoughts are not yet completely filtered through the intellect but rather felt (and understood) mostly through the body and other nonrational mechanisms. Such a stage allows a "freedom" (*The Stream* 81) that cannot be achieved when one is imprisoned in the inflexible Reian "prison house of language." In sum, Reis's poetry does not drink the reality of life; it is not inserted into the Lévinasian "element." In this sense then, we can say that the Pessoan Reis is an absolute idealist who grounds his ontology and epistemology on an a priori intellectual paradigm, which is unrelated to (or greatly deviates from) reality. In order for him to write poetry that is inserted into the "element," he ought to start off by apprehending knowledge from all of his senses (i.e., hear, touch, smell, taste, vision) and emptying his mind of purely intellectual thoughts: he must become more of a phenomenologist and less of an idealist. In other words, rather than merely "thinking what he feels," Reis ought to start "feeling what he thinks."

Given Reis's poetic ideals and his belief in the superiority of the intellect over the emotions, it is no surprise that the women in his poetry appear as ethereal, ideal companions rather than real people with whom he has or has had any carnal love relationship. The poetry of Ricardo Reis is saturated with images and allusions to the "ideal" woman—the bodiless, absent, unengaged, and spiritual being, who in some ways seems to allow Reis to experience the ideal, platoniclike and pure love. Reis's female characters tend to be aristocratic women, who are described as being physically and spiritually beautiful, but who must remain at a distance. They are mere objects of adoration and idealization, that is. Female names such as Chloe, Neaera, Lydia, and Marcenda are common in his poetry, the first three being in fact direct borrowings from Horace's poetry. This reinforces the idea that Reis is not referring to real women with whom he has had encounters, but, rather, female literary archetypes or ideals—women once loved and also idealized by Reis's similarly detached Roman counterpart. Lídia is the most often occurring woman in Reis's poetry, and like the others, she comes across as a noncarnal figure, as someone whose physical features are never (or very seldom) mentioned or described. Lídia's physical beauty is frequently hinted at in Reis's poetry, in the sense that she is often compared (directly and indirectly) with the roses she holds on her lap or the roses of the Adonis's garden, for example. And yet, it is very difficult to discern any of Lídia's bodily specificities, making her a quasi—if not entirely—metaphysical presence. Reis must not touch or even hold hands with his "ideal" Lídia, for those acts would corrupt not only Lídia's serene frozenlike beauty, but also the notion (and remembrance) the poet has (or will have) of her and his love for her—all these being of course figments of the poet's imaginative and speculative mind. In order to achieve the intellectual and idealized love so appreciated by Reis, both the poet and his lover must remain untouched by each other. As the poet says in the poem "Lydia, Come and Sit with Me, by the Riverside" ("Quintanilha" 75) ("Vem sentar-te comigo Lydia, à beira do rio") ("Quintanilha" [74]) they must remain "grown-up children" ("crianças adultas"), which is to say, they must both remain virgins. The poem suggests that Reis wants to teach Lídia how to leave the world of matter and carnal desire so that she can enter a superior state of existence and being. Reis comes across as a domineering man who merely wants the idealized Lídia to follow his advice and internalize his own voice, values and ideals. To use a Lévinasian language, Reis refuses to consider Lídia's alterity (otherness) and merely wants to transform her into a mirror of himself. He commits the self-indulging "crime" of totalization, the "crime" of incorporating the other into self or sameness, remaining thus at the "gaze" level and proving incapable of reaching what Lévinas refers to as the "face":

> The way in which the other presents himself, exceeding the *idea of the other in me*, we here name face. This *mode* does not consist in figuring as a theme under my gaze, in spreading itself forth as a set of qualities forming an image. The face of the Other at each moment destroys and overflows the plastic image it leaves me, the idea existing to my own measure and to the measure of its *ideatum*—the adequate idea. It does not manifest itself by these qualities, but *kath auto*. It expresses *itself*. The face brings a notion of truth which, in contradistinction to contemporary ontology, is not the disclosure of an impersonal Neuter, but *expression*: the existent breaks through all the envelopings and generalities of Being to spread out in its "form" the totality of its "content," finally abolishing the distinction between form and content. (*Totality and Infinity* 50-51).

As António Ferreira states, the Lídia of the Pessoan Reis is,

> most of all, a traveling companion, a silent and silenced presence who listens to the wise advice of the domineering masculine voice, without answering and acting. . . . Lídia never has a voice in the poetry of Ricardo Reis. Let us take a look, for instance, at the ode "Lydia, Come and Sit with Me, by the Riverside"—one of the most known, and, for that reason also one of the responsible for reactions opposing that of Ricardo Reis. The poem is dominated by an imperative tone which opens with the initial verse "Come" and continues in the verbal forms of "let us stay watching," "let us understand," "let us think," "put your hand in mine," "let my hands go," etc. It is quite clear from the very first strophe, that the invitation "Come and sit with me . . . by the riverside" has a pedagogical intention, for in the second verse— "Let us stay watching the water go calmly by and let us understand"—the conjunction "and" is equivalent, at the stylistic level, to a final proposition.

> sobretudo, uma companheira de viagem, uma presença silente e silenciada que ouve, sem responder e sem agir, os concelhos sapientes de uma voz masculina dominadora. . . . Lídia nunca tem voz na poesia de Ricardo Reis. Veja-se, como exemplo, a ode "Vem sentar-te comigo, Lydia, à beira do rio"—uma das mais conhecidas, e, também por isso, uma das responsáveis pelas reacções que outras vozes têm contraposto à de Ricardo Reis. O poema é dominado por um tom imperativo que abre o verso inicial— —"Vem"—e continua nas formas verbais "fitemos," "aprendamos," "enlacemos," "desenlacemos," etc. Fica bem claro, logo na primeira estrofe, que o convite "Vem sentar-te comigo . . . à beira do rio" tem uma intenção pedagógica pois no segundo verso—"Sossegadamente fitemos o seu curso e aprendamos"—a conjunção "e" equivale, no plano estilístico, a uma proposição final. (259-60)

The poetry of Reis places great emphasis on contemplating the world (and by extension Lídia) passively and from afar. By inviting Lídia to sit with him by the river in the poem cited above, Reis is inviting her to experience (and enter) what he considers to be a higher kind of love and to let go of all carnal desires and passions, as well as their ephemeral, painful, and unsatisfying nature. The presence of the image of the flowing river in this poem plays an important and complex role. If we accept the idea that the eye is often perceived as the window to a person's spirit or soul and the window to connect deeply with someone, then Lídia and Reis remain closed off from each other. Not only are they not holding hands, but they are also not looking into each other's eyes: they are merely sitting side by side, contemplating the flowing river. A closer contact between the two would probably require them to make some eye contact, in which case they would need to be facing each other and not the river. Moreover, by looking at the river and not at each other, they are also looking at the reflection of each other on the water: Reis sees Lídia as she is reflected in the water and vice versa. In sum, they see one another through a meditating substance: the water. The water is the barrier between the two, the substance that impedes them from getting a more realistic perception of one another. In the end, then, both are only looking at themselves; they are like two Narcissus figures enamored with themselves, egocentric creatures who cannot reach outside their individual shell. The other seen in the water is not the real other, or the other in his or her most original self, but rather the other seen only through the eye (mind) of the self.

As Lévinas would say, Reis is practicing the role of the same; he is allowing his self to totalize and annihilate the other and its possibility of existence. In order for the other to remain other, the other can not be totally understood and disclosed by the analyzing subject, for that would correspond to the annihilation of the other and the committing of psychological murder. The other must remain hermeneutically undisclosed: she or he must remain in the realm of the infinitum, the fluid and the uncanny (see Lévinas, *Totality and Infinity* 48-52; Avram, "The Priority of 'Ethics'"; Blum, "Emmanuel Lévinas's Theory of Commitment"). Thus, Lídia is merely a creation of Reis's idealist, intellectual, and artistic mind. She is a creation of Reis, but also a creation that has been passed onto him by other artists (i.e., Horace). Reis's mind or intellect has been fed ideal (and false) archetypes of women and it continues to reproduce such archetypes. Reis has entered a "parroting" (uncritical) cycle which prevents him from experiencing real intimacy with women, a cycle that alienates him both from himself and from women, and thus also alienates women, impeding the nurturing of genuine relationships between the two sexes. The image of the flowing river suggests something else. Apart from not being able to see the real other in the reflection of the river waters, Lídia and Reis are also not able to see their real selves: they only see a reflection of their selves, which is not faithful to the nature of their true selves. The image projected onto the water is only an imitation of their real self, a mirage of sorts, which if attained will not have substance or body: it is an image as empty as the one Reis sees of Lídia projected into the river waters. If we take into account the fact that identity is forged through contact with the other, through interrelational encounters, then both Reis and Lídia are left without identity, as if they were empty shells. As Lévinas puts it, "It is as if in going towards the other I met myself and implanted myself in a land, henceforth native, and I were stripped of all the weight of my identity. A native land owing nothing to enrootedness, nothing to first occupation; a native land owing nothing to birth" (Lévinas, *Proper Names* 44-45).

The fecundity of the relational ontological search versus the sterility of the individual ontological search

Saramago is well known for reinventing, rewriting, and questioning not only the veracity of history in general as it has been traditionally told in the West (see Gómez Aguilera 267-76; Amorim 83-108) but also the very existence of religious sacred icons of Christianity such as God himself, Jesus Christ, and the Virgin Mary. The author has openly admitted several times that he does not believe in God, any God, in fact (see Arnaut 57, 196) and part of his project in his fiction is to demystify religion, to dismantle (deconstruct) the idea that indeed a God exists. He wants people to come to the realization that they have been indoctrinated to believe in something that does not exist and that is why the world is in the sorry condition it is. He wants people to question, to reflect, to see without the cloud of Christianity (or any other religion), so that they can become fully engaged individuals who can make the world work for the better (see Gómez Aguilera 123-36). This position is explored at length in his novel, *O Evangelho Segundo Jesus Cristo* (*The Gospel According to Jesus Christ*). In this work, God, Jesus Christ, and the Virgin Mary are depicted in a very human (physical way) in the sense that they perform sexual acts: they act out their instinctual drives and are grounded in their bodies. And in *Blindness*, the divinity and existence of God are questioned, and humans are seen as the only agents responsible for their own destiny and actions. Saramago portrays God as blind—as symbolized by the white cloth covering Christ's and all the saints' eyes in the final church scene. God is blind because he does not exist and thus people become blind because they do not realize they are adoring (and relying on) a nonexisting entity, therefore failing to take charge of their lives. The fact that Saramago calls the novel *Ensaio Sobre a Cegueira* (which literally means "essay about blindness") and not just *Cegueira* (*Blindness*), as the English translation conveys, shows that the author intends to teach his readership something. In Portuguese the word "ensaio" ("essay") implies the teaching of something by someone who knows a lot about the subject and thus wins the argument, or at least makes the addressee think quite deeply about the subject matter at hand. See also António José Borges's book *José Saramago: Da Cegueira À Lucidez* (José Saramago: From Blindness to Lucidity) for a discussion of Saramago's use of the word "essaio" in the titles of his novels and how that relates to the author's intent on having a deep intellectual and rational debate and reflection about certain ideologies that society has come to accept blindly. His intention is to make us rethink and deconstruct our views. Here we should note that Saramago has published a second novel titled *Ensasio Sobre a Lucidez* (Essay on Lucidity), which again engages the reader in similar debates and exercises of the mind. The Saramaguian authorial voice is therefore bold, political, unwavering, and didactic.

Just like he reinvents and rewrites history and religious figures, Saramago also often reinvents women portraying them as positive role models. As Gómez Aguilera puts it, "Saramago's oeuvre is one sustained by exceptional female figures, which appear as shinning incarnations of the best in the human condition" ("A obra de

Saramago é ... uma literatura sustentada por excepcionais figuras femininas, presentes nos seus romances como fulgurantes encarnações do melhor da condição humana" [277]). And in Saramago's own words, "I feel that women are generally better than men." (Gómez Aguilera 279). In his novels, women often achieve "sainthood" (earthly sainthood, that is) by doing deeds that serve to ameliorate the human condition (see also Amorim 69-77). Moreover, they are not devoid of a body and sexual desires, unlike the Virgin Mary or any other women depicted throughout history who could only be whores or saints but never both. The Saramaguian women make illicit (unwed and sexual) love with men while still managing to be respected and valued. And this is especially evident in *The Year of the Death of Ricardo Reis*. A central part of the novel revolves around the love affair between Reis and Lídia Martins, a maid at the Hotel Bragança in Lisbon where Reis is staying. Unlike the Pessoan Reian original Lídia, who is depicted in Reis's poetry as the absent, goddesslike, asexual, unengaged, untouchable figure, Lídia Martins is present, human, sexual, engaged, and touchable. In *O Ano*, the Reian Pessoan ideal Lídia is always present. Reis often refers to her in his poems and compares her to the "real" Lídia he is now faced with:

> down on her knees, her body wriggling, [she] did her vigorous best to remove the offending moisture {from the waxed wooded floor}. Tomorrow she will give the floor another coat of wax. Can I do something else for you, Doctor. No, much obliged. They looked straight into each other's eyes. Beating heavily on the windowpanes, the rain's rhythm accelerated, riffling like a great drum, causing those who were asleep to wake up in alarm. What is your name, Lydia, sir, she replied, she adds, at your service, Doctor. . . . The Doctor made no reply, he appeared to be whispering the name Lydia in case he should need to call her again. There are people who repeat the words they hear, because we are all like parrots repeating one another, nor is there another way of learning. This reflection is inappropriate, perhaps, since it was not made by Lydia, who is the other interlocutor and already has a name, so let us allow her to leave, take her mop and bucket with her. Ricardo Reis remains there smiling ironically, moving his lips in a way that deceives no one. Lydia, he repeats, and smiles, and smiling goes to the drawer to look for his poems, his Sapphic odes, and read the verses which catch his eye as he turns the pages. {*And so, Lydia, sitting by the hearth, Lydia, let the image be thus, Let us show no desire, at this hour, When our autumn comes, Lydia, come sit with me, Lydia, on the riverbank, Lydia, the most abject existence is preferable to death.* There is no longer any trace of irony in his smile, if the word *smile* is an apt description for those parted lips exposing his teeth, when inside the skin the game has altered itself, now a contortion or a painful grimace, as we would say in a constrained style.} (*The Year* 34-35)

> a criada ... posta de joelhos, serpeando o corpo ao movimento dos braços, restituiu quanto possível a secura que às madeiras enceradas convém, amanhã lhe deitará um pouco de cera, Deseja mais alguma coisa, senhor doutor, Não muito obrigado, e ambos se olharam de frente, a chuva batia fortíssima nas vidraças, acelerava-se o ritmo, agora rufava como um tambor, em

sobressalto os adormecidos acordavam, Como se chama, e ela respondeu, Lídia, senhor doutor, e acrescentou, Às ordens do senhor doutor. . . . mas ele não respondeu, apenas pareceu que repetia o nome, Lídia, num sussurro, quem sabe se para não o esquecer quando precisasse de voltar a chamá-la, há pessoas assim, repetem as palavras que ouvem, as pessoas, em verdade, são papagaios umas das outras, nem há outro modo de aprendizagem, acaso esta reflexão veio fora de propósito porque não a fez Lídia, que é o outro interlocutor. . . . Lídia, diz, e sorri. Sorrindo vai buscar à gaveta os seus poemas, as suas odes sáficas, lê alguns versos apanhados ao passar das folhas, *E assim, Lídia, à lareira, como estando, Tal seja, Lídia, o quadro, Não desejemos, Lídia, nesta hora, Quando Lídia, vier o nosso outono, vem sentar-te comigo, Lídia, à beira do rio, Lídia, a vida mais vil antes que a morte,* já não resta vestígio de ironia no sorriso, se de sorriso ainda justificam o nome dois lábios abertos sobre os dentes, quando por dentro da pele se alterou o jogo dos músculos, ricto agora ou doloroso esgar se diria em estilo chumbado. (*O Ano* 47-48)

This passage describes the first encounter between Lídia Martins and Reis at the Hotel Bragança. The scene is reminiscent—in reverse—of the original poem, "Lydia, Come and Sit with Me, by the Riverside." As in the original poem, we have a meeting between Reis and Lídia, involving water, albeit not the calming water of the flowing river, but the turbulent, unstable, and violent water of the thunderstorm that has entered Reis's room, through the window he had inadvertently left open. Rather than merely looking at the river, and not directly at each other, as in the original poem, Reis and Lídia now directly look at one other. The water is no longer mediating their encounter and impeding them from getting a closer look at each other: the water is in fact mopped from the floor by Lídia, as if symbolizing her willingness to be an active feminine agent who wants to clear up the misunderstandings that might exist between her and Reis, so that both can see each other in a clearer manner. It is this frontal (direct) look between the two, and the eye contact that it involves, that gives rise to the sexual energy between them: "They looked straight into each other's eyes. Beating heavily on the windowpanes, the rain's rhythm accelerated, riffling like a great drum, causing those who were asleep to wake up in alarm" (34) ("ambos se olharam de frente, a chuva batia fortíssima nas vidraças, acelerava-se o ritmo, agora rufava como um tambor, em sobressalto os adormecidos acordavam" [47]).

When finding out that the name of the maid is Lídia, Reis smiles ironically: the reader familiar with the Pessoan intertext permeating Saramago's novel will know that Reis is thinking about his ideal Lídia and comparing the two, for right after this brief first encounter, Reis searches for the odes he had written about the ideal Lídia and reads them. We get the impression Reis is afraid of the feelings the real Lídia awoke in him, and thus retreats into the calm nature of his neoclassical poetry, so that his feelings and sexual energy towards the real Lídia can be tamed and controlled. The severe, controlled, and calm tone of his poetry functions as an appeasement for his awakened physical senses and sexual desires: "There is no longer any trace of irony in his smile, if the word *smile* is an apt description for those parted lips exposing his teeth, {when inside the skin the game has altered itself, now a contortion or a painful grimace, as we would say in a constrained style}" (35) ("já não resta vestígio de ironia no sorriso, se de sorriso ainda justificam o nome dois lábios abertos sobre os dentes, quando por dentro da pele se alterou o jogo dos músculos, ricto agora ou doloroso esgar se diria em estilo chumbado" [48]). The smile Reis has after reading his poems about the ideal Lídia, which are written in a constrained neoclassical style, is also a constrained and lifeless smile, as ironically mirrored by Saramago's own second description of it: "now a contortion or a painful grimace, as we would say in a constrained style" (35) ("ricto agora ou doloroso esgar como se diria em estilo chumbado" [48]).

Rather than concentrate on the Lídia that he has just encountered and directly faced, Reis prefers to retreat to the protection of the odes kept in the drawer so that he can try to hold on to his ideal Lídia. He refuses to live in the present and to connect with real people, and prefers to hide himself behind his neoclassical poetry, behind words that try to control his carnal desires. The drawer can be seen as symbolizing the old, the dead, the absent, the hidden; as symbolizing an ancient poetic style that Reis had subscribed to, in other words, someone else's ideas, passed on to him by ancient poets for generations and generations. Reis acts as if he has no freedom of choice, as if he were an automaton: doing, saying, and writing what he has been taught and told by previous generations of poets. As Saramago suggests, Reis is no more than a parrot who is repeating another parrot: "There are people who repeat the words they hear, {in reality, people are parrots of one another"} (35) ("há pessoas assim, repetem as palavras que ouvem, as pessoas, em verdade, são papagaios umas das outras" [47]). Reis is a parrot repeating the name of Lídia, a name which represents a character from another poet's art, a name grounded in idealist conceptions of women and love—conceptions which do not "feed" into the spatio-temporal present and its realities. Despite the fact that Lídia tells Reis that she is at his disposal, which could be interpreted as an offer of sexual favors (traditionally, in Portugal, chambermaids have often been perceived as "maids for all services" ["criadas para todos os serviços"], in other words, loose women who easily give into the sexual advances of the clients or bosses) he does not acknowledge her response and instead starts whispering the name Lídia, as if he were in a reverie. He is oblivious to the present Lídia and does not seem to hear (understand, acknowledge even) what she says. This view of lower-class women as "maids for all services" is reminiscent of that held in England between the seventeenth and nineteenth centuries as discussed by Dijkstra, and as previously noted, where lower-class women often became easy prey for the middle-class men whose wives had become "household nuns." In his novel, *O manual dos inquisidores* (The Inquisitor's Manual), contemporary Portuguese writer António Lobo Antunes also addresses the issue of the sexual abuse of the maid or the lower-class woman by the upper-class man, and specifically by the members of the fascist regime, as well as the abundant existence of prostitution in Portugal during that time, a time when religious puritanism was extremely high.

Contrary to Reis, the Saramaguian narrator does acknowledge Lídia as being an interlocutor, as someone who partakes in a dialogue—an entity who should speak

The Politics of Agency in Saramago 69

and be heard without having the narrative voice constantly interrupt or control her thoughts, words and voice: "She could have expressed it more formally, saying, for example, in a louder voice, I was instructed to my utmost to please the doctor, for the manager said, Look here, Lídia, take good care of the guest in room two hundred and one, Doctor Reis . . . This reflection is inappropriate, perhaps, since it was not made by Lydia, who is the other interlocutor" (34) ("poderia ter dito de outra maneira, por exemplo, e bem mais alto, Eis-me aqui, a este extremo autorizada pela recomendação do gerente, Olha lá, ó Lídia, dá tu atenção ao hóspede do duzentos e um, ao doutor Reis, e ela lha estava dando, mas ele não respondeu . . . acaso esta reflexão veio fora de propósito porque não a fez Lídia, que é o outro interlocutor" [48]). Despite the general belief that chambermaids perform sexual favors for the clients, as suggested by the narrative voice here which guesses or speculates about what the hotel manager would have told her and the connotations behind it, the narrator makes a point of stating that what he is insinuating does not necessarily correspond to what Lídia says or to what she might be thinking or feeling: the narrator is merely speculating and even excuses himself for taking such a liberty, indicating that his comment is likely inappropriate. This narrative voice, then, is one that shows respect for the characters and does not want to silence them, or act as if it knows everything about them. In other words, it gives them the opportunity to be seen outside of the traditional, stereotypical, and male lens, and ultimately, outside of the totalizing gaze in the Lévinasian sense.

Saramago counterposes the two Lídias in a highly satiric way and mocks the Pessoan Reian idealistic conception of women and love. Lídia Martins is the figure depicted in the most positive manner in the novel. She is the person who tries to live life as it comes to her and who is grounded in the spatio-temporal present and realities (grounded in the Lévinasian "element"); she is someone who, despite her limited sociocultural resources and formal education, often offers much sharper insights regarding the enigmas of life than Reis, someone who tries to reach outside herself by relating to, connecting with, and helping others. In sum, she is the person who practices an ethics of relationality and phenomenology. The Reian ideal, phantomlike, absent, physically unoccupied (unengaged) and asexual upper-class Lídia is very different from the real Lídia. The latter is a figure of flesh and bone; she is sexual, and physically engaged; she is a useful person who performs physical and visible deeds as a maid at the Hotel Bragança. The novel gives us many details not only about Lídia's physical features and how she enjoys the pleasures of the flesh, but also about what she does and how she cares for Reis when he is ill:

> We already know the maid who brings breakfast, it is Lydia, who also makes the bed and cleans and tidies up the room. . . . Lydia must be about thirty years of age, a mature {and nicely shaped young woman, a Portuguese brunette,} short rather than tall, if there is a point in mentioning the physical traits of an ordinary woman who so far has done nothing but scrub floors, serve breakfast. . . . Ricardo Reis noticed the birthmark at the side [of her] nostril. (68-69); She put the tray on the table and approached the

bed, and quite spontaneously put her hand on his forehead, You have a fever. . . . He placed a hand over Lydia's and closed his eyes, If there are only these two tears, I will be able to keep them back, he thought, holding Lydia's work roughened, almost coarse hand, so different from the hands of Chloe, Neaera, and that other Lydia, and from the tapered fingers, manicured nails, and soft palms of Marcenda. From Marcenda's one living hand, I should say, because her left hand is anticipated death. (141-42); Lydia insisting he take one more spoonful of chicken broth, but he refuses, he has no appetite, he also wants her to plead with him, a game which would seem absurd to {anyone in a state} of perfect health. To tell the truth, Ricardo Reis is not so ill that he is unable to feed himself. (143); Lydia is happy. A woman who goes to bed so willingly with a man is deaf to gossip, let voices slander her in hallways and courtyards. (260)

Já conhecemos a criada que traz o pequeno-almoço, é a Lídia, ela é também quem faz a cama e limpa e arruma o quarto. . . . Lídia tem quê, os seus trinta anos, é uma mulher feita e bem feita, morena Portuguesa, mais para o baixo que para o alto, se há importância em mencionar os sinais particulares ou as características físicas duma simples criada que até agora não fez mais que limpar o chão, servir o pequeno-almoço . . . Ricardo Reis notou o sinal que ela tinha perto da asa do nariz. (86-87); pousou o tabuleiro na mesa, aproximou-se da cama, num gesto simples pôs-lhe a mão na testa, Está com febre . . . colocou uma das mãos sobre a mão de Lídia, fechou os olhos, se não for mais que estas duas lágrimas poderei retê-las assim, como retinha aquela mão castigada de trabalhos, áspera, quase bruta, tão diferente das mãos de Cloe, Neera e a outra Lídia, dos afuselados dedos, das cuidadas unhas, das macias palmas de Marcenda, da sua única mão viva, quero dizer, a esquerda é morte antecipada. (168); Lídia insistindo, Só mais esta colher, é o caldo de galinha que ele se recusa a acabar, por fastio, para ser rogado também, jogo que parecerá ridículo a quem estiver de perfeita saúde . . . que em verdade não está Ricardo Reis tão doente que não possa alimentar-se por suas próprias mãos e forças. (170); Lídia sente-se feliz, mulher que com tanto gosto se deita não tem ouvidos. (303)

In Saramago's text, Lídia Martins is a "real" living person who lives in the present and not some "ideal" character from ancient Greece about whom Horace once also wrote about. Moreover, the physical characteristics of Saramago's Lídia emphasize the beauty of the classic Portuguese woman: the olive skin and dark-haired woman. As Ceres Fernandes points out, this type of woman had traditionally occupied a peripheral position in the imaginary of European (and Iberian) literature at least since the Middle Ages, for she was seen as the very opposite of the Christian woman usually described as having lighter skin and hair and perceived as being more pure and spiritual. The darker woman—the Moor in the Iberian Peninsula and the Gipsy and Jewish woman in the rest of Europe—was regarded as more prone to sensuality and less pure (Fernandes 92-98). Lídia Martins is someone with whom Reis comes to interact at many levels: sexual, emotional, and even intellectual. The fact that Lídia is a maid makes her an even more real and grounded figure. She is someone who continuously works with her body, cleaning, sweeping, serving, and moving rapidly to perform the many tasks her job requires. Not only does Lídia work with her body literally, in the sense that she uses it in order to earn a living, but she also uses it in the sexual way: she responds to the physical and sexual advances of Reis (and two other clients) and enjoys the sexual act for, as she puts it, "this life is so sad" (78) ("esta vida [é] tão triste" [97]). Being able to enjoy her own sexuality seems to be for Lídia a way to find relief from the existential nausea and solitude we humans are all bound to experience. One could in fact argue that the existential nausea and solitude that constantly assail Ricardo Reis are tied to the fact that he refuses to fully give into the pleasures of the senses and fails to see that those pleasures might indeed be the door to the fulfillment of the soul. I am not suggesting that Lídia's empowerment relies solely on her openness to sexual love, but rather that, contrary to Reis, she seems to recognize the importance of that type of love in one's existence and is thus able to unburden her individual ego during the process. As Mark Epstein puts it,

> [Otto] Rank moved the theory from genital orgasm to a kind of ego orgasm, describing how the ego seeks to "unburden itself" through its love relationships, freeing itself from inner tensions and inhibitions by "making use" of another person in sex or love. "The ego," said Rank, is "always ready to unravel its ego structure in object relations as soon as it finds objects and situations suitable for its purpose." When the ego is not able to "unravel its structure," when the capacity for love is shut down because of fear, insecurity, or confusion, then the person becomes isolated by and imprisoned in individuality. Where there is no rhythm of tension and relaxation, there can be no freedom to bond, no surrender of ego boundaries, and no merging of the kind that characterizes all forms of love. (51-52)

This inability of Reis to break down his individual ego boundaries during the sexual love act is well depicted in the novel during the act of lovemaking between Lídia and Reis. This act is indirectly compared with the earthquake that is taking place in Lisbon. Lídia feels no fear of the earthquake (the death of the individual self) because she is able to unburden her ego during lovemaking, in other words, she is able to die, to let go of her individual self. Reis, on the other hand, feels afraid of the earthquake because he is not able to truly unburden his ego and reach the "ego orgasm." The physicality of the real Lídia in all its dimensions—her hard, physical work and her openness towards sexual love—serve as constant reminders to Reis, reminders that there is a material reality, a tangible way of being and "finding" oneself, a phenomenological life always happening before his eyes. Lídia's class and the narrator's frequent focus on (and detailed description of) the many physical tasks she has to perform as a maid reinforce the idea of the need to work against material exploitation, the need to work within one's own community, the need not to be blind to the material reality, so that a more egalitarian society can emerge. Contrary to Reis, who merely stares at the world passively, abstractedly, and intellectually, and contrary, too, in some ways to Marcenda—the upper-class, educated young virgin with whom Reis is involved mostly on a platonic level—Lídia is grounded in her immediate world and reality. The latter not only cleans Reis's room and serves him breakfast, but she is also the one who gives him what other women have not been able to do: the presence, reality, warmth and ecstasy of physical and emotional love. Yet, the fact that she is the "maid of all services" is not presented in a negative way in Saramago's novel, since she is depicted in many ways not only as a female role model but also a role model for Reis himself. Lídia is a self-sufficient and engaged woman who is assertive on her own terms and within the limits of her own society, someone who is not afraid to love an upper-class man, even if the latter does not (or cannot) love her fully because he is imprisoned in all kinds of social clichés (pertaining to class and gender) and idealist conceptions of love. Despite her limited formal education, Saramago's Lídia is undoubtedly quite savvy, unconventional, and resourceful, and is often depicted as being smarter and more liberated than the educated Ricardo Reis. For example, she seems unconcerned about the fact that she has premarital sex and with more than one man, and she is even distrustful of the advantages of being a married woman—all uncommon behaviors and reactions for a Portuguese woman living in the highly conventional, patriarchal, and religious society of the mid-1930s:

> Do you want me to come and spend my days with you when you have a place of your own, Would you like that, Of course I would, Then you must come, until such time as, Until you find someone of your own station. That was not what I was going to say. When that happens, you need only say to me, Lydia, I don't want you to come anymore. Sometimes I feel I don't really know you. I'm a hotel chambermaid. But your name is Lydia, and you have a curious way of saying things. When people start talking their hearts, as I'm doing now with my head on your shoulder, the words aren't the same, {even I can feel it.} I hope you find yourself a good husband someday. It would be nice, but when I listen to other women, those who say they have good husbands, it makes me wonder. You think they're not good husbands, Not for me, What is a good husband, in your opinion, I don't know, You're hard to please. Not really, lying here without any future, I'm happy with what I have now. (171)

> Se quer que eu vá ter consigo quando tiver casa, nos meus dias de saída, Tu queres, Quero, Então irás, até que, Até que arranje alguém da sua educação, Não era isso que eu queria dizer, Quando tal tiver de ser, diga-me assim Lídia não voltes mais a minha casa, e eu não volto, Às vezes não sei bem quem tu és, Sou uma criada de hotel, Mas chamas-te Lídia e dizes as coisas de uma certa maneira, Em a gente se pondo a falar, assim como eu estou agora, com a cabeça pousada no seu ombro, as palavras saem diferentes, até eu sinto, Gostava que encontrasses um bom marido, Também gostava, mas ouço as outras mulheres, as que dizem que têm bons maridos, e fico a pensar, Achas que não são bons maridos, Para mim, não, Que é um bom marido, para ti, Não sei, És difícil de contentar, Nem por isso, basta-me o que tenho agora, estar aqui deitada, sem nenhum futuro. (200-01)

When Lídia finds out that she is pregnant, with what she insists will be a boy, she tells Reis she will have the child and that he does not have to assume any of the emotional, moral, or financial responsibilities of fatherhood—further signs of her personal strength, identity, and capacity to overcome the strong social stigmas associated with single motherhood. Her decision, is of course, a great relief to Reis, who is not ready to accept his baby, the unmistakable sign of the life his body can

The Politics of Agency in Saramago

generate, much less one whose mother is a maid, a woman of a very different class from his own. The class distinction is sharp between the two and thus an open union between Reis (a man of letters and a doctor) and Lídia (a hotel chambermaid) would be very unlikely. However, as Saramago suggests, affairs between male bosses and maids are in fact common in Lisbon: "these {associations between master and servant, all too common in this Lisbon city of ours, but in disguise}" (308) ("estas misturas de patrão e criada, aliás muito comuns nesta nossa cidade de Lisboa, mas com disfarce" [356]). As the narrative voice tells us, Reis would rather have Lídia perform an abortion, although he does not openly suggest this:

> Ricardo Reis searches for the right words but all he finds within himself is {an estrangement, an indifference, as if, though aware that he is obliged to help solve the problem, he does not feel implicated in its cause in any immediate or remote fashion.} Rather, he sees himself in the role of the doctor to whom a patient has blurted out her guilty secret, Ah, Doctor, what is to become of me, I am pregnant and this could not have happened at a worse moment. He {cannot} tell her, Have an abortion, don't be a fool. On the contrary, he puts on a grave air... But Ricardo Reis cannot speak with such neutrality, {for he is, at the very least, the putative father, since} there is no evidence that in the last few months Lydia has slept with any man but him. {So,} Ricardo Reis makes a decision, he must know her intentions, there is no point in evading the issue any longer, Are you thinking of having the child. Just as well that there is no one eavesdropping, otherwise Ricardo Reis would find himself accused of suggesting an abortion, but before the witnesses have been heard and the judge passes the sentence, Lydia steps forward and declares, I am going to have the {baby boy.} For the first time, Ricardo Reis feels a finger touch his heart. It is not pain he experiences, or a twitch or chill, but a sensation like no other, like the first handshake of men from two different planets, both human beings yet completely alien to each other, {or worse yet, knowing each other in their difference}.... a great anger now surges inside, I've got myself into a fine mess, he is thinking, if she doesn't have an abortion, I'll end up with a child in my hands, I'll have to acknowledge it as mine, I am morally obliged, what a mess, I never thought anything like this could happen to me. Snuggling up closer, Lydia wanted him to hold her tight, because it felt good, and casually she uttered these incredible words, If you don't want to acknowledge the child, I don't mind, the child can be illegitimate, like me. Ricardo Reis felt his eyes fill with tears, some tears of shame, some of pity, if anyone can tell the difference. (306-07)

> Ricardo Reis procura as palavras convenientes, mas o que encontra dentro de si é um alheamento, uma indiferença, assim como se, embora ciente de que é sua obrigação contribuir para a solução do problema, não se sentisse implicado na origem dele, tanto a próxima como a remota. Vê-se na figura do médico a quem a paciente disse por desabafo, Ai senhor doutor, que vai ser de mim, estou grávida e nesta altura não me convinha nada, um médico não pode responder, Desmanche, não seja parva, pelo contrário, mostra uma expressão grave... Não se admite que o declare assim, com falsa naturalidade, Ricardo Reis, que é pai pelo menos putativo, pois não consta que Lídia nos últimos meses se tenha deitado com outro homem que não seja

> ele ... Então Ricardo Reis decide-se, quer perceber quais as intenções dela, não há mais tempo para subtilezas de dialéctica, salvo se ainda o for a hipótese negativa que a pergunta esconde mal, Pensas em deixar vir a criança, o que vale é não haver aqui ouvidos estranhos, não faltaria ver-se acusado Ricardo Reis de sugerir o desmancho, e quando, terminada audição das testemunhas, o juiz ia proferir a sentença condenatória, Lídia mete-se adiante e responde, Vou deixar vir o menino. Então, pela primeira vez, Ricardo Reis sente um dedo tocar-lhe o coração. Não é dor, nem crispação, nem despegamento, é uma impressão estranha e incomparável, como seria o primeiro contacto físico entre dois seres de universos diferentes, humanos ambos, mas ignotos das sua semelhança, ou, mais perturbadoramente conhecendo-se na sua diferença ... nessa altura se está formando uma grande cólera dentro de Ricardo Reis, Meti-me em grande sarilho, pensa ele, se ela não faz o aborto, fico para aqui com um filho às costas, terei de o perfilhar, é minha obrigação moral, que chatice, nunca esperei que viesse a acontecer-me uma destas. Lídia aconchegou-se melhor, quer que ele a abrace com força, por nada, só pelo bem que sabe, e diz as incríveis palavras, simplesmente, sem nenhum ênfase particular, se não quiser perfilhar o menino, não faz mal, fica sendo filho de pai incógnito, como eu. Os olhos de Ricardo Reis encheram-se de lágrimas, umas de vergonha, outras de piedade, distinga-as quem puder. (354-56)

Lídia is given a certain sainthood in Saramago's novel, and one that is counterposed to the religious Christian view of female sainthood and virtue, usually requiring one to be chaste or perform sexual acts only within marriage. Notwithstanding the fact that Lídia is not chaste, she is put on a pedestal and even compared to the Virgin Mary—not the ethereal, spiritual and aphysical Virgin Mary, traditionally depicted by the Christian religion, but rather a more realist Virgin Mary, who possesses a body, has sexual desires and is capable of performing her own (real and visible) miracles:

> These are days of bliss. On vacation from her job at the hotel, Lydia spends nearly all her time with Ricardo Reis ... The apartment is celebrating Resurrection Saturday and Easter Sunday by the grace and labor of this humble servant who passes her hands over things and leaves them spotless and gleaming, not even in the days of Dona Luísa and the Appeals Court Judge, with a regiment of maids to do the shopping and the cooking, did these walls and furniture shine with such luster, blessed be Lydia among women ... A few days ago the place smelled of mildew, dust, blocked drains, and now light penetrates, the most remote corners, makes all the glass look like crystal, polishes every surface, the ceiling itself becomes starlit with reflections when the sun enters the windows, a celestial abode, a diamond within a diamond, and it was through menial housework {that these superior, sublime transformations were achieved}. Perhaps also the abode is celestial because of the frequency with which Lydia and Ricardo Reis make love, such is the pleasure in giving and taking, I cannot think what has come over these two that they are suddenly {carnally} so demanding and so generous with their favors. Could it be the summer that is heating their blood, could it be the presence of that tiny ferment in her womb, {perhaps the result of a distracted union, the new cause of resuscitated ardors,} the ferment is nothing in this world as yet, yet already it has some influence in governing it. (308-09)

> Estes dias são bons. Lídia está de férias do hotel, passa quase o tempo todo com Ricardo Reis ... A casa vive o seu sábado de aleluia, o seu domingo de páscoa, por graça e obra desta mulher, serva humilde, que passa as mãos sobre as coisas e as deixa lustralmente limpas, nem mesmo em tempos de Dona Luísa e juiz da Relação, com seu regimento de criadas de fora, dentro e cozinha, resplandeceram com tanta glória estas paredes e estes móveis, abençoada seja Lídia entre as mulheres ... Ainda há poucos dias cheirava a bafio, a mofo, a cotão rolado, a esgoto renitente, e hoje a luz chega aos mais remotos cantos, fulge nos vidros e nos cristais ou faz de todo o vidro cristal, derrama grandes toalhas sobre os encerados, o próprio tecto fica estrelado de reverberações quando o sol entra pelas janelas, esta morada é celeste, diamante no interior de diamante, e é pela vulgaridade de um trabalho de limpeza que se alcançam estas superiores sublimidades. Talvez também por tão amiúde se deitarem Lídia e Ricardo Reis, por tanto gosto de corpo darem e tomarem, não sei que deu a estes dois para de súbito se terem tornado tão carnalmente exigentes e dadivosos, será o verão que os aquece, será de estar no ventre aquele minúsculo fermento, efeito duma união acaso distraída, causa nova de ressuscitados ardores, ainda não somos nada neste mundo e já temos parte no governo do mundo. (356-57)

The bliss and goodness that Lídia brings to Ricardo Reis through her household domestic activities, the act of lovemaking, the individual attention, tenderness, care, and presence are presented by Saramago as sublime actions, for they can achieve great, visible, and immediate effects. It is the immediacy of life and the experiences that it gives us (the now and the here) that are valued, rather than the remembrance of the past or the speculations about the future. Life is depicted as something which is always happening, always in the present, the reason why one must grasp it and enjoy it. It is the physical, emotional, and sensual side of Lídia that are seen as great values, values which will lead to spiritual realization and ecstasy, an ecstasy grounded in the immediate and material world. It is through the physical work performed by Lídia that Reis's house becomes alive; it becomes enlightened, sublime, celestial, blessed, and blissful; it attains a terrestrial sanctity much grander than any other type of abstract conception of sanctity normally attributed to invisible divine entities. Lídia is in fact compared to a priestess or a goddess herself: the one who through her magical abilities (as cleaner, lover and caregiver) can transform Reis's house into a sanctuary, or even a cathedral of great beauty and celestial dimensions. She is described as a "diamond within a diamond" (309) ("diamante no interior de diamante" [375]) suggesting thus that she is an entity with great strength and powers who possesses the ability to erect her own world. She is the builder of a better world, the maker of a more humane and livable society, the engaged individual who makes life happen, contrary to the highly fatalistic and passive Reis, who mostly observes the world, just awaiting for his destiny to realize itself.

Lídia can be seen as a replacement for the absent, invisible (and thus blind) God of Saramago's other novel *Blindness*. She becomes very much like the nameless female protagonist of this novel, the only character not affected by the plague of blindness, the person who literally guides and helps others, in other words, the person who displays empathy and love for others, and who aids and shows concern for the well-being of the collectivity. Unlike Reis, these two women are not blind because they take charge of their lives and those of others, and they in fact try to change the oppressive social circumstances so that humans can live in a better world. Contrary to Reis, whose favorite verse is "Wise is the one who contents himself with the spectacle of the world" (Introduction, *The Year*) ("Sábio é aquele que se contenta com o espectáculo do mundo" [Introdução, *O ano*]), these women are wise precisely because they do not "content themselves with the spectacle of the world" and make attempts to change such a spectacle, especially because it is one that is oppressive and destructive. As noted earlier, Saramago does not hold much believe in the existence of God and places the responsibility of human well-being in the hands of humans themselves. As he states,

> But I always come back to a citation by Mark and Engels in *The Holy Family*—in reality only half a dozen words, and not more than that, and I think we can summarize in a few words an entire system, an entire philosophy, an entire hope. Those are very simple words: "If man is formed by circumstances, then it is necessary to form the circumstances humanly." And this is not being done by capitalism and socialism, the so-called real socialism, did not do it either. Thus, it is only still a project, but one that demands, and I go back to what I said before, to the so-called state of mind, which makes people, because they know that man is formed by circumstances, to think and act in ways that will bring about humanly formed circumstances.
>
> Mas eu volto sempre a uma citação do Marx e do Engels na *Sagrada Família*— são meia dúzia de palavras, no fundo, e não são mais do que isso—e creio que se pode resumir em poucas palavras todo um sistema, toda uma filosofia, toda uma esperança. São palavras muito simples: "Se o homem é formado pelas circunstâncias, então é preciso formar as circunstâncias humanamente." E isso nem o capitalismo o faz nem o socialismo, o chamado socialismo real, o fez. Portanto é um projecto que continua como projecto mas que exige, e voltamos àquilo que eu tinha dito antes, o tal estado de espírito que leva as pessoas, sabendo que o homem é formado pelas circunstâncias, a pensar e a agir no sentido de que as circunstâncias que formam o homem têm, elas mesmas, de ser formadas humanamente. (*Uma voz* 38)

When Lídia's visits to Reis's house become rare and then finally stop, the house becomes lifeless, dark, dirty, and difficult to discern, as if it were literally disappearing. Reis himself starts to lose his physicality and identity. Without Lídia's continuous and assiduous presence, Reis initiates his fall into nothingness for he has no one to see, hear, touch, feel, and smell:

> But now Lydia's vacation is over and everything returns to normal, she will come, as before, once a week on her day off. Now, even when the sun finds an open window, the light is different, weaker, and the sieve of time has started once more to sift the impalpable dust that makes outlines fade and blurs features. When Ricardo Reis turns down the bedcover at night, he barely sees the pillow where he will rest his head, and in the morning he cannot rise without first identifying himself with his own hands, line by

line, what he can still find of himself, like a fingerprint partially obliterated by a large, {profound} scar. (309); Having reverted, after Lydia's vacation, to his habit of sleeping practically until lunchtime, Ricardo Reis must have been the last to learn of the military coup in Spain. Blearyeyed, he went to pick up the morning newspaper off his doormat and returned to his bedroom yawning, {one more day that starts, Ah, this long, existential tedium, this pretense of calling it serenity}. (320)

Acabaram as férias de Lídia, tudo voltou ao que dantes era, passará a vir no seu dia de folga, uma vez por semana, agora, mesmo quando o sol encontra uma janela aberta, a luz é diferente, mole, baça, e o tamiz do tempo recomeçou a peneirar o impalpável pó que faz desmaiar os contornos e as feições. Quando, há noite, Ricardo Reis abre a cama para se deitar, mal consegue ver a almofada onde pousará a cabeça, e de manhã não conseguiria levantar-se se com as suas próprias mãos não se identificasse, linha por linha, o que de si ainda é possível achar, como uma impressão digital deformada por uma cicatriz larga e profunda. (357-58); Regressado, depois de terminadas as férias de Lídia, ao seu hábito de dormir até quase há hora do almoço, Ricardo Reis deve ter sido o último habitante de Lisboa a saber que se dera um golpe de estado em Espanha. Ainda com os olhos pesados de sono, foi à escada buscar o jornal, do capacho o levantou e meteu debaixo do braço, voltou ao quarto bocejando, mais um dia que começa, ah, este longo fastídio de existir, este fingimento de lhe chamar serenidade. (371)

Lídia's presence functioned as an affirmation of Reis's own life, suggesting that human identity is always relational, dialectical, and intrinsically tied to others, those others who are there acknowledging us and making us realize (and reflect on) who we are in relation to them, reinforcing again the idea of the Lévinasian ontological relationality. Lídia was Reis's real connection to the world and his own self. Without her, he is unable to stay in touch with either reality. Lídia's absence causes Reis to enter a phase of gradually accelerating self-erasure: he starts to lose his vision, becomes unalert and even needs to touch his body continuously to make sure it is still there. Alone in the large apartment, now totally unoccupied, Reis loses track of time and becomes increasingly lethargic. Cut off from the world, and constantly living in his head, he loses himself in himself. His constant sleepiness is related to his inability to create (and give) meaning to his life and relate to the exterior world, his inability to "make" time. As Lévinas argues in *Time and the Other*, "The situation of the face-to-face would be the very accomplishment of time; the encroachment of the present on the future is not the feat of the subject alone, but the intersubjective relationship. The condition of time lies in the relationship between humans, or in history" (79). The "serenity" characterizing Reis's life is not the serenity felt by someone living a peaceful, fulfilled, and content existence. On the contrary, it indicates a lack, an emptiness, a void, an anxiety, and this is the reason why Saramago refers to it as "tedium" ("fastídio"). This tedium can only be diminished by the self's immersion into phenomenological reality, "in-the-element," into relational and purposeful—in the sense of being occupied—enterprises. This Reian "serenity" is similar to the angst and anxiety described by Camus in *L'Etranger* and experienced by the protagonist of the novel, Meursault. It is also similar to what Séan Hand calls the "unbearable weight of existence" in referring to Lévinas's *Time and the Other* (*The Lévinas* 37). Like Mr. Meursault in Camus's novel, Reis's actions (or better yet, lack thereof) are very nihilistic. In the face of a seemingly absurd world, where God no longer exists, or in Reis's case, where the gods are imperfect like humans and fate is inescapable, and where certainty and unified epistemological systems have been lost, both Meursault and Reis ultimately prove incapable of exiting the sterility of their own existence by creating sense for their own lives. Put differently, they fail to properly exercise freedom and the responsibility that always comes with it (Sartre 707-11). They prove unable to overcome what could be termed the ontological and epistemological abysses, the existential angst and anxiety so proper to the shattered and destabilized subject living in a modern world, where God is absent (dead), and humans become the sole makers of their destiny, and thus cannot blame divine forces for what happens to them (see also Frier 197). As Pessoa says to Reis in the novel, the function of men is "To challenge order, to change fate . . . For better or for worse, it makes no difference, the point is to keep fate from being fate" (288) ("Perturbar a ordem, corrigir o destino . . . Para melhor ou para pior, tanto faz, o que é preciso é impedir que o destino seja destino" [334]). The point is to take charge of one's life and not merely "content [oneself] with the spectacle of the world." And the point is also to relate to others through meaningful, responsible and ethical interaction—an interaction attentive to the well-being not only of the self but also of others.

As David Frier points out, most of Saramago's novels, including *O Ano,* display a central idea of love, life, and relational ethics (the latter often entailing a close encounter with the female or poor other_and an effort to know the other without the judging eye of phallocentrism or classism), which is comparable to the idea of Christian charity, even though, Saramago is a self-professed atheist. There is a central world view running through the author's novels which constantly reinforces the idea that is it the human subject's responsibility to make his or her life better through meaningful activities, direct engagement in the world and relations with the other:

> Love thus becomes central to the functioning of almost all of Saramago's work: most often this is expressed in the traditional sense of an adult relationship between a man and a woman . . . but it may also take some unusual and more interesting forms which contribute to an overall vision of the need for real commitment to the other in order for life to be at all satisfactory for all of us. In the case of *Cegueira,* for instance, the example set by the doctor's wife (who declares herself to be blind early on in the text in order not to have to abandon her husband on his solitary fate in the asylum; see *Cegueira*, p. 44) is ultimately seen to spread to others, as she thinks globally and acts locally by extending a helping hand to those around her encouraging them to emerge from the isolationist mindset which has plagued the unknown city in its hour of need. Thus, when (in another positive example of language as meaningful action within the world) she declares all images in the church are blindfolded (pp. 301-02), the people taking shelter there flee the premises and set about constructing their own positive solutions to the crisis rather than waiting for a messianic savior whom the author clearly

sees as having no reality behind the form of His (overused) name. Surprisingly, therefore, this constitutes an example of something very much like Christian charity in action. (Frier 197-98)

And in the words of Gómez Aguilera. "The political thinking of Saramago is supported by a strong ethical charge. It is habitual for people to allude to the author as an ethical reference and a moral authority or to note the vigor of his principles." ("O pensamento político de Saramago apoia-se em uma forte carga ética. É habitual [que pessoas] aludam ao autor como referência ética e autoridade moral ou se sublinhe a pujança dos seus princípios." [115]).

Reis's decision to move into a large, old apartment by himself is the first sign that he is doomed to end up alone and erase himself into nothingness. While at the Hotel Bragança, he had the presence of other people around him (i.e., the waiter, the manager, other guests) who would talk to and acknowledge him, and who in fact became almost like his family, his relations. And he also had daily and very important interaction with Lídia. In opposition to the hotel where people existed, laughed, spoke, and could be seen in all their physical and immediate manifestations, Reis's newly rented apartment is an empty, big entity, an impersonal site, where he can only hear the noises created by his own movements, the echo of his own voice or other impersonal sounds associated with domestic life:

> Here is the apartment, spacious, adequate for a large family, furniture made of dark mahogany, an enormous bed, a tall closet, a fully furnished dining room, a sideboard, a credenza for silver or china according to one's means, an extending table, and the study paneled with maple, the desk covered with green baize like a billiard, threadbare in one corner, and a kitchen, and a bathroom rudimentary but adequate. Every item of furniture was bare, empty, not a single utensil, dish, ornament, no sheets or towels, The last tenant was an old woman, a widow. (175-76); The apartment filled with noises, the running of water, the vibration of the pipes, a tapping sound from the meter, then gradually silence was restored . . . he finally said loud, like a message he must not forget, I live here, this is where I live, this is my home, this, I have no other, and suddenly he felt fear, the terror of a man who finds himself in a deep cave and pushed open a door that leads into the darkness of an even deeper cave, or to a void, an absence, a nothingness, the passage to nonbeing. {He took off his raincoat and jacket and felt cold.} (186)

> esta é a casa, vasta, ampla, para numerosa família, numa mobília também de mogno escuro, profunda cama, alto guarda-fato, uma sala de jantar completa, o aparador, o guarda-prata, ou louças, dependendo das posses, a mesa extensível, e o escritório, de torcido e tremido pau-santo, mesa de bilhar, puído num dos cantos, a cozinha, a casa de banho rudimentar, mas aceitável, porém todos os móveis estão nus e vazios, nenhuma peça de louça, nenhum lençol ou toalha, A pessoa que aqui viveu era uma senhora idosa, viúva. (206); a casa encheu-se de rumores, o correr da água, o vibrar dos canos, o bater do contador, depois o silêncio voltou . . . e afinal, disse-o em voz alta, como um recado que não deveria esquecer, Eu moro aqui, é aqui que eu moro, é esta a minha casa, é esta, não tenho outra, então cercou-o um súbito medo, o medo de quem, em funda cave, empurra uma porta que

abre para a escuridão doutra cave ainda mais funda, ou para a ausência, o vazio, o nada, a passagem para o não ser. Despiu a gabardina e o casaco, e sentiu frio. (219)

Even the streets surrounding the apartment are empty, desolate, only a few people looking at the sky—as if expecting some divine intervention—and the few ships at the port, as if reminiscing about the Portuguese early empire when great wealth would regularly arrive at the Tejo shore in many ships. Like Reis, these people fail to live in the present and find happiness in their immediate surroundings: "He returned to the front of the apartment to look out at the grimy bedroom window at the deserted street, {the sky was now cloudy}. There stood Adamastor, livid against the dull clouds, a giant raging in silence. Some people are watching the ships, they look up from time to time as if expecting rain, and seated on the bench, the two old men lost in conversation" (186) ("Voltou à parte da frente da casa, ao quarto, olhou pela janela suja a rua deserta, o céu agora coberto, lá estava, lívido contra a cor plúmbea das nuvens, o Adamastor bramindo em silêncio, algumas pessoas contemplavam os navios, de vez em quando levantavam a cabeça para ver se a chuva vinha, os dois velhos conversavam sentados no mesmo banco" [219]). The old men, reminiscent of Velho do Restelo, and the statue of Adamastor are both mythical figures of Camões's epic long poem *Os Lusíadas*, which is an apology of the Portuguese ultramarine expansions and colonial enterprises. This further indicates that Portugal (and Reis) are immersed in past glories; they have delusions of grandeur or happiness that are grounded in the past and are unable to live or be in the present. Everything and everyone seems to be dormant, old and silent, as if in a permanent state of immobility and frigidity. People do not act or move to "make" their lives happen. Instead they seem to be expecting a message from above, a message from a higher force coming from afar, from beyond their immediate horizon. This is why people look to the sky to see if rain will come, but the sky is "cloudy" and "dull." The sky does not send any clear message; it remains closed off to the people, suggesting thus that God is indeed blind. God is dead. Throughout the novel, Reis is often visited by his creator, the dead Fernando Pessoa, which further suggests that he is mostly immersed in his own self: his many selves (alter-egos or personalities) are constantly confronting each other—a sign that Reis is involved in an individual ontological search. There are many other examples throughout the novel that further point to the fact that Reis is an isolated, fragmented, and very unstable self—a self cut off from the rest of the world (the other selves)—and for that very reason, a self who cannot find its identity and give purpose to its life. For example, although Reis eats alone all the time, he likes to have an extra plate and glass on his dinning table, as if to pretend that he is indeed with someone:

> the impression made by the doctor was that of someone refined, he would come in, wish everyone good afternoon or good evening, would order immediately what he wanted, and then it was almost as if he wasn't there. Did he always eat alone, Always, but he did have a curious habit, What was that, Whenever we began to remove the setting of the opposite side of the table,

he always asked us to leave it there, he said that the table looked more attractive set for two, and on one occasion when I was serving him there was a strange little incident. When I poured his wine, I made a mistake of filling both glasses, his and that of the {absent person}, if you know what I mean. Yes, I see, and then what happened. He said it was perfect {like that}, and from then on he always insisted that the other glass should be filled, and at the end of the meal he would drink it on the go, keeping his eyes closed as he drunk. How odd. {You must know, sir, that we waiters see many curious sights.} Did he do this in all other restaurants he frequented, Ah, that I couldn't tell you, you would have to ask around. Can you recall if he ever met a friend or an acquaintance, even if he did not sit at the same table. Never, he always gave the impression of someone who had just arrived from abroad, just like when I first came here from Xunqueira de Ambia, if you get my meaning. I know exactly what you mean, we all have had that experience. (230)

a ideia com que nós ficámos, na nossa cabeça, é que o senhor doutor era uma pessoa educada, entrava, dava as boas-tardes ou boas-noites, dizia logo o que queria comer, e depois não se dava mais por ele, era como se aí não estivesse, Comia sempre sozinho, Sempre, o que tinha era um costume, Qual, Quando nós íamos a tirar o talher da mesa, o que estava defronte dele, pedia que o deixássemos ficar, que assim parecia a mesa mais composta, e uma vez, comigo, até se deu um caso, Que caso, Quando lhe servi o vinho, enganei-me e enchi os dois copos, o dele e o da outra pessoa que lá não estava, não sei se está a perceber, Estou a perceber, estou, e depois, Então me disse que estava bem assim, e a partir daí tinha sempre o outro copo cheio, no fim da refeição bebia-o duma só vez, fechava os olhos para beber, Caso estranho, Saiba vossa excelência que nós, criados, vimos muitas coisas estranhas, E fazia o mesmo em todos os restaurantes aonde ia, Ah, isso não sei, só perguntando, Lembram-se de alguma vez ter encontrado um amigo ou um conhecido, mesmo que não se sentassem à mesma mesa, Nunca, era como se tivesse acabado de chegar de um país estrangeiro, assim como eu quando vim de Xunqueira de Ambia, não sei se me entende, Entendo muito bem, todos nós já passámos por isso. (270)

The extra plate and the full glass on the table give Reis the illusion that there is in fact another person there. But in reality, there is no one else there but himself, or "his multiple selves." The plate and the full glass are mere fragmented reflections of the Reian self, mirrors reflected back to a mirror, a mirror that has no real mirror (people or other "Is") to see itself in (through). Thus, the plate and the glass function as "returns" of the self to the self. The Reian self is an isolated self, a self not engaged with other real others (people): a self who is merely immersed in individual ontological reflections (searches) and makes little or no attempt to interrelate with external others or with otherness. The fact that Reis drinks the wine of the "absent person" (230) ("pessoa que lá não estava" [270]), as the waiter ironically puts it, is further indication that he is constantly "drinking" himself in and thus has difficulty knowing who he is: he is isolated from the feedback that other people would give him about who he is, were he to be immersed in relational experiences. On a more obvious level, when the narrator tells us that Reis is drinking the wine of the "absent person" he is also obviously referring to Reis's own creator: the dead Fernando Pessoa. But even this reading suggests that Reis is dead not just because his creator is literally dead but also because he (Reis) is a creation of Pessoa, he is an "I" created by that same "I," and thus a being with no grounds in a reality outside of the "mind" of the self, an "I" with no body and no "real" (outside) other with which to compare himself. The fact that Reis drinks the wine of the second glass with his eyes closed further reinforces the idea that he is closed off to the world. His senses are not really awakened: they are overshadowed (or tamed) by the abstract nature of the intellect. Stated otherwise, he is not aware of his surroundings (e.g., the people, the sounds, the colours, the smiles, the sensations, the trees). He is blind to the real (phenomenological) world constantly pulsating in front of him because he is encapsulated in his egotistical self. He is like a dead person, who has no friends, no connections at all, as if his real life lay somewhere else, in another spatio-temporal reality. As the hypothetical conversation between the waiter and the narrator suggests, Reis is like someone "who just arrived from abroad" (230) ("acabado de chegar de um país estrangeiro" [270]). And he is so, because he lives in the detached, abstract, and inner life of the intellect, as if his real life were in some other land and time frame, as if he were only passing through and could not bother to truly leave the mark of his presence. We have the impression he is searching for the infinite (or the absolute, the divine) and fails to realize that the access to that very world might be via his insertion into the finite (immediate) world.

The Reian self-centeredness, his intra-personal and introverted attitude is constantly present (and repeated) throughout Saramago's novel in the form of what I choose to call metaphors of the "mirror," "dark," and "lifelessness": "In this light, or because of these somber faces, the mirror resembles an aquarium, and when Ricardo Reis crosses the lounge on the far side and comes back by the same route in order not to turn around and make a beeline for the doorway, he sees himself in the greenish abyss as if he were walking on the ocean floor amid wreckage and drowned corpses. He must live this space {now, reach the surface, breathe}. (85); Ricardo Reis smiled, {while mentally he considered} these sad irreverences. It is not pleasant to see a man smiling to himself, particularly if he is smiling into {the mirror}, a good thing there is a closed door between him and the rest of the world" (208) ("A esta luz, ou por causa destes rostos apagados, o espelho parece um aquário, e Ricardo Reis, quando atravessa a sala para o lado de lá e pelo mesmo caminho de volta, questão de não virar as costas e fugir logo à entrada da porta, vê-se naquela profundeza esverdeada como se caminhasse no fundo do oceano, entre destroços de navios e gente afogada, tem de sair já, vir ao de cima, respirar" [105]; "Ricardo Reis sorria, enquanto mentalmente, desafiava estas irreverências tristes, não é agradável ver um homem sorrir sozinho, pior ainda se é ao espelho que sorri, o que vale é haver uma porta fechada entre ele e o resto do mundo. Então pensou, E Marcenda, que mulher será Marcenda, a pergunta é inconsequente, mero entretém de quem não tem com quem falar" [244]). As these passages suggest, Reis is only an intellect that ponders, analyzes, and reflects about the ways in which Marcenda might act and about what kind of woman she might be. Rather than approaching Marcenda directly by talking to her, asking her questions about herself and feeling (knowing) her physically, he prefers to "remain" in his mind and imagine her. This situation is a déjà vu: it mirrors the ways Reis dealt with his imaginary Lídia, as depicted, for instance, in the poem "Lydia, Come and Sit with Me, by the Riverside." Reis is a solitary man who ruminates about the way women might be, a man who "does not get out of his mind" to really meet women and see how they might be in their most real dimensions. He is a person immersed in constant "cogito": a mirror looking at his mirror, a face looking at his face. The mirror becomes a "greenish abyss" (85) ("profundeza esverdeada" [105]) giving Reis the impression that he is "walking on the ocean floor amid wreckage and drowned corpses" (85) ("caminha[ndo] no fundo do oceano, entre destroços de navios e gente afogada" [105]). The mirror is described in such a negative and deadly mode precisely because it returns Reis to himself: it returns his own image to himself, like a deadly, perpetual, and endless game, a game which can only end when Reis decides to come to the surface and meet other "Is"—the "Is" who will assure (and remind) him of who he (really) is. It is as if Reis were the only person who exists in the world, for he refuses to see (meet) others, and by doing so, he also fails to meet his most real or assured self, thus living in a constant state of self-doubt, as someone on the verge of dying or disappearing. The mirror image Reis receives of himself resembles a person, walking amidst "drowned corpses" (85) ("gente afogada" [105]), precisely because Reis is living in himself and not with (and through) other people. All the corpses at the bottom of the ocean symbolize Reis's many selves fighting against one another, fighting for grounded, stable, and stabilized identity: Who is real, who is not real, who or what am I, what must I believe in, and think, and do in order to "meet" (find, anchor) my self? Those are the questions the fragmented (and unsure) self is struggling with.

These ontological and epistemological questions (dilemmas) are all going through the Reian mind in the course of the novel, yet they are never answered or resolved. The Reian self becomes more and more fragmented because it does not attempt to find unity, identity, and meaning for its life outside of the solitary cogito. In a fashion similar to Descartes, Reis believes that he can find his self in himself and that he exists because he thinks. Ironically, it is this excessive thinking (over-cogitation) that makes Reis lose his identity. Rather than just believe that "he is because he thinks," Reis ought to also believe that "he is because he feels, or sees, or touches." Reis inhabits his own isolated, intra-personal and individualistic self, a place where there is no room for sociability and interaction with others and otherness. In order to find life (meaning, coherence for his self and his life) Reis must "live this space {now}, reach the surface" (85) ("sair já, vir ao de cima" [105]) so that he can "breathe" (85) ("respirar" [105]), in other words, find life and meaning outside of his self. Reaching the surface would equate to the Reian entrance into the real world and the commencement of his social and interpersonal engagement.

Throughout the novel, Reis is in fact depicted as someone who lives in what I call the "mirror stage" (not in the Lacanian sense) or the "moon-light stage" rather that the "real stage" or the "day-light stage." Reis lives in a "mirror stage" because he isolates himself from the real people, which would function as his real mirrors—the "Is" who would remind him of who he is. We all need mirrors (people) to tell or remind us of who we are. But because Reis isolates himself he becomes his own mirror and thus an empty one, a mirror without the real mirror (a type of archetype) in the background to reaffirm and reflect its truest identity (presence). Thus, in reality, the Reian self becomes a charade, a false reflection, or many false reflections:

> Leaning over the barrister, Ricardo Reis sees her [Marcenda]. Halfway up the first flight of stairs, she looks up, anxious to make sure that the person she seeks really lives here, {she is smiling, he also smiles, these are smiles that have a future}, unlike those reflected in a mirror, that is the difference. Ricardo Reis backs towards the door, Marcenda is climbing the last flight of stairs, only now does he notice that the light in the stairwell is off, that he is about to receive her almost in darkness, and while he vacillates, on another level of thought he wonders with surprise, {How was it possible for her smile to seem so radiant when seen from above, now that she stands} before me, what should I say, I cannot ask, How have you been, nor exclaim in an even more plebeian fashion. (209)

> Debruçado do corrimão, Ricardo Reis vê-a [Marcenda] subir, a meio do primeiro lanço ela olha para cima, a certificar-se de que mora realmente ali a pessoa que procura, sorri, ele sorri também, são sorrisos que têm um destino, não são feitos ao espelho, essa é a diferença. Recuou Ricardo Reis para a porta, Marcenda sobe o último lanço, só então ele repara que não acendera a luz da escada, vai recebê-la às escuras, e enquanto hesita sobre o que deve fazer, acender, não acender, há outro nível de pensamento em que se exprime uma surpresa, como foi possível parecer tão luminoso o sorriso dela, visto de cá de cima, diante de mim agora, que palavras irão ser ditas, não posso perguntar, Então como tem passado, ou exclamar plebeiamente. (245)

The nature of the smiles displayed by Marcenda and Reis is different from the nature of the Reian smile previously alluded to, when Reis is thinking and pondering about what type of woman Marcenda might be, instead of directly confronting her. That smile was described by the narrator as being a smile "into the mirror" (208) ("no espelho" [244]), and one that was unpleasant. In opposition, the smiles displayed by Reis and Marcenda in the above passage are described as "smiles that have a future, unlike those reflected in a mirror" (209) ("sorrisos que têm um destino, não são feitos ao espelho" [245]). While the first one symbolizes the Reian isolated cogito pondering about other cogitos, the second actually symbolizes the encounter between the two cogitos (people). This time the smile is meeting another real smile; this time the smile has a future precisely because it has a receiver outside of the individual self. Both Reis and Marcenda are senders and receivers outside of themselves. They are not merely smiling at themselves, smiling about their conjectures of others: what they might be or think or how they might act. However, as the narrator ironically points out, Marcenda's smile seemed more radiant to Reis when he was receiving it from above. Now that Marcenda is in front of him, he seems surprised that her smile had indeed seemed so radiant. In other words, he had seen Marcenda (and her smile) from his own cogito again, from afar and beyond the reality that she represents. Now that her body is in front of him, he seems to have lost interest in her smile. The fact that he thinks he is going to receive Marcenda in the dark and that he hesitates between turning on the lights or leaving them off are again indications of the Reian confusion about where to find love and existential fulfillment: in the here and the now, or in the isolation and abstraction of his own mind (in the light/life of the present/physical or the dark/dead of the absent/abstract)? We could say that in this instance Reis is in the moon-light stage: he seems to be close to the real stage, or at least be able to have a glimpse of the pleasure that such stage might entail. Yet, he reverts to the mirror stage, to his reflective self and his idealist conceptions of love and women.

Throughout the novel Reis displays other moon-light stages as he seems to be going in the direction of exiting his cogito and making real connections with other people or with the physical world, yet he always ends up by retreating into his own self, thus never reaching the real stage or day-light stage, in other words, never being able to form his identity relationally. While at the hotel for example, Reis had, to a certain extent, exited the mirror stage and entered the moon-light stage. Through his regular (even if often superficial) relationships and interactions with the others, he had attempted to "forget himself" so that he could recognize or realize himself through others. Reis's solitary confinement in a large and old house is a step back in his ontological search. It is a reentrance into the mirror stage:

> Ricardo Reis has got into the habit of rising late. He has learned to suppress any desire to eat in the morning. The opulent trays Lydia used to bring to his room at the Hotel Bragança now seem to belong to someone else's past. He sleeps late, wakes up and goes back to sleep again, he studies his own sleeping, and after numerous attempts has succeeded in fixing his mind on a single dream, always the same dream, about one who dreams that he does not wish to conceal one dream with another, like erasing telltale footprints, It is simple, all you have to do is drag the branch of a tree behind you, leaving only scattered leaves and pieces of twig, which soon wither and merge with the dust. When he gets up, it is time for lunch. Washing, shaving, dressing are mechanical acts in which the {conscience} barely participates. This face covered with lather is a mask that could fit any man's face, and when the razor little by little reveals what is underneath, Ricardo Reis is intrigued by what he sees, and disturbed, as if afraid that some evil emerge. He examines himself carefully in the mirror, comparing his face with {another face he has stopped seeing for a while now, but his conscience denies him that, he tells} himself that as long as he shaves every day, sees every day these eyes, this mouth, this nose, this chin, these pale cheeks, these crumpled, absurd appendages called ears, that such a change is impossible, and yet he feels certain he spent years in some place without mirrors, because today he looks in the mirror and does not recognize himself. (298-99)

> Ricardo Reis, agora, levanta-se tarde. Deixou de tomar o pequeno-almoço, habituou-se a dominar o apetite matinal, ao ponto de lhe parecerem memória doutra vida não sua as bandejas opulentas que a Lídia lhe levava

ao quanto nos abundosos tempos do Hotel Bragança. Dorme pela manhã adentro, acorda e readormece, assiste ao seu próprio dormir, e, após muitas tentativas, conseguiu fixar-se num único sonho, sempre igual, o de alguém que sonha que não quer sonhar, encobrindo os sonhos com o sonho, como quem apaga os rastos que deixou, os sinais dos pés, as reveladoras pegadas, é simples, basta ir arrastando atrás de si um ramo de árvore ou uma palma de palmeira, não ficam mais do que folhas soltas, agudas flechas, em breve secas e confundidas com o pó. Quando se levanta são horas de almoçar. Lavar-se, barbear-se, vestir-se são actos mecânicos em que a consciência mal participa. Esta cara coberta de espuma não é mais do que uma máscara de homem, adaptável a qualquer outro rosto de homem, e quando a navalha, aos poucos, vai revelando o que está por baixo, Ricardo Reis olha-se perplexo, um tanto intrigado, inquieto, como se temesse que dali pudesse vir algum mal. Observa minuciosamente o que o espelho lhe mostra, tenta descobrir as parecenças deste rosto com um outro rosto que terá deixado de ver há muito tempo, que assim não pode dizer-lho a consciência, basta que tem a certeza de barbear-se todos os dias, de todos os dias ver estes olhos, esta boca, este nariz, este queixo, estas faces pálidas, estes apêndices ridículos que são as orelhas, e no entanto é como se tivesse passado muitos anos sem se olhar, num lugar sem espelhos, sequer os olhos de alguém, e hoje vê-se e não se reconhece. (345)

Alone in the house, Reis loses touch with his psychological and physical identity. Even though he often looks himself in the mirror, his facial features seem alien to him, for there are no other eyes to see them, except his own. He becomes a mask because he has no real archetype (other people) to see himself through, to compare himself with. He becomes a dream within a dream for he is the one attempting to create an image of himself, an image that has no external (real) copy to be compared with. At the hotel, Reis's self had been face to face with the other, and so his identity had been reassured of its existence, outside of the self. This is why he now feels "he spent years in some place without mirrors" (299) ("como se tivesse passado muitos anos sem se olhar" [345]). The "mirrors" here refer to the people he had interacted with daily while at the hotel Bragança. Now that Reis is alone in his large apartment where there are no "real" mirrors to remind him of who he is, he no longer recognizes himself when looking into the mirror. Alone with his self, Reis's identity becomes shattered, fragile, and fragmented. He feels fear when looking into the mirror because he senses he is losing grasp of who he is: it is as if he knows that he is about to die. While at the hotel, Reis was not merely looking into himself, but rather, he was having a real, unmediated glimpse at the other others, and thus also a truer glimpse at himself. He had been, if not totally in the real stage or day-light stage, at least in the moon-light stage. While immersed in relationships, Reis was in the arena of sensibility, immediacy, and phenomenological and interrelational apprehension; he was living rather than merely thinking (or reflecting). He was in the Lévinasian "element":

> To-be-in-the-element does indeed disengage a being from blind and deaf participation in a whole, but differs from a thought making its way outward... It is to be within, to be inside of... This situation is not reducible

to a representation, not even an inarticulate representation; it belongs to sensibility, which is the *mode* of enjoyment. It is when sensibility is interpreted as representation and mutilated thought that the finitude of our thought has to be invoked so as to account for these "obscure" thoughts . . . One does not know, one lives sensible qualities: the green of these leaves, the red of this sunset . . . Sensibility, essentially naïve, suffices to itself in a world insufficient for thought . . . Sensibility establishes a relation with the pure quality without support, with the element . . . Sensibility is not an inferior theoretical knowledge bound however intimately to affective states: in its very *gnosis* sensibility is enjoyment; it is satisfied with the given, it is contented . . . This earth upon which I find myself and from which I welcome sensible objects or make my way to them suffices me. The earth which upholds me does so without my troubling myself about knowing what upholds the earth. I am content with the aspect this corner of the world, universe of my daily behavior, this city or this neighborhood or this street in which I move, this horizon within which I live, turn to me; I do not ground them in a more vast system. (*Totality and Infinity* 135-37)

As many have argued, Lévinas did not directly extend his "sensibility" and his "be[ing]-in-the-element" to erotic, sexual love, and, in fact, saw this type of love as "profanation" (259), "animality" (259), "violation" (260), "indecency," "lasciviousness," "pleasure and dual egoism" (263), and as "a return to oneself" (266). For example, Sonia Sikka argues that, "given the fact that *eros* is for [Lévinas] redeemed not by its own nature but by the engendering of the son, it would seem that the erotic relation is here also depicted as a form of intercourse, less than fully human and bordering the shameful, with a faceless other in order to reproduce oneself" (102). In her "correction" of Lévinas's "Phenomenology of Eros" as depicted in *Totality*, Irigaray also attacks Lévinas's concept of sexual love. She extends the Lévinasian "sensibility" and the "being-in-the-element" to erotic love. In fact, Irigaray sees nonpossessive, interrelational erotic love between a man and a woman as the fountain of divinity, infinity, and dwelling; as the site where subjectivity erases itself, but where it also finds the space to be reborn, born in difference. This difference allows the man and the woman to maintain their otherness, and at the same time, continuously discover or rediscover each other and themselves in each other's bodies (borders). As she nicely puts it in "The Fecundity of the Caress,"

> Before orality comes to be, touch is already in existence. No nourishment can compensate for the grace or work of touching. Touch makes it possible to wait, to gather strength, so that the other will return to caress and reshape, from within and from without, a flesh that is given back to itself in the gesture of love. The most necessary guardian of my life is the other's flesh. Approaching and speaking to me with his hands. Bringing me back to life more intimately than any regenerative nourishment, the other's hands, these palms with which he approaches without going through me, give me back the borders of my body and call me to the remembrance of the most profound intimacy. (121); Both fulfilling the cycles of their solitude to come back to the other. (131); Touching can also place a limit on the reabsorption of the other in the same. Giving the other her contours, calling her to them,

amounts to inviting her to live where she is without becoming other, without appropriating herself. (134); To give back to the other the possible site of his identity, of his intimacy: a second birth that returns one to innocence. (136); Dwelling with the self, and with the other—while letting the other go . . . Remembering the act not as a simple discharge of energy but for its characteristic intensity, sensation, color, and rhythm. (140); A kind of house that shelters without enclosing me, untying and tying me to the other, as to one who helps me to build and inhabit. (142); Scent or premonition between my self and the other, this memory of the flesh as the place of approach means ethical fidelity to incarnation. To destroy it is to risk the suppression of alterity, both God's and the other's. Thereby dissolving any possibility to access to transcendence. (143)

The "Phenomenology of Eros," as described and understood by Irigaray is, as I have already shown, enough for and appreciated by Lídia. She loves to make love because life is "so sad" (78) ("tão triste" [97]); she wants Ricardo Reis to hold her tight "{only} because it {feels} good" (307) ("só pelo bem que sabe" [356]) and she finds it satisfying enough to simply lie in bed with Reis, after the act of lovemaking: "lying here without any future, I'm happy with what I have now" (171) ("basta-me o que tenho agora, estar aqui deitada, sem nenhum futuro" [201]). She is grounded in reality and thus is able to experience perhaps the best happiness humans can feel: an ecstasy even, a dwelling, such as described by Irigaray. Lídia respects, appreciates, welcomes, and understands what Irigaray calls the "memory of the flesh." And at moments, we have the impression that Reis, too, appreciates this "memory of the flesh" and the happiness that can come from tangible things: from being with people, from eating and drinking, from simply walking through the streets of Lisbon and experiencing its smells, its noises, its life. And yet, he ultimately fails to be at peace with such reality of human life and to reconcile body and soul, human and divine, finite and infinite, and so, he ultimately fails to tame his existential tedium and to find his truer self and the truer other.

It is true that the Saramaguian Reis appears as a much more sympathetic figure than the original Pessoan Reis. The former experiences moments of what seems to be genuine tenderness towards Lídia, often showing respect and admiration for her. He enjoys her company, and not merely during the sexual act; he sees her as an intelligent person with many strengths and qualities, frequently asking for her opinion on different matters and being generally interested in listening to what she has to say. Sometimes Reis is even able to see her outside of his intellectual (restricted and totalizing) paradigm of femininity, otherness, and class, or at least, come near to the questioning of such paradigm: "Because it caught Lydia's head at a favorable angle, Ricardo Reis noticed the birthmark at the side of one nostril. It becomes her, he thought, although later he could not say if he was referring to the birthmark or to her apron, or to the starched cap on her head, or to the embroidered collar she wore around her neck" (69) ("e como a cabeça de Lídia estava em posição favorável Ricardo Reis notou o sinal que ela tinha perto da asa do nariz, Fica-lhe bem, pensou, depois não soube se ainda estava a referir-se ao sinal, ou avental branco, ou ao adorno engomado da cabeça, ou ao debrum bordado que lhe cingia o pescoço" [87]). At first glance, the passage gives us the impression that Reis tends to take the part as the whole, that is, look at one aspect of Lídia's appearance and use it as the synecdoche to define her entire self. However, a second reading will show that at this point Reis actually becomes confused about Lídia's true identity: he no longer knows whether it is the birthmark, or the apron, or the starched cap, or the embroidered collar that define her. Is it one of these marks and which one exactly? Or is it rather all of them that define her? Thus, in reality, Reis is at this point questioning his reductive (totalizing) definition (gaze) of women, and even more specifically, of maids: the feminine and the class paradigms are no longer static and entirely graspable to the observer's eye. Is Lídia just a woman? Is she rather just a hotel chambermaid, as the apron and the cap seem to indicate? Or is she in fact a unique type of woman, as the birthmark on the nostril seem to indicate, and thus one who cannot be defined in a straightforward manner and be put in a simple and totalizing category? Reis does not seem to know. The fact that he looks at the birthmark and the physical appearance (the clothes) of Lídia further suggests that he is attempting to be grounded in the phenomenology of life: to see the physical marks of people, to appreciate and live via the sensible, and distrust what the mind tells him. His confusion about what looks good on Lídia indicates his deviation from the mind's rhetoric and his attempt to make sense of phenomenological reality: his attempt to start "clean" and understand life via phenomenon. The birthmark can also be seen to function as a symbol that conveys doubt and mystery, in other words, a symbol of what lies beyond one's logical comprehension and rational grasp: the unreachable, the infinitum, the exterior, the other as other and different from the observing self. Thus, in these instances we can suggest that Reis is entering, or close to entering, the Lévinasian notion of alterity and otherness: he is able to see the "face" and go beyond the "image" or the "gaze." Unlike the original Pessoan Reis, who merely gives Lídia guidance and advice and does not even allow her to speak, Saramago's Reis recognizes that in order to get to know a woman, one needs to be physical with her, to listen to her language (be it silence or spoken words) and witness her emotions:

> If you were alive and found yourself in my shoes, with an unwanted child and, its mother from a lower class, you would have the doubts I have. The very same. The doubts of a cad. That's right, dear Reis, a cad. I may be a cad, but I have no intention of abandoning Lydia. Perhaps because she is making things easy for you. True enough, she told me there was no need for me to acknowledge the child as mine. Why are women like this, Not all of them, Agreed, but only women can be like this. Anyone listening to you would think you had a great deal of experience with women. The only experience I have is that of a spectator, {who sees them pass}. No, one has to sleep with them, make them pregnant, even if it ends in abortion, one has to see them when they are sad and happy, laughing and weeping, silent and talkative, one has to watch them when they do not know that they are being watched. And what does an experienced man see at such moments? An enigma, a labyrinth, a charade. I was always good at charades, But a disaster when it came to women, My dear Reis, {you are not being kind}. (312)

> Portanto, se você estivesse vivo e o caso fosse consigo, filho não desejado, mulher desigual, teria as mesmas dúvidas, Tal e qual, Um safado, Muito bem feito, caro Reis, Seja como for, não vou fugir, Talvez porque a Lídia lhe facilite as coisas, É verdade, chegou-me a dizer que não tenho que perfilhar a criança, Por que será que as mulheres são assim, Nem todas, De acordo, mas só mulheres o conseguem ser, Quem o ouvisse, diria que você teve uma grande experiência delas, Tive apenas a experiência de quem assiste e vê passar, É grande engano o seu se continua a julgar que isso basta, é preciso dormir com elas, fazer-lhes filhos, mesmo que sejam para desmanchar, é preciso vê-las tristes e alegres, a rir e a chorar, caladas e falando, é preciso olhá-las quando não sabem que estão a ser olhadas, E que vêem então os homens hábeis, Um enigma, um quebra-cabeças, um labirinto, uma charada, Sempre fui bom em charadas, Mas em mulheres um desastre, Meu caro Reis você não está a ser amável. (361-62)

This conversation between Pessoa and Reis tells us that although the original Pessoa wrote a lot about women, he never in fact had any sexual (physical) relations with any—and so, some might say, cannot really be trusted in his account of them. Pessoa was good with "charades," good at pretending and acting; in other words, good with intellectual and unreal accounts of women, but never good with "real" women. He could not get out of his ungrounded and biased artistic creation, a creation that did not "drink" in the reality of women. As the contemporary Portuguese writer António Lobo Antunes has put it, when referring to Pessoa's art and its enormous influence, "I distrust someone who never had sexual relations" ("Desconfio de alguém que nunca teve relações sexuais"[qtd. in Carvalho 3]) someone who is too intellectual, and who has been "sanctified" and "sacralized" (qtd. in Carvalho 3) by everyone, he adds (see also Crespo 239-50). Reis does come to the realization that it is impossible for a man to ever completely understand the "otherness" of a woman: she will always remain an "enigma, a labyrinth, a charade" (312), as he says. Or, to use Lévinasian language, she will remain hermeneutically undisclosed, impossible to truly understand or discern by the observing male eye. What the male will see (perceive) in his encounter with the woman is not the real woman but rather the charade; in other words, the persona she puts on and acquires when faced with the encounter with the male other. This is why Reis says to Pessoa that "one has to watch [women] when they do not know they are being watched" (312), suggesting that it is at those moments that the male eye might have a truer glimpse at the female nature: truer perhaps, but never complete, for that would equate with incorporation and totalization.

The Reian process of self-erasure finally comes to a climax when Reis decides to accompany the already dead Pessoa into the cemetery, rather than make any final attempt to contact Lídia and assume his paternal responsibilities. His inability to attach himself to a real woman and his own baby—his flesh and blood—are the final indications that Reis is unable to take charge of his own life, to form his identity interrelationally and accept his body as the house of his soul. It is clear then that Saramago values relational ontological searches rather than individual ontological searches, for the former bring contact with others and make us realize that we can find fulfillment in our most human qualities, and furthermore, that we have the power and responsibility to build a better world and life for ourselves and others; the power to be fecund, to find happiness in the immediacy of life, and with and within our community. Saramago's message regarding the nature of ontological inquiry is thus different from that of Sartre, Hegel, and Heidegger and close to that of Lévinas, as Anthony Macri argues:

> The existentialist ontologies of both Heidegger and Sartre are intensely individualistic; though they discuss the encounter with the Other, they do not make interpersonal relations the cornerstone of their systems. Rather the individual being-in-the-world engages the world from the standpoint [of his or her] subjectivity as a meaning-making agent, providing meaning to that which has none in-itself. For Heidegger, the ability to create meaning for the world ends in death, and it is the anticipation of death that results in anxiety for the self, destabilizing it. In Sartre's philosophy, simply the possibility of creating meaning in complete and total freedom destabilizes the self, hurling it into a state of anxiety. The individual comes to a realization of his existential anxiety, for both thinkers in an act of self-reflection. (1-2); Levinas, attacking both the ontological idealism of Hegel and the individualistic concepts of existential thought, stresses the incoming of the Other as the moment of de-totalization. The other is the reminder of the infinite that prevents notions of totality. (6); [For Lévinas, ontology] is constantly involved in the concrete relationships of the world. It is not based on deep personal and individualistic reflection, but rather one that erupts from a notion of the self as the one who meets the Other in a tenuous and at times volatile relationship... The Otherness of selfhood, developed through existential inquiry into Levinas, can be the starting point for a more exhaustive and comprehensive understanding of reality suited for the contemporary postmodern world. This ontology merits consideration as taking human relationality to be the core of existence, and will no doubt yield meaningful outlooks through future exploration. (7-8)

The very beginning and end of the novel are indications of Saramago's phenomenological message, a message that preaches about the need to ground ourselves to the spatio-temporal present and realities: "Here the sea ends and the earth begins" (1) ("Aqui o mar acaba e a terra principia" [1]), reads the opening of the novel. And the end reiterates the same message: "Here, where the sea {has ended} and the earth awaits" (358) ("Aqui, onde o mar se acabou e a terra espera" [415]). The earth refers to Portugal, a country that must leave the past behind, with all its maritime and intercontinental enterprises, and concentrate on strengthening itself within its own frontiers. But the earth also refers to the human body, a house that we all have and must cherish so that we can finally be at home.

Female and male sterility and the alienating rhetorical entanglement

Salazar's constitution proclaimed everyone equal by the law "except for women, the differences resulting from their nature and for the good of the family" ("salvas, quanto à mulher, as diferenças resultantes da sua natureza e do bem da família"

[221])—legally making them subjects of men, denying them the right to divorce and (with a few exceptions) even the right to vote. In *O Ano* the oppressive situation of women in Portugal during the fascist regime is widely explored and constitutes a very important aspect of the novel. In direct opposition to Lídia who, as already discussed, is described by Saramago as someone who is able to maintain her dignity as a woman and to mix the pleasures of the body with the pleasures of the soul, many other women of the novel are often mocked and portrayed in a negative light by Saramago. These women are depicted as aiding and supporting the oppressive, fascist, highly religious and patriarchal regime of Salazar. In this sense, they literally become like the tragic female dog Ugolina, described in the novel as eating her own puppies (her own self). Like Ugolina, these women are eating their own selves because they are erasing or silencing their own voices, their difference and value, and further entangling themselves in the complex web of a male dominated society:

> {Dear voracious reader,} the cannibalism of bitches is generally due to malnutrition during the gestation period. The dog must be fed with meat as her staple diet and supplemented with milk, bread, and vegetables, in brief, a well-balanced diet. If this does not change {her} habits, there's no remedy, either destroy the dog or do not allow her to mate, let her put up with being in heat or you can have her spayed. Now let us try to imagine what would happen if women suffering from malnutrition during pregnancy, starved of meat, {milk, bread and cabbage}, which is fairly common, were also to begin eating their infants. After trying to image it and having concluded that such crimes do not occur, it becomes easy to see the difference between people and animals. The editor did not add {this comment}, nor did Ricardo Reis, who is thinking about something else, a suitable name for the bitch. (18-19)

> O canibalismo das cadelas, prezado leitor e consulente, é no geral devido ao mau arroçamento durante a gestação, com insuficiência de carne, deve-se--lhe dar comida em abundância, em que a carne entre como base, mas a que não faltem o leite, o pão e os legumes, enfim, um alimentação completa, se mesmo assim não lhe passar a balda, não tem cura, mate-a ou não a deixe cobrir, que se avenha com o cio, ou mande capá-la. Agora imaginemos nós que as mulheres mal arroçadas durante a gravidez, e é o mais do comum, sem carne, sem leite, algum pão e couves, se punham também a comer os filhos, e, tendo imaginado e verificado que tal não acontece, torna-se afinal fácil distinguir as pessoas dos animais, este comentário não o acrescentou o redactor, nem Ricardo Reis, que está a pensar noutra coisa, que nome adequado se deveria dar a esta cadela. (30)

As indicated here, it is not the editor of the newspaper Reis is reading who adds the comments regarding the malnourished pregnant women and their potential to act like Ugolina by eating their own offspring. Nor is it Ricardo Reis himself, and so it is obvious that it is the narrator who does so. The narrator is not merely telling a story without stating his opinion, but rather letting the reader know his position regarding the situation of women in Portugal. By hypothesizing a comparison between women and Ugolina, the narrator is telling us to read beyond what the newspaper openly says;

The Politics of Agency in Saramago

he wants us to "see" what lies beyond the page of the paper, beyond the story being openly told about Ugolina. Given that women are living under the highly repressive regime of Salazar, it is likely that the newspaper would be controlled by the state, so that the socioeconomic realities affecting most people (i.e., censorship, poverty, exploitation, and physical and psychological violence) could be kept in the shadows. Salazar's regime was famous for its use of violence with its many political prisoners and with the people in general. The PIDE (*Polícia Internacional e de Defesa do Estado* ["International and State Defense Police"]) was its most repressive and controlling agent, often resorting to the use of physical torture and psychological intimidation.

The narrator points out the fact that the newspaper Reis is reading tells the story of the cannibal bitch "calmly" (19) ("tranquilamente" [30]) and that Reis in fact falls asleep while reading. These narrational details are crucial to the understanding of the Saramaguian political message. Reis's falling asleep is indicative of his disinterest in the violence and oppression literally killing people around him, or at least of his incapacity to see beyond the "calm" words of the newspaper. The narrator, on the other hand, keeps pointing to the extremely violent physical aspects, which characterize the cannibal act of the bitch eating her own puppies. This illustrates his interest in telling the reader about the reality beyond the surface, the reality, beyond the "calm" words of the newspaper's editor, beyond the naming, in other words, the phenomenological reality,

> Therefore let the {mother who eats her own children} be called Ugolina, so unnatural that her heart suffers no compassion as she tears the warm and tender skin of the defenseless jaws, slaughtering them, causing them their delicate bones to snap, and the poor little puppies, whining, perish without realizing who is devouring them, the mother who gave them birth. Ugolina, do not kill me, I am your offspring. The page which calmly relates these horrors falls onto the lap of Ricardo Reis. He is fast asleep. A sudden gust of wind rattles the windowpanes, the rain pours like a deluge. Through the deserted streets of Lisbon prowls the bitch Ugolina slavering blood, sniffing in doorways, howling in squares and parks, furiously biting at her own womb, where the next litter is about to be conceived. (19)

> chame-se pois Ugolina à mãe que come os seus próprios filhos, tão desnaturada que não se lhe movem as entranhas à piedade quando com as suas mesmas queixadas rasga a morna e macia pele dos indefesos, os trucida, fazendo-lhes estalar os ossos tenros, e os pobres cãezinhos, gementes, estão morrendo sem verem quem os devora, a mãe que os pariu, Ugolina não me mates que sou teu filho. A folha que tais horrores explica tranquilamente cai sobre os joelhos de Ricardo Reis, adormecido. Uma rajada súbita fez estremecer as vidraças, a chuva desaba como um dilúvio. Pelas ruas de Lisboa anda a cadela Ugolina a babar-se de sangue, rosnando às portas, uivando em praças e jardins, mordendo furiosa o próprio ventre onde já está a gerar-se a próxima ninhada. (30-31)

When the narrator says, "Ugolina, do not kill me, I am your offspring" (19) ("Ugolina não me mates que sou teu filho" [30]), his message is at least four-dimensional. The story becomes a story within a story with a story within a story: a plural mise en abyme. On one level, the narrator is obviously referring to the bitch. On a second level, he is referring to the sociopolitical reality of Portuguese women in general, a reality unfavorable to their well-being and not conducive to their existence (and emergence) as real women, for there are laws classifying them as being less than men. Like Ugolina, these women are being "fed" improper and insufficient food, and this is the reason why they then come to hate (eat) themselves and align themselves with men. On a third level, the narrator is also referring to the actions of naming undertaken by Reis, the poet obsessed with words and their capacity to tame, understand and make sense of reality: the poet who is more worried about naming the bitch than feeling (understanding and seeing) the atrocities that she is in fact committing against her own flesh and blood. In some ways Reis becomes comparable to the fascist regime itself, a regime which suppresses the rights of women and even forges a constitution (a discourse, a rhetoric) that entangles women in false rhetoric and classifies them according to male views (ideals) of womanhood—classifies them as others, who exist not for themselves but for their husbands and children, others whose model is the male, the only full subject, the same, who uses them as convenient appendices. This argument makes sense if we take into account the fact that Reis is a man who continues to nourish the idea of the ideal woman (love) and tries to tame his carnal desires towards the real Lídia, as we recall, by going to the drawer and reading about his ideal Lídia—a Lídia also invented by an ancient male artist. The reality escapes Reis and so he constantly reverts to the security of words to his mind where myths about female subjectivity abound. In a fashion similar to the constitution, then, Reis is totalizing that which cannot or should not be totalized: he is "eating" the women, and thus becoming an Ugolino, just like "Ugolino della Gherardesca, that most {cannibal and macho count} who ate his children and grandchildren" (19) ("Ugolino della Gherardesca, canibalíssimo conde macho que manjou filhos e netos" [30]). The fact that Reis relies on historical and literary accounts to name the bitch is further indication that he is always immersed in the rhetoric of the past, a past which has forged myths about female subjecthood, rather than living in the present and really looking at women in an attempt to see what they might really be like:

> He did not call her Diana ou Lembrada, {but what's the use of giving a name to the crime or its motives if the wicked creature is going to die} from eating poisoned food or from the riffle shot fired by her own master. Ricardo Reis persists and finally finds the right {appellative}, one which comes from Ugolino della Gherardesca, that most {cannibal, macho count} who ate his children and grandchildren, {and} there are testimonies and {guarantees} to this in the *History of the Guelphs and Ghibellines* and also in the *Divine Comedy*, {canto} thirty-tree of the *Inferno*. Therefore let the {mother} who eats {her own children} be called Ugolina. (19)
>
> Não lhe chamará Diana ou Lembrada, e que adiantará um nome ao crime ou aos motivos dele, se vai o nefando bicho morrer de bolo envenenado ou tiro de caçadeira por mão do seu dono, Teima Ricardo Reis e enfim encontra o certo apelativo, um que vem de Ugolino della Gherardesca, canibalíssimo

conde macho que manjou filhos e netos, e tem atestados disso, e abonações, na História dos Guelfos e Gibelinos, capítulo respectivo, e também na Divina Comédia, canto trigésimo terceiro do Inferno, chame-se pois Ugolina à mãe que come os seus próprios filhos. (30)

On a fourth level, and if we take into account the Irigarian philosophy of sexual ethics, the story is telling us that when Reis and the patriarchal fascist regime "kill" their women, they are also killing themselves. And they are doing so because women are the entities that would in fact remind men of who they are: the others, who in their difference, make men realize their subjecthood more fully—just like women are also reminded of who they are through men. The very fact that the narrator uses the word "appellative" (19) ("apelativo" [30]), defined grammatically as the name used to refer to the many elements of the same species, when referring to the name Ugolina, further reinforces the idea that he wants us to read beyond the story of Ugolina and see the many connections (associations) that exist within the story. The story of the bitch does, however, also offer a solution for the cannibalism of both dogs and human beings. The story tells us that the cure lies in giving the proper food to the animal. When extended to the situation of women, what this entails is that men must allow women to be what they are, without imposing on them their views or considering them less than full subjects, who exist only to complement men's lives and have no purpose in and by themselves. If that is done, women will not turn against themselves, for they will feel valued and appreciated for who they are. Society must thus create the proper conditions for women to be valued and considered equals of men, equals in difference. Such a solution would allow both men and women to nourish their differences, to be more self-assured and find more fulfillment: to learn from and complete one another. What the narrator is implying, then, is that we must work towards the eradication of the conditions that give rise to sexist societies where men and women are kept apart and classified in discriminatory, dichotomist terms. To use Saramago's own words, and since we are all formed by circumstances, what is needed is "to think and act in ways that will bring about humanly formed circumstances" ("pensar e agir no sentido de que as circunstâncias [sejam] formadas humanamente" [*Uma voz* 38]). The fact that the story about Ugolina tells us that she must be killed if her behavior does not change with proper nutrition further reinforces the idea that we must work towards the eradication of oppression and violence in our society, even if that also entails the use of violence. Ugolina's story, then, can be seen as a very Marxist and revolutionary one. On the grander level of the novel, the story can be read as an argument against material poverty, against the exploitation of one class by another, and against the oppressive fascist regime. The story then becomes a statement for the overthrow of the class system and the Fascist dictatorship, whereby the oppressed would use force to take the oppressors, for all else has failed. Isaura de Oliveira has also argued that Ugolina functions as a metaphor for the violence perpetrated by Salazar's regime (7-8).

If, on the one hand, women were legally considered inferior to men during the fascist regime, it is also true that they were often depicted as Marian incarnations and for different reasons. For one, and as already noted, the Virgin Mary archetype which has influenced many Christian societies in the world was well alive in Portugal at the time since we are dealing with a highly religious society. Moreover, Salazar's regime had very strong ties with the Catholic Church and the two worked hand in hand to maintain the regime for nearly fifty years. In addition, the fact that Portugal is the place where Marian apparitions are said to have occurred in 1917 in Fátima for over a period of six months, might also play a role in the association of women with sainthood. In a paper entitled "Marian Apparitions in Fátima as Political Reality: Religion and Politics in Twentieth-Century Portugal," Christopher Manuel argues how the Marian apparitions in Fátima served as a political tool to defeat republicanism in Portugal and bring back the conservative and religious regime which led to the installment of the fascist regime. The apparition of the Virgin Mary reinforces the idea that Portugal was indeed the chosen country, a place of salvation—a country that should serve as a model of conduct for other countries. In in the novel, Marcenda and her father both go to Fátima hoping for a miraculous cure for Marcenda's handicapped hand and Reis follows them, pointing to the fact that the power of Our Lady of Fátima was very much alive. Furthermore, the Portuguese nation is in fact described by an archbishop as "Portugal is Christ, Christ is Portugal" (240) ("Portugal é Cristo, Cristo é Portugal" [281]). It should therefore not be surprising that women would be seen as being neither holy, nor full subjects, and yet also seen as possessing certain sainthood: the old virgin/whore dichotomy. Saramago's novel further utilizes and challenges that dichotomy. In the novel women are often represented as figures who possess the capacity to help men reach their spiritual height and moral redemption—even if often that simply means that they are deviating them from communist thoughts and activities, and bringing them back to the defense and aid of Salazar's *Estado Novo* ("New State"):

> Holy women, angels of mercy, Portuguese nuns, daughters of Mary and pious sisters, be they in convents or brothels, in palaces or in hovels, the daughters of some boarding house landlady or of a senator, what astral and telepathic messages must they exchange among themselves, so that from such varied circumstances and conditions there should result so concerted an effect, which is nothing more or less than the redemption of a man in danger of losing his soul, {who contrary to what the saying affirms, is always waiting for advice}. As the supreme reward, these women offer him their sisterly friendship, or sometimes their love, even their bodies and all the other advantages a beloved spouse can provide, and this sustains a man's hope in the happiness that will come, if it comes at all, in the wake of the good angel descended from the altars on high, for ultimately, let us confess it, this is nothing other than a secondary manifestation of the Marian cult, {we would call them the Seconds in the word could be authorized}. Marília and the daughter of the landlady, both incarnations of the Most Holy Virgin, cast pitying glances and place their healing hands on physical and moral sores, working the miracle of health and political conversion. Humanity will take a step forward when such women begin to rule. (207-08)

> Santas mulheres, agentes de salvação, religiosas portuguesas, sorores marianas e piedosas, estejam lá onde estiverem, nos conventos ou nos alcou-

> ces, nos palácios ou nas choupanas, filhas de dona de pensão ou de senador, que mensagens astrais e telepáticas trocarão entre si para que, de tão diferentes seres e condições, segundo os nossos terrenos critérios, resulte uma acção tão consertada, igualmente conclusiva, resgatar-se o homem perdido, que ao contrário do que afirma o ditado sempre espera concelhos, e, como supremo prémio, umas vezes lhe dão a sua amizade de irmãs, outras o amor, o corpo e as conveniências de esposa estremecida. Por isso o homem mantém viva e perene a esperança da felicidade, que virá, vindo, nas auras do anjo bom descido das alturas e dos altares, porque, enfim, confessemo-lo de uma vez, tudo isto não é mais que manifestações segundas do mariano culto, secundinas, se a palavra fosse autorizada, Marília e a filha da dona da pensão humanos avatares da Virgem Santíssima, piedosamente mirando e pondo as mãos lenitivas nas chagas físicas e morais, obrando o milagre da saúde e da conversão política, a humanidade dará um grande passo para a frente quando esta espécie de mulheres começar a mandar. (243-44)

For Irigaray, the type of woman alluded to here would fall into the category of the woman who, "Inside the male territory, even if she plays at disguising herself in various showy and coquettish poses which he 'strips away' in the act of love . . . still lacks both the identity and the passport she needs to traverse or transgress the male lover's language. Is she some more or less domesticated child or animal that clothes herself in or takes on a semblance of humanity? Takes on the subject's unconscious and involuntary movements, veils them is softness, in folds, in spaciousness to give him back some room. Wraps herself up in the remainder of what he has taken in and from love" (*An Ethics* 196). In the above quotation from *O ano*, it is Reis himself who is attacking women who support a regime that annihilates them and sees them as peripheral beings. Ironically, although Reis, like the narrator, seems to despise the women who support a system that abuses and uses them, he fails to recognize that his conception and treatment of women is in fact quite similar to that of the fascist state: "Ricardo Reis smiled as he thought about these sad irreverences. There is something disagreeable about watching a man smile to himself, particularly if he is smiling into {the mirror}, a good thing there is a closed door between him and the rest of the world. Then he asked himself, And Marcenda, what kind of woman is Marcenda. The question is beside the point, a mere mental game for one who has no one to talk to" (208) ("Ricardo Reis sorria, enquanto mentalmente, desafiava estas irreverências tristes, não é agradável ver um homem sorrir sozinho, pior ainda se é ao espelho que sorri, o que vale é haver uma porta fechada entre ele e o resto do mundo. Então pensou, E Marcenda, que mulher será Marcenda, a pergunta é inconsequente, mero entretém de quem não tem com quem falar" [244]). Reis is smiling "into {the mirror}" and does not even know it. He is not much different from the patriarchs ruling Portuguese society and fails to see that he, like the Catholic Church and Salazar's state, has also created, engendered, and nurtured a type of woman who is sterile, one who is merely used for the benefit of men and who cannot show her real self. In fact, Reis is just like the artist responsible for the film *The May Revolution* ("Revolução de Maio") and the novel *Conspiracy* (Conspiração), which in the novel function as artistic propaganda media used by the fascist state to engender and create a type of woman who is very spiritual and close to God, and in fact saves man from sin. The poet, novelist, and filmmaker are thus portrayed in Saramago's novel as three types of artists who keep reproducing and creating a false conception of woman, therefore contributing to the perpetuation of old myths regarding the female self:

> they have started filming *The May Revolution*, which tells the story of a refugee who arrives in Portugal to foment revolt, not this one, {the other one}, and he is won over to the Nationalist cause by the daughter of the landlady at the boarding house where is staying incognito. This last item Ricardo Reis read once, twice, three times, in an effort to rid himself of a faint echo buzzing deep inside his memory, but all three times his memory failed him, and it was only when he moved on to another news story, the general strike in La Coruña, that this tenuous thought became clear and defined. It was nothing distant, it was the *Conspiracy*, that book, that Marília, that story of another conversion to Nationalism and its ideals, apparently the tale has it most effective propagandist among women, with such magnificent results that literature and the seventh art pay tribute to these angels of chastity and self-sacrifice who seek out the wayward if not lost souls of men. No one can resist them when they place a hand upon a shoulder or cast a chaste glance beneath a suspended tear. (207)

> começaram as filmagens da Revolução de Maio que conta a história de um foragido que entra em Portugal para fazer a revolução, não aquela, a outra, e é convertido aos ideais nacionalistas pela filha da dona da pensão onde vai hospedar-se clandestino, esta notícia leu-a Ricardo Reis primeira, segunda e terceira vezes, a ver se libertava um impreciso eco que zumbia no fundo recôndito da memória, Isto lembra-me qualquer coisa, uma das três vezes não conseguiu, e foi quando já passara a outra notícia, greve geral na Corunha, que o ténue murmúrio se definiu e tornou claro, nem sequer se tratava de uma recordação antiga, era a Conspiração, esse livro, essa Marília, a história dessa outra conversão ao nacionalismo e seus ideais, que, a avaliar pelas provas dadas, sucessivas, têm nas mulheres activas propagandistas, com resultados tão magníficos que já a literatura e a sétima arte dão o nome e merecimento a esses anjos de pureza e abnegação que procuram fervidamente as almas masculinas transviadas, se perdidas ainda melhor, nem um lhes resiste, assim possam elas pôr-lhe a mão em cima, e o olhar puríssimo sob a lágrima suspensa. (242-43)

Reis is eventually able to put all the events together and see that all these artistic media are working for the state by fabricating an image of a woman who is saint-like. And yet again, he fails to see that he does the very same in his relationships with women by refusing carnal love and looking for love in the infinite. The filmmaker, the poet, and the novelist are also depicted by Saramago as being similar to the advertising industry. For example, the ad displayed in the paper Reis is reading advertises creams which promise to make women's breasts larger, smaller, or firmer, thus giving women the message that they are not good enough as they are and need to perfect their bodies in order to become more appealing to men. Ironically, the ad gives the impression that the idea for bust enhancement comes from a woman, thus making it seem natural, justifiable and noncoercive. Yet, the reality is that men are eating women, and women then go on to eat themselves and other women. Put differently, women are shown as being unable or incapable of bringing to the surface their most real self, for they, like the cannibal bitch Ugolina, are not fed the proper food: "Poor solitary creature, he is flabbergasted when confronted with an advertisement that promises women a perfect bosom within three to five weeks using the Parisian method, Exuber, which combines those three fundamental desiderata, Bust Firmer, Bust Developer, and Bust Reducer. This {Arabian} Franglais is translated into concrete results under the supervision of Madame Hélène Duroy of the Rue de Miromesnil, which is in Paris, of course, where ravishing women firm up, develop, and reduce their busts, successively or all at the same time" (206) ("pobre homem solitário, pasma diante de um anúncio que promete às mulheres um peito impecável em três a cinco semanas pelos métodos parisienses Exuber, de acordo com os três desideratos fundamentais, Bust Raffermer, Bust Developer, Bust Reducer, algaravia anglo-francesa de cuja tradução em resultados se encarrega Madame Hélène Duroy, da Rue de Miromesnil, que é, claro está em Paris, onde todas aquelas esplêndidas mulheres aplicam estes métodos para endurecer, desenvolver e reduzir, sucessivamente ou ao mesmo tempo" [241-42]). The very name of Madame Duroy ("du" plus "roi") is ironic, for it suggests that she is working for and is owned by the patriarchal order (the king). She is literally the lady of (and for) the king, although she appears to be working for the good of women and to be a free agent in the making of her own life, identity, and subjectivity. In a similar fashion, the name of the street where Madame Duroy runs her beauty business further reinforces the idea that she is working against female empowerment. The name "Miromesnil" which appears to be mixing Portuguese and French words, can be broken down as follows: "miro" (first tense of the verb "to watch," "to gaze") or the short version of the French word "mirroir" ("mirror") plus "mes" (short for the Portuguese word "mesmo" ("same") or French "même") plus "esnil," which turns into the Portuguese word "senil" ("senile") or "sénile" in French if we invert (or add) the "e" and the "s." Thus, the name "Miromesnil" contains multiple feminist messages. It implies that women are being told by men what to be and how to look and thus cannot be themselves and nurture their differences (they are merely the other of the same, the same being the male); it implies that men are objectifying women and literally "making" their bodies according to what they think is desirable; that men are merely gazing at women and unable to operate under what Lévinas calls "face"; that women are the mirror of men, a mirror that reflects only the male self or identity and discards the feminine self or the possibility of it being different or independent from the male self; and that both men and women are literally "senil" ("senile"), for they are not allowing each other to emerge in their differences and thus become less sure of who they are, so unsure in fact that they reach the point of madness or alienation. In other words, because the other is incorporated into sameness and because the reminder (assuror) of the individual identity relies only (or primarily) on the internal (the isolated individual), both men and women become less sure of their subjectivity or identity. The name of the street could thus be translated as follows: "Je regarde le même, ou à moi-même et je deviens sénile," or in Portuguese, "Eu miro o mesmo, ou a mim mesmo e fico senil" ("I watch the same, or myself and I become senile"). The fact that the cream is developed in Paris and by a French woman further suggest that Reis (and Portuguese men) are looking for the ideal woman outside of their immediate reality (outside of Portugal); they are absent from their most immediate phenomenological reality and look for satisfaction in the distant, absent, and abstract. The beauty of the typical Portuguese woman (brunette) seems to be discarded and so the feminine subject tries to imitate the French woman, thus further alienating herself. This can further be linked to European cultural dichotomies whereby northern European countries have tended to be seen as superior and more advanced when compared to their Southern neighbors—which leads of course to all kinds of other Ugolina stories or mise en abymes present in the novel.

On the one hand, women are supposed to be saints and remind men of the chaste and spiritual Virgin Mary; on the other hand, they are supposed to be physically enticing to men. They are supposed to both be whores and saints, bodies and souls, seductresses and virgins. Yet, they cannot be the two at the same time and be fully and openly accepted and appreciated as such, for carnal love is still seen as inferior to, and corrupting of, spiritual love. But as Saramago suggests, unconsciously what in fact draws men to women is the power of sexual and physical desire, and not so much the Virgin Mary and goddesslike qualities women are seen as possessing. The latter are a cover-up for the real desires of men, a cover-up necessary when living in a highly religious society that still sees carnal love as inferior to divine and spiritual love, a cover-up forged by the complex workings of the human mind, which, despite all that it has been "fed" with by society, still returns to the biological, the phenomenological, the sensible. What men seem to want, even if they are not consciously aware of this, is a woman who can be both a virgin and a whore. Men become confused and unable to see what they really want because of the many contradictory messages they receive about women. They become lost in an "(Arabian) Franglais" (206) ("algaravia anglo-francesa" [241]), lost in a language full of contradiction and confused voices that entangles them in a paradoxical, complex and alienating discursive web. The word "algaravia" refers to the Arabic language but also to a language that contains several voices in it and various traces of different languages, thus becoming very difficult to understand: "[These spiritual and moral] feminine {arts exceed and multiply} the abovementioned techniques of making firm, developing, and reducing, although it might be more correct to say that {these arts initially derive from these three, as much in the literal sense as in the concurrent and incurrent senses, including the impassioned outbursts and} exaggerated metaphors, and wild association of ideas" (207) ("São plurais estas [espirituais e morais] femininas artes, excedem, multiplicando, as outras, já mencionadas, de endurecer, desenvolver e reduzir, se não seria mais rigoroso dizer que todas se resumem limiarmente nestas, tanto nos seus sentidos literais como nas decorrências e concorrências, incluindo os arrojos e exageros da metáfora, as libertinagens da associação de ideias" [243]). Again, Saramago is inviting us to see the connections between men's physical desires and their emotional and spiritual perception of women; between the conscious and the unconscious forces driving the desires of men. Literally, what Saramago is saying is that the physical sexual instinct is the one which "makes firm, develops and reduces" (207) ("endurece, desenvolve e reduz" [243]) the moral and spiritual attraction of men to women. There is a high level of irony here, since the choice of words can be seen as directly mirroring the physical reaction of men when sexually aroused: the verb "endurecer" ("making firm") being a direct reference to the male erection. The other two verbs can similarly be seen as mirroring the change in the size of the penis according to degree of arousal. This is why the narrator tells us to read what he is saying in a literal, concurrent, and incurrent sense and to watch for the "exaggerated metaphors" ("exageros de metáfora") and "wild association of ideas" ("libertinagens de associação de ideias"). Such associations and exaggerated metaphors constantly take place throughout the novel: they are a type of mise en abyme that exists at the semantic, structural, morphological and symbolical levels, in a similar fashion to what happens in the stories of Couto (see also Amorim for an exposition on the use of the mise en abyme in *O ano* and in Saramago's other novels 211-19).

O ano contains in fact a larger mise en abyme and one that informs all other mise en abymes of the novel. In a similar manner to Samuel Coleridge, Saramago seems to believe that language and thought are inseparable and that ideas and theories are a "commerce," "an industry" of sorts, a human-made product—but also a product that imprisons its own producer, whether the producer is or is not aware of his or her action or position as consumer:

> When one idea is drawn from another, we say that there has been an association. Some are even of the opinion that the whole human mental process derives from this succession of stimuli, sometimes unconscious, {sometimes not quite} unconscious, which achieves original combinations, new relationships of thoughts interlinked by the species and together forming what might be called a commerce, an industry of ideas, because man, apart from all the other things he is, has been, or will be, performs an industrial an commercial function, first as producer, then as retailer, and finally as consumer, but even this order can be shuffled and rearranged. I am speaking of ideas and nothing else. So, then, we can consider ideas as corporate entities, independent or in partnership, perhaps publicly held, but never with limited liability, never anonymous, for a name is something we all possess. (49-50)

> Quando uma ideia puxou outra, dizemos que houve associação delas, não falta mesmo quem seja de opinião que todo o processo mental humano decorre dessa sucessiva estimulação, muitas vezes inconsciente, outras nem tanto, outras compulsiva, outras agindo em fingimento de que o é para poder ser adjunção diferente, inversa quando calha, enfim, relações que são muitas, mas entre si ligadas pela espécie que juntas constituem e parte do que latamente se denominará comércio e indústria dos pensamentos, por isso o homem, entre mais que seja, tenha sido ou venha a ser, é lugar comercial e industrial, productor primeiro, retalhista depois, consumidor finalmente, e também baralhada e reordenada esta ordem, de ideias falo, de al não, então

> lhe chamaríamos, com propriedade, ideias associadas, com ou sem companhia, ou em comandita, acaso sociedade cooperativa, nunca de responsabilidade limitada, jamais anónima, porque, nome todos o temos. (64)

Thus, one of the central messages of the novel is that language is also a trickster, a medium which will trick us into believing in something that has no basis in the "real" and "sensible" reality, to use Lévinas's own words. The message, then, is also that we ought to distrust language, theories, and rhetoric, for they are often used in tricking and unproductive fashions to exploit human beings, to reduce them to discriminatory categories and to argue and justify oppressive regimes. Thus, the need to question and study language attentively in all its "commercial" uses, to use Saramago's own expression, the need to be deconstructive and to return to the sensible, to point zero as it were, to that which is not yet corrupted with words, discourse and rhetoric. As Lévinas puts it,

> This world, in which reason recognizes itself more and more, is not inhabitable. It is hard and cold, like those supply depots where merchandise which cannot satisfy is piled up: it can neither clothe those who are naked nor feed those who are hungry; it is impersonal, like factory hangars and industrial cities where manufactured things remain abstract, true with the truth of calculations and brought into the anonymous circuit of the economy that proceeds according to knowledgeable plans that cannot prevent, though they can prepare, disasters. This is the spirit in all its masculine essence. It lives *outdoors,* exposed to the fiery sun which blinds and to the winds of the open sea which beat it and blow it down, in a world that offers it no inner refuge, in which it is disoriented, solitary and wandering, and even as such is already alienated by the products it had helped to create, which rise up untamed and hostile. (*Difficult Freedom* 32-33)

Part Two

The Deeper Politics of Agency

Chapter Three

Authenticity of Being as the Politics of Agency in Lispector

Being political on her own terms

Perhaps not surprisingly, Clarice Lispector has earned the reputation of being an introverted, self-centred, difficult, romantic, and apolitical writer. When she published her first novel, *Perto do coração selvagem* (*Near to the Wild Heart*), in 1944, Lispector received some negative criticism from important critics of the time. Álvaro Lins situated her book in the category of "feminine literature" ("literatura feminine") and qualified it as a text full of "lyricism" ("lirismo") and "narcissism" ("narcisismo") (qtd. in Guidin 14) and lacking in structure. Although such comments might not be interpreted as totally negative, they carry a pejorative connotation, especially if we take into account that factual and explicitly and socially committed literature was so much in vogue during this time and was seen as the type of literature needed in Brazil if social change for the better were to occur. However, Lins also praised Lispector's book for its originality, comparing her with avant-garde writers such as Joyce and Woolf. Sérgio Millet, another important critic of the time, said that when he first read Lispector he thought of her as a "little girl who would die of an attack when faced with the most serious critique" ("mocinha que morreria de ataque diante da crítica mais séria"[qtd. in Guidin 14]), a condescending and patriarchal comment, to say the least. On the other hand, Millet also praised her book for its aesthetic quality. Several other critics would say that Lispector's style was "difficult" (see Scott-Buccleuch and Teles de Oliveira 328) and would thus be rejected by and impossible to understand for a large number of readers, or that her work was "separated from the social context" ("desliga[do] do contexto social" [Lucas 32]).

Lispector was a contemporary of the so-called regionalist writers such as Raquel de Queiroz (1910-2003) and Jorge Amado (1912-2002), who were concerned with social justice issues and the development of a national identity, and who sought to found a national literature reflecting themes, forms, and modes of expression that would be "truly Brazilian." The prose fiction of these writers, commonly referred to as the *Romance Regionalista* ("Regionalist Novel") tended to be documentary, often addressing the issues of poverty, drought, illiteracy, and isolation faced by the northeasterners of the "Back Lands" ("Sertão"), and denouncing the bribery and corrupting systems of "clientelism" ("compadrismo") and "patronage" ("coronelismo") regulating Brazilian society. Such fiction was considered to be openly committed literature, putting the social in the forefront, and realistically and openly describing the sociopolitical mechanisms that were perceived as responsible for the oppression and exploitation of the Brazilian people. This type of committed literature was well accepted by most Brazilian intellectuals, who were conscious of the multitude of problems affecting their country, problems which they felt they needed to address so that a better and more egalitarian society could be engendered. As Márcia Guidin explains, "The celebrated regionalist novel (cf. Pécaut, 1990) was for the Brazilian intellectuals, a precise instrument to understand the country. A new documentary realism was triumphing. This realism would show the individual inserted in a collectivity as well as his familial and clientelistic structures. To reveal the social reality of the country was the word of order for the intellectuals, who were seen as powerful political interventionists. In 1934, Jorge Amado affirmed that no author could abstract himself from engagement" (85) ("O festejado romance regionalista (cf. Pécaut, 1990) era, para a intelectualidade brasileira, um instrumento preciso do conhecimento do país. Um novo realismo documental triunfava. Mostrava-se um indvíduo inserido numa coletividade e as suas estruturas familiares e de compadrio. Revelar a realidade social do país era a palavra de ordem para os intelectuais, vistos como poderosos interventores políticos. Jorge Amado em 1934 afirmava que nenhum autor poderia subtrair-se ao engajamento" [13]) (see also Grob-Lima 236-46).

But contrary to what many of her critics have suggested, it would be unfair to say that Lispector's writing constitutes only a self-indulgent and self-reflecting exercise, totally alienated from and uninterested in social causes. It would be inaccurate to say that Lispector did not use her writing to fight and uncover the social injustices governing Brazilian society. The notion of what constitutes the political novel has changed quite dramatically within the last sixty years. Today political writing is not merely the type of writing which factually, openly, and objectively describes the mechanisms of oppression and alienation governing people's lives. Today, in order for one to detect the political(ity) of a novel it is necessary to go beyond explicit content. One needs to look at the form used in a given novel (i.e., the type of language, punctuation, structure, and the use of ambivalent metaphors) or even—as Pierre Macherey has pointed out—at what and whom the novel omits from the narrative (82-97). Within this enlarged concept of the political, then, all of Lispector's novels are political, even if generally in a covert and implicit way—and deeper, too, as I demonstrate throughout this chapter.

The writer's inability to portray the poor other and the failure of literature

Marta Peixoto has indicated that "Lispector questions the dubious moral and psychic forces at work in the representation of oppression. She points to the absurd hubris of the well-off writer who imagines the position of someone who goes hungry, stressing—and giving into—the urge to engage in just such an act of the imagination . . . To tell stories, for Lispector, is to give up the very possibility of innocence and to enact a knowing, guilt-ridden struggle with the mastering and violent powers of narrative" (98-99). This "absurd hubris" of the socially and culturally integrated and economically well-off writer trying to portray the other and his or her harsh reality is brought up by Lispector several times and in different ways in *A hora*. Being a contemporary of the openly committed writers mentioned above, Lispector could not help but feel (and be made to feel) that her literature was not sufficiently engaged or concerned with the Brazilian "social problem." In fact, she came to feel a profound guilt of her ineptitude as writer and expresses it quite touchingly in her chronicle "Literature and Justice" ("Literatura e Justiça"):

> Today, quite unexpectedly, as in any real discovery, I found that some of my tolerance towards others was reserved for me as well (but for how long?). I took advantage of this crest of the wave to bring myself up to date with forgiveness. For example, my tolerance in relation to myself, as someone who writes, is to forgive my inability to deal with the "social problem" in a literary vein (that is to say, by transforming it into the vehemence of the art). Ever since I have come to know myself, the social problem has been more important to me than any other issue: in Recife the black shanty towns were the first truth that I encountered. Long before I felt "art," I felt the profound beauty of human conflict. I tend to be simple in my approach to any social problem: I wanted "to do" something, as if writing were not doing anything. What I cannot do is to exploit writing to this end, however much my incapacity pains and distresses me. The problem of justice for me is such an obvious and basic feeling {that it does not bring me any surprise}. . . . Also because for me, to write is a quest. I have never considered any feeling of justice as a quest or as a discovery, what worries me is that this feeling {for} justice should not be so obvious to everyone else . . . But {today} out of tolerance towards myself, I am not entirely ashamed of contributing nothing human or social through my writing. It is not a matter of not wanting to, it is a question of not being able to. What I am ashamed of is of "not doing, " of not contributing {with actions}. (*The Legion* 124-25)

> Hoje, de repente, como um verdadeiro achado minha tolerância para com os outros sobrou um pouco para mim também (por quanto tempo?). Aproveitei a crista da onda para me pôr em dia com o perdão. Por exemplo, minha tolerância em relação a mim, como pessoa que escreve, é perdoar eu não saber como me aproximar de um modo "literário" (isto é transformado na veemência da arte) da coisa social. Desde que me conheço o fato social teve em mim importância maior do que qualquer outro: em Recife os mocambos foram a primeira verdade para mim. Muito antes de sentir "arte," senti a beleza profunda da luta. Mas é que tenho um modo simplório de me

> aproximar do fato social: eu queria "fazer" alguma coisa, como se escrever não fosse fazer. O que não consigo é usar escrever para isso, por mais que a incapacidade me doa e me humilhe. O problema de justiça é em mim um sentimento tão óbvio e tão básico que não consigo me surpreender com ele . . . E também porque para mim escrever é procurar. O sentimento de justiça nunca foi procura em mim, nunca chegou a ser descoberta e o que me espanta é que ele não seja igualmente óbvio em todos . . . Mas, por tolerância hoje para comigo, não estou me envergonhando totalmente de não contribuir para nada humano e social por meio de escrever. É que não se trata de querer, é questão de não poder. Do que me envergonho, sim, é de não "fazer," de não contribuir com ações. (*A Legião* 149)

Despite this deeply felt guilt, Lispector does not believe in the power of literature to change society. Unlike the regionalist writers, she thinks that in order for Brazilian society to change in the real sense, people, including herself, need to engage themselves directly; they need to take action outside of the written word, that is, action that will truly lead to the change of the oppressive structures of Brazilian society. As she notes above, she feels ashamed of "not doing," "not contributing with actions." In *A hora*, the male narrator, named Rodrigo S.M., whom Lispector the writer openly identifies with, attacks directly and mocks those writers who see themselves as capable of changing the oppressive status quo through their writing, those who see their writing as crucial for the betterment of the Brazilian society and who firmly believe that their art is capable of accurately portraying the reality of the poor other:

> I do not intend to write anything complicated, although I am obliged to use {words} that sustain you. The story—I {determine with false} free will—should have seven characters, {I being one of the more important ones of course}. I, Rodrigo S.M. A traditional tale for I {do not want} to be modish and invent colloquialisms under the guise of originality. So I shall attempt, contrary to my normal method, to write a story with a beginning, a middle, and a 'grand finale' followed by silence and falling rain . . . Like every writer, I am clearly tempted to use succulent terms: I have at my command magnificent adjectives, robust nouns, and verbs so {slender that they can sharply pierce the atmosphere} as they move into action. For surely words are actions, {wouldn't you agree}? Yet I have no intention of adorning the word, for {if I touch the girl's bread, that bread will} turn to gold—and the girl (she is nineteen years old) the girl will not be able to bite it, and consequently die of hunger. (13-15)

> Proponho-me a que não seja complexo o que escreverei, embora obrigado a usar palavras que vos sustentam. A história—determino com falso livre--arbítrio—vai ter uns sete personagens e eu sou um dos mais importantes deles, é claro. Eu Rodrigo S.M. Relato antigo, este, pois não quero ser modernoso e inventar modismos à guisa de originalidade. Assim é que experimentarei contra os meus hábitos uma história com começo, meio e "gran finale" seguido de silêncio e de chuva caindo . . . É claro que, como todo escritor, tenho a tentação de usar termos suculentos: conheço adjectivos esplendorosos, carnudos substantivos e verbos tão esguios que atravessam

Authenticity of Being as the Politics of Agency in Lispector

agudos o ar em vias de ação, já que palavra é ação, concordais. Mas não vou enfeitar a palavra pois se eu tocar no pão da moça esse pão se tornará em ouro—e a jovem (ela tem dezanove anos) e a jovem não poderia mordê-lo morrendo de fome. (13-15)

The narrator becomes one of the most important characters because he has the power to choose what to say, how to say it, who and what to omit from the story, which implies that the narrator is not impartial. On the other hand, even if he wanted to be impartial and tell the truth about the other, he could not, for his own voice always supersedes (and guides) the voices of everyone else. The narrator cannot completely control his "I" when writing, for that "I" will always be the filter through which everything and everyone will be portrayed. This is precisely why he says he "determines with false free will" the number of characters the novella will have, and that he will be "one of the most important ones." The narrator says he intends to write a simple and uncomplicated story; yet he also says that he is forced to use words that "sustain you" (13) ("usar palavras que vos sustentam" [15]). To whom is he speaking here? Who is the "you" implied in the "vos"? The use of the verb "sustentar" (sustain, support, maintain, uphold) in the second-person plural seems to suggest that the story the narrator is about to tell is one that will in no way contribute to change the oppressive structures regulating Brazilian society or accurately "tell" the voice of the other. It is also a story that "fabricates" the poor other, thus contributing to unfair, stereotypical, and fruitless classifications of that same other. Rather than deconstructing and challenging standard and hegemonic ideas (ideals, views), this classification of the other leaves nothing changed. In fact, it reinforces the hegemonic discourse that regulates the society in question. The writer, then, becomes the hegemonic figure (voice) par excellence for she or he is classifying the other according to her or his values, according to what she or he thinks or perceives as being misery, happiness, self-realization, fulfillment, and so on. As Peixoto further states, "The narrator constructs Macabéa and the other characters by calling upon openly displayed class prejudice. The characterisation of Olímpico and Glória, especially, relies with strident glee on the clichés through which the upper classes typically view the poor: Olímpico's gold tooth, proudly acquired, and greasy hair ointment; Glória's cheap perfume disguising infrequent baths, her bleached egg-yellow hair" (93).

In addition, Glória is also described as "swinging her hips as she walked, no doubt due to some strain of African blood" ("amaneirada no bamboleio do caminhar por causa do sangue africano que trazia Escondido" [59]), someone who "although white . . . displayed that vitality one associates with a mulatta" ("apesar de branca tinha em si a força da mulatice" [59]). This description carries a pejorative value, for it seems to imply that the Afro-Brazilians are more passionate, more inclined to have sexual promiscuous relationships, and closer to the world of nature, the body, the instinct, and passion, closer to animals even, as the expression "força da mulatice" suggests. Glória is indeed portrayed as a very sexually active woman who has had several abortions. The association of blackness with sexual promiscuity was quite common during the European encounters with the Africans. In his article "Black

Bodies, White Bodies," Sander Gilman explains how such stereotypes came about: "[In] the eighteenth century, the sexuality of the black, both male and female, becomes an icon for deviant sexuality in general. . . . Buffon comments of the lascivious, apelike sexual appetite of the black, introducing a commonplace of early travel literature into a 'scientific' context. He stated that this animal sexuallike appetite went so far as to lead black women to copulate with apes . . . Buffon's view was based on a confusion of two applications of the great chain of being to the nature of black. Such a scale was employed to indicate the innate differences between the two races: in this view of mankind, the black occupied the antithetical position to the white on the scale of humanity" (225-31).

The narrator openly admits that his narration is incomplete and incapable of speaking the other: "See how apprehensive I have become since putting down words about the girl from the northeast. The question is: how do I write? I can verify that I write by ear, just as I learned English and French by ear. My antecedents as a writer? I am a man who possesses more money than those who go hungry, and this makes me in some ways dishonest" (18) ("E eis que fiquei agora receoso quando pus palavras sobre a nordestina. E a pergunta é: como escrevo? Verifico que escrevo de ouvido como aprendi inglês e francês de ouvido. Antecedentes meus de escrever? sou um homem que tem mais dinheiro do que os que passam fome, o que faz de mim de algum modo um desonesto" [18]). He is demonstrating his uneasiness and inability to write about the other, for that other belongs to a lower social class that never "comes to [him]" (18) because he has no way of directly knowing and experiencing the life of the other, and thus is only understanding that other vaguely and indirectly. The narrator says he learns about Macabéa by ear, just as he learned how to speak French and English, suggesting that his perception of the other is only based on what he has heard (and seen) about her: in other words, his knowledge of the other is secondary, indirect, and therefore corrupted. The other remains a foreign language, like French or English, languages which the narrator describes as having learned only by ear, thus suggesting that he was never able to feel or understand them deeply—contrary to one's mother tongue which one tends to learn gradually from one's parents at a very early age, enabling one to identify with it in a more complete and deep manner. Put differently, the narrator's social class is his mother tongue (his primary language), whereas the language of the poor will always remain his second language—for it was not properly felt, learned, and incorporated from infancy through the many capacities humans possess: sensual, spiritual, physical, emotional, and intellectual. In sum, it was not "lived" through his own skin.

The narrator's inability to accurately narrate the other is brought up several other times throughout the novella:

> How do I know all that is about to follow if it is unfamiliar and something I have never experienced? (12-13); But the idea of transcending my own limits suddenly appealed to me. {It was then that I thought of writing about the reality}, since reality exceeds me. (17); In order to speak about the girl I mustn't shave for days. I must acquire dark circles under my eyes from

lack of sleep: dozing from sheer exhaustion, I become a manual laborer. Also wearing threadbare clothes. I am doing all this to put myself on the same footing as the girl from the northeast. Fully aware that I might have to present myself in a more convincing manner to societies who demand a great deal from {those who are typing at this very moment}. (19); In order to draw the girl, I must control {myself and in order to be able to capture her soul}, I must nourish myself frugally on fruit and drink chilled white wine because it is stifling in this cubby-hole where I have locked myself away and where {I have the vain pretension of wanting} to see the world. I've also had to give up sex and football. And avoid all human contact. . . . I should also mention that I read nothing these days for fear that I might adulterate the simplicity of my language with useless refinements. (22); (But what about me? {What about me?}) Here I am telling a story about events that have never happened to me or to anyone known to me. I am amazed at my own perception of the truth. Can it be that it's my painful task to perceive in the flesh truths that no one wants to face?) (56)

Como é que sei tudo o que se vai seguir e que ainda o desconheço, já que nunca o vivi? (12); Transgredir porém os meus próprios limites me fascinou de repente. E foi quando pensei em escrever sobre a realidade, já que essa me ultrapassa. (17); para falar da moça tenho que não fazer a barba durante dias e adquirir olheiras escuras por dormir pouco, só cochilar de pura exaustão, sou um trabalhador manual. Além de me vestir de roupa velha rasgada. Tudo isso para me pôr ao nível da nordestina. Sabendo no entanto que talvez eu tivesse que me apresentar de modo mais convincente às sociedades que muito reclamam de quem está neste instante mesmo batendo à máquina. (19-20); Para desenhar a moça tenho que me domar e para poder captar sua alma tenho que me alimentar frugalmente de frutas e beber vinho branco gelado pois faz calor neste cubículo onde me tranquei e de onde tenho a veleidade de querer ver o mundo. Também tive que me abster de sexo e de futebol. Sem falar que não entro em contacto com ninguém.... Vejo agora que esqueci de dizer que por enquanto nada leio para não contaminar com luxos a simplicidade de minha linguagem. (22-23); (Mas e eu? E eu que estou contando esta história que nunca me aconteceu e nem a ninguém que eu conheça? Fico abismado por saber tanta a verdade. Será que o meu ofício doloroso é o de adivinhar na carne a verdade que ninguém quer enxergar?) (57)

These quotations contain high levels of irony and contradiction. The narrator, Rodrigo S.M., talks about his attempt to lower himself to the level of his protagonist by eating and drinking frugally, dressing poorly, sleeping little, and working continuously (as a hard manual laborer would do) until the point of exhaustion, by not having sex or even reading anything that would possibly contaminate the accurate narrative portrayal of Macabéa. He does all this and yet he remains in his cubicle from where he has the "vain pretension of wanting to see the world." Rodrigo cannot know the other because he closes himself off from the world inhabited by that same other, that world filled with poverty and hunger. He closes himself from the other by writing in isolation, as most writers do, but also by not being familiar with the life of the lower classes, not living it, not experiencing it. He sees the other from his golden castle, as it were, where there are no flies, no cries, no hunger, and no rats—the rats from Acre Street which scare and disgust him a great deal. He only catches a glimpse of Macabéa, seeing her from a "glance" (12) ("relance"[12]), meaning that his apprehension of Macabéa is partial, brief, and thus incomplete. Here the narrator is operating according to the Lévinasian concept of "face" as already discussed in chapter 2, for he admits Macabéa's reality surpasses his comprehension. The narrator considers himself more of an actor, someone who instead of portraying the reality of the other as it is—and thus helping that other to be seen (understood) accurately by the readership—ends up by fabricating a fictional and artificial character. Rather than liberating, our narrator oppresses and violates the "sanctity" (21) ("santidade" [21]) and the "bread" (15) ("pão" [14)] of Macabéa. Writing is perceived as being an oppressive way of capturing the other, even when one writes using a very careful (sensitive) language, something our narrator strives to do: "For as explained, the word is my instrument and must resemble the word. Or am I not a writer? {In truth I am more actor than writer, for with a mere system of punctuation I juggle with intonation and oblige} another's breathing to accompany my text" (22-23) ("Pois como eu disse a palavra tem que se parecer com a palavra, instrumento meu. Ou não sou um escritor? Na verdade sou mais ator porque, com apenas um modo de pontuar, faço malabarismos de entonação, obrigo o respirar alheio a me acompanhar o texto" [23]). Here the narrator sees writing as an act of violence, an act that "obliges" (incarcerates, subdues, forces) the "breathing" (voice) of the other into same, an act that "obliges" the other to be told and imagined through the writer's own syntax, a syntax that chooses to emphasize certain words and consequently also certain aspects of the narrative while discarding or underplaying others. Thus, in lieu of helping the voice of the other to be propagated, the narrator (writer) ends up by imprisoning the other in his own narrative, and consequently, in his perception of what constitutes happiness, self-realization, fulfilment, poverty, and oppression: "I see the girl from the northeast looking into the mirror and—the ruffle of a drum—in the mirror there appears my own face, weary and unshaven. {For} we have reversed roles so completely" (22) ("Vejo a nordestina se olhando ao espelho e—um rufar de tambor—no espelho aparece o meu rosto cansado e barbudo. Tanto nós nos intertrocamos" [22]). In a similar fashion to what happens to Ricardo Reis and his ideal Lídia, the image projected onto the mirror (and consequently Lispector's narrative) is not the image of the real Macabéa but rather the image the Lispectorian narrator creates of Macabéa. Like Ricardo Reis, the narrator of the novella becomes entangled in his own *cogito*, in his own mental reality, his art becoming alienated from phenomenological reality. Thus, it seems improbable that any writer can ever write a totally objective and accurate story, and those who believe they can are only deluding themselves and imposing their reality onto others—in one word, only committing the "hubris" mentioned by Peixoto. In "Textual Cross-Gendering of the Self and the Other in Lispector's *A hora da estrela*," Lesley Feracho also offers a good exposé of Lispector's narrative techniques in the novella by discussing the entanglement between author, narrator, and protagonist and how such entanglement is important to create a narrative that serves both to reaffirm the hegemonic discourse that tries to bring Macabéa to the center but also to counterpose such discourse. This zig-zag, if you will, of narrative voices or perspectives creates a fragmented narrative that defies enclosure and problematizes the telling of the poor other, leaving her untold or unknown.

There are other problems relating to the political efficacy and accuracy of writing. Who is it that in fact reads literature? Is it the ones who go hungry, the ones about whom the traditional self-proclaimed engaged writer often claims to be writing for, so that they can gain consciousness of their state of oppression and then take the necessary action to change it? It is not. The majority of Brazilian readers are from the upper and middle classes, for as our narrator states, the ones who are hungry have no time to read or even feel sad, since those are superfluous things which only the wealthy can afford to experience: "If the reader is financially secure and enjoys the comforts of life, he {might sometimes} step out of himself and see how others live. If he is poor, he will not be reading this story because what I have to say is superfluous for anyone who {permanently} feels the pangs of hunger. Here I am acting as the safety valve for you and the tedious bourgeoisie." (30); "sadness was the privilege of the rich, of those who could afford it, of those who had nothing better to do. Sadness was a luxury" (61) ("Se o leitor possui alguma riqueza sairá de si para ver como é às vezes o outro. Se é pobre, não estará me lendo porque ler-me é supérfluo para quem tem uma leve fome permanente. Faço aqui o papel da vossa válvula de escape e da vida massacrante da média burguesia" [30]; "tristeza era coisa de rico, era para quem podia, para quem não tinha o que fazer. Tristeza era luxo" [61]). The poor and oppressed do not have sufficient formal education to identify and understand the mechanisms of oppression that regulate their lives, a fact which in turn prevents them from understanding political literature. Thus, what is most needed is not the production of literature about oppression, but, rather, the development of the proper infrastructures and mechanisms that would permit the presently poor uneducated person to identify his or her oppression and then fight against it. For example, the development of schools and their accessibility to everyone could allow people to gain consciousness of their oppression. The indication that the Brazilian poor are often unaware of their sociopolitical oppression—and thus unprepared to fight against it—comes across very clearly in *A hora* when Macabéa comes face to face with a book bearing a highly political title—*The {Humiliated} and Oppressed* (*Humilhados e Ofendidos*): "One day, however, she saw something that, for one brief moment, she dearly wanted: it was a book that Senhor Raimundo, who was fond of literature, had left on the table. The book was entitled *The Humiliated and Oppressed*. The girl remained pensive. Perhaps for the very first time she had established her social class. She thought, {thought}, and thought! She decided that no one had ever oppressed her and that everything that happened to her was inevitable. It was futile trying to struggle. Why struggle?" (40) ("Mas um dia viu um livro que por um leve instante cobiçou: um livro que Seu Raimundo, dado a literatura, deixara sobre a mesa. O título era "Humilhados e Ofendidos." Ficou pensativa. Talvez tivesse pela primeira vez se definido numa classe social. Pensou, pensou e pensou! Chegou à conclusão que na verdade ninguém jamais a ofendeu, tudo que acontecia era porque as coisas são assim e não havia luta possível, para quê lutar?" [40]). If Macabéa were able to read and understand the book properly, perhaps she would be able to gain awareness of her condition as an oppressed person. Possessing only a grade three education, Macabéa often displays great difficulty in understanding many of the words used in the everyday life or culture of cosmopolitan Rio de Janeiro, including the very word "culture." For Macabéa, things are the way they are and there is really no other way for them to be: she accepts reality as it is and sees no need or point in changing it. Without being able to identify those oppressive mechanisms—which would constitute the very first step to change the oppression taking place—Macabéa remains an unconcious prisoner of oppression.

The book in question does not belong to Macabéa. It belongs to her boss, Raimundo, who functions as her immediate oppressor, the one who most likely would be aware of the mechanisms of oppression and yet does not do anything to change the situation. In fact, Raimundo exploits Macabéa by paying her less than the legally established minimum wage. Again, Lispector seems to be pointing to the fact that there is no point in creating books that deal with the mechanisms of oppression if those books are not accessible to the exploited class. The middle and upper classes read and write about oppression and they are aware that it exists: "So, dear readers, you know more than you imagine it, however much you may deny it" (13) ("Assim é que os senhores sabem mais do que imaginam e estão se fingindo de sonsos" [12]). The question is: are they prepared to take any real action to help the poor other? Are they prepared to give away the comfort of their lives so that the poor other can also have enough to eat? It does not seem so, for that would entail the loss of their privileged status and position. Lispector's protagonist writes in his cubicle from a privileged position, while being isolated from the world. Raimundo reads at his leisure in his office, while being part of the immediate exploitative mechanism by paying Macabéa less than the minimum wage. The narrator of *A hora* writes that he "possesses more money than those who go hungry, and that makes [him] in some ways a dishonest" (18) ("tem mais dinheiro do que os que passam fome, o que faz [dele] de algum modo [um] desonesto" [18]). The boss reads because he can buy books and because he owns a business and does not have to follow orders from others. He reads because he too has more money (and time) than most people—and he has it precisely because he exploits those same people.

Both the writer and Raimundo write and read (respectively) about the other but only to appease their guilt: "{I play the role of your safety valve here and the slaughtering life of the middle class}" (30) ("Faço aqui o papel da vossa válvula de escape e da vida massacrante da média burguesia" [30]). In other words, the books our writer writes function as an antidote to appease not only his guilty conscience, but also that of those who can but do nothing to change the status quo, those who in fact want to maintain the status quo for their own benefit; those who do not go hungry, who exploit, in sum, all of Lispector's readership composed mostly of the middle and upper classes. For the others (the poor and oppressed) have more fundamental concerns to deal with (e.g., finding food and shelter) and thus cannot afford to read. By writing and reading about oppression, the narrator and the boss (both representative of the bourgeoisie or the upper and middle classes) can make themselves believe that they are in fact doing something to help the other, when in fact the reality of the other will remain the same, since the structures of the society remain unchanged. The very act of writing and reading literature which addresses issues of poverty and oppression appears to have a therapeutic effect for both the writer and the reader. In other words, the mere act of dealing with and exploring the issue in one's mind (in an abstract way, and to a certain extent, mediated by the use of an aesthetic or beautiful language) gives the illusory impression that one is dealing or even resolving (and addressing) the problem at hand. However, in reality the misery and poverty of the reality of Acre Street where Macabéa lives and where hunger, prostitution, and rats abound will continue to exist, not at all appeased by the "courageous" efforts of the well-off writer and reader. As we have already seen, our narrator is aware of the traps that the use of beautiful language can generate in literature and thus he tries to curb his own language so that the reality of Macabéa might remain in some ways intact: "Like every writer, I am clearly tempted to use succulent terms: I have at my command magnificent adjectives, robust nouns, and verbs so {slender that they can sharply pierce the atmosphere} as they move into action. For surely words are actions, {wouldn't you agree}? Yet I have no intention of adorning the word, for {if I touch the girl's bread, that bread will} turn to gold—and the girl . . . will not be able to bite it, and consequently die of hunger" (15) ("É claro que, como todo escritor, tenho a tentação de usar termos suculentos: conheço adjectivos esplendorosos, carnudos e verbos tão esguios que atravessam agudos no ar em vias de ação, já que palavra é ação, concordais? Mas não vou enfeitar a palavra pois se eu tocar no pão da moça esse pão se tornará em ouro—e a jovem . . . poderia mordê-lo morrendo de fome" [15]). Here, the narrator points to the fact that writers should not put art above the fray, otherwise they risk becoming blind, risk seeing the world through rose-colored glasses which filter the colors that are agreeable to the eye and to the heart, leaving out the ones which are unpleasant. The view of the narrator is close to that of Theodore Adorno, who has claimed that the beauty of lyric poetry can be dangerous in the sense that it tends to reinforce escapism and inaction. Adorno claims that the aestheticizing impulse of lyrical writing can have the effect of transforming atrocity in such a way that the horror of what is being described (in this case, the Holocaust) is removed, leaving the reader with the feeling of having dealt with or solved the problem, when in fact the reality of the problem remains unchanged (*Marxist Literary Theory* 187-03). In a similar manner, W.H. Auden has also lamented the fact that poetry "makes nothing happen" (553). In his now famous poem, "In Memory of W.B. Yeats," he undermines the power of Yeats's lyrical political poetry, which despite its undeniable beauty, did not in any way change Ireland's political situation. Although both Adorno and Auden were referring specifically to poetry, one can apply such principles to literature in general, since such writing is in one way or another lyrical and uses metaphoric language (it beautifies language) to describe reality, thus producing also an aestheticizing and even therapeutic effect—which can lead to the erasure or decrease of the horror (or injustice) of the issue in question and potentially make the writer (and reader) feel morally vindicated or relived.

The narrator's critique of the writer as an accomplice and supporter of the capitalist (and imperialist) system responsible for the oppression of the poor is present in other ways in *A hora*: "I forgot to mention that the record that is about to begin—for I can no longer bear the onslaught of facts—the record that is about to start is written under the sponsorship of the most popular soft drink in the world . . . a soft drink that is distributed throughout the world. It is the same soft drink that sponsored the recent earthquake in Guatemala. Despite the fact that it {has the taste} of nail polish, toilet soap, and chewed plastic. None of this prevents people from loving it with servility and subservience" (23) ("Também esqueci de dizer que o registro que em breve vai ter que começar—pois já não aguento mais a pressão dos fatos—o registro que em breve vai ter que começar é escrito sobre o patrocínio do refrigerante mais popular do mundo . . . refrigerante esse espalhado por todos os países. Aliás foi ele quem patrocinou o último terramoto em Guatemala. Apesar de ter gosto do cheiro de esmalte de unhas, de sabão Aristolino e plástico mastigado. Tudo isso não impede que todos o amem com servilidade e subserviência" [23]). By claiming that his narrative account is being sponsored by the most popular soft drink sold worldwide (Coca-Cola), the narrator appears to be implying at least two things. On the one hand, he seems to be suggesting that the writer writes because he needs the money in order to live a comfortable life in a highly capitalist and technological society. Writing becomes therefore a way of fulfilling the capitalist dream and even a way of acquiring intellectual recognition. As a participating member of the capitalist system, the writer sells his product because he wants to obtain either material goods or fame, and not because of genuine concern for others. Writing then becomes equated with the act of selling Coca-Cola: the writer writes because he wants to acquire personal gains and not because he wants to help the oppressed person exit his or her condition. In a similar manner, the owner of Coca-Cola industries produces Coca-Cola because he is interested in making large amounts of money, even if he knows that the product being sold is in fact not healthy and lacks quality, or as our narrator puts it, it {has the taste} of nail polish, toilet soap, and chewed plastic" (23).

On another level, the narrator is implying that there is really no point in writing, since the very act of writing is being supported (sponsored) by the agent responsible for the problem being discussed in the first place. Put differently, under the disguise of democracy and genuine concern for the poor, the capitalist system pays a writer to discuss and study the problem of poverty and oppression while knowing very well that the real problem is the system itself. In a similar manner, we have television stations which often praise themselves for having frequent debates about the evils of capitalism, or about the reasons behind the eating disorders affecting many women today and then often interrupt these programs with paradoxical commercials where we see a Mercedes Benz being caressed by a thin young woman (not to mention the fact that the television stations are being paid by the firms whose products are being advertised). In other words, the television station might in fact be doing a good job in unmasking the evils of society, but that effort is then annihilated by the very fact that the commercials showing the Mercedes and the thin woman are paying for the airing of those programs. The problem is the very capitalist system—a system that exploits the majority of people by paying them extremely low salaries, making them live well below the poverty line in order for others to make mega-profits. The narrator tells us that it is the Coca-Cola corporation that makes earthquakes happen in Guatemala, further suggesting that capitalism is so pervasive and influential that it not only exploits people across borders and makes poor nations dependent on rich nations, but it can also cause natural disasters. The earthquake could be read as a metaphor for the damage big corporations have caused to our atmosphere, our water and our soil, for example. Ironically, Macabéa's favourite drink is also Coca-Cola, another indication that she is the victim of the exploitation exerted by a capitalist and imperialist economy system but does not realize it, and even comes to like that system or see it as natural. In, *O Humanismo em Clarice Lispector: Um Estudo de Ser Social em a hora da estrela*, Ana Aparecida Arguelho de Sousa argues that one Lispector's main goals in *A hora* is in fact to denounce the political machinery of Brazil during the time it put forward the idea that the liberal economics that promoted capitalism and international trade was the way to go, the necessary tool to modernize Brazil and bring it to the level of the world's powerful economies. *A hora*, Arguelho de Sousa, argues puts forward a counter-ideology that shows the misery, exploitation, and mental alienation caused by this economic ideology.

Macabéa is trapped but cannot identify the trap, for the very system oppressing her has a way of making things seem natural, legitimate, and democratic, a way of covering the "holes" and showing an "even surface." In a similar fashion to Macabéa, Olímpico does not understand the structures that keep him oppressed, and even if he knows he is being exploited, he is not interested in changing the structures responsible for such oppression, but only in moving up in the social ladder, so that instead of being the oppressed he can become the oppressor:

> Olímpico de Jesus was a metal worker and Macabéa failed to notice that he never once referred to himself as "worker" but always as a "metallurgist." Macabéa was delighted with his professional standing just as she was proud of being a typist, even if she did earn less that the minimum salary. She and Olímpico had social status. "Metallurgist and typist" {made them a couple with social prestige}. Olímpico's job had the flavor one tastes when smoking a cigarette the wrong way round. His job was to collect the metal rods as they came off the machine and load them underneath on top of a conveyor belt. Olímpico never asked himself why he put the rods {at the bottom}. He didn't have such a hard life and he even managed to save some of his wages: he had free shelter at night in a hut that was due for demolition because of his friendship with the night watchman. (45)

> Olímpico de Jesus trabalhava de operário numa metalúrgica e ela nem notou que ele não se chamava de "operário" e sim de "metalúrgico." Macabéa

ficava contente com a posição social dele porque também tinha orgulho em ser datilógrafa, embora ganhasse menos que o salário mínimo. Mas ela e Olímpico eram alguém no mundo. "Metalúrgico e datilógrafa" formavam um casal de classe. A tarefa de Olímpico tinha o gosto que se sente quando se fuma um cigarro do lado errado, na ponta da cortiça. O trabalho consistia em pegar em barras de metal que vinham deslizando de cima da máquina para colocá-las embaixo, sobre uma placa deslizante. Nunca se perguntara por que colocava a barra embaixo. A vida não lhe era má e ele até economizava um pouco de dinheiro: dormia de graça numa guarita em obras de demolição por camaradagem do vigia. (45)

This quotation has clear Marxist undertones. Both Macabéa and Olímpico are obvious victims of the capitalist system—a system based on sharp class distinctions—and one that makes the values (and interests) of the oppressive class prevail and seem natural. The couple is being exploited by the system, yet the two think they are lucky to have the jobs they have. As Macabéa puts it, they are a "casal de classe" (literally meaning a "couple with class," denoting they have social status); they have "posição social" ("social prestige"), and that makes her happy. Their class is the very sign that they live in a society where exploitation of many sorts takes place, one that is highly stratified, where one group takes over and imposes its views and values onto others, either directly or indirectly. Nevertheless, Macabéa feels happy because they belong to a social class, they are given a "name," a position and a recognized place in their world. Olímpico calls himself a "metalúrgico" ("metallurgist, metal worker") rather than an "operário" ("worker, labourer") which suggests several things about the capitalist system Olímpico lives in and also how he positions himself in it. First, he is unable to clearly see the connection between his job and the capitalist system at large. "Operário" is the general name given to those who work in factories and thus is a name that connotes capitalism in a more encompassing, general manner. "Metalúrgico" on the other hand, is a name given to someone who does a specific job inside the capitalist system and thus a name seemingly unrelated to the global capitalist framework: it separates (dissects) workers through specialization, which makes it more difficult for them to see themselves as part of the larger capitalist entity. The naming (classifying) here functions as a repressive and controlling mechanism. Second, Olímpico wants to see himself as someone with more power than he has, which means he sees the capitalist system as legitimate and wants to be part of that system, preferably in a position of power. Third, he does not realize that as a working-class person, he is working constantly to sustain the capitalist system that is oppressing him. This last point is further supported by the fact that Olímpico's work consists of collecting the metal rods from a machine and putting them at the bottom. His work as a metallurgist is an excellent metaphor for the entire capitalist system, a system designed to appear natural: it is a "deslizante" ("sliding") system that runs (slides) smoothly, just as the metal rods do on the conveyor belt. Olímpico also fails to question the reasons for his task, which consists of putting the metal bar at the bottom, suggesting that he fails to see he is at the very bottom of the class system that regulates the capitalist society he is part of. He is at the bottom, even though that bottom is in fact the very pillar of the entire system, a system that has the vast majority of the population working very hard for a small minority, so that the latter can make a fortune. The implication here is that Olímpico fails to see that the working class has a lot of power and were it to decide to stop working, the entire system would collapse. He does not understand that the power coming from above is unnatural, illegitimate, and coercive. A better understanding of the coerciveness (and unfairness) of the capitalist system would allow workers to fight for more rights through organized labor movements, such as unions, for example.

Not only is Olímpico unaware of his role in perpetuating and aiding the exploitative capitalist system—which prevents him from fighting it—but he also seems to be using whatever methods he has at his disposal to receive favors and to make it to the top. He wants to become the oppressive agent that is now oppressing him by entering the "desirable clan of the South" (59) ("ambicionado clã do sul") [59]), and will do all he can to attain his goal, even killing people (we are told that he killed a man while living in the northeast). In fact, his grand dream is to become a deputy, a sign that he is indeed only interested in achieving power himself, in exploiting others and not in changing the status quo. Olímpico's behavior is indicative of the patronage and clientele systems regulating Brazilian society, a society where people try to move up in the social ladder using whatever means they can rather than fight the oppressive structures. Yet, the fact that they do not usually fight these structures is also often related to the fact that they do not understand the oppressing system well and tend to see it as legitimate. Olímpico's own name, reminiscent of an Olympian god, suggests that he wants to achieve power, which within the structures of his society equates to him being an oppressor. Ultimately, what Lispector is suggesting is that literature is part of what Louis Althusser would classify as ideological state apparatuses (ISAs), for it operates in a fashion that, although not immediately seen or understood, is very pervasive and repressive, and ultimately reflects and promotes the values and interests of the ruling class (Althusser 146). Furthermore, our narrator seems to be suggesting that in order to change the state of affairs, people need to rebel against this capitalist system, and writers need to refuse to continue supporting and being part of such a system. People need to wake up from their state of lethargy and unconsciousness, from their "servility and subservience" (23) ("servilidade e subserviência" [23]). In other words, they must stop drinking Coca-Cola, for that is the drink that keeps them dependent on the repressive capitalist system. In sum, people must stop writing or reading literature that brings no real change or that is directly or indirectly being sponsored by the capitalist system, even if that literature is also pointing to the fallacies of the capitalist system itself and thus undermining it.

Writing as search for the writer's authentic self and as remedy for the malaises of the soul

For Lispector, writing becomes less an exercise about justice and for the benefit of the poor other than an exercise aimed at achieving personal mental and psychic well-being. Writing becomes a way of connecting with her authentic self, of exiting the "death" of everyday language, of being symbolically renewed (reborn) and of dealing with her existential anguish and possibly, even with her neurosis. Writing becomes the arena where the writer's most intense struggles, regarding the nature of her being and the attainment of existential fulfilment, are brought to the forefront. In this sense, Lispector's narration becomes very autobiographical: it becomes a self-indulgent exercise where the needs of the poor other often become secondary. Our writer-narrator writes not because of the "girl from the northeast but {because} of a much more serious reason of '*force majeure*' or as they say in formal petitions by 'force of law'" (18) ("nordestina mas por motivo grave de 'força maior,' como se diz nos requerimentos oficiais, por 'força de lei'" ([18]); he writes because he has "nothing to do in this world" (21) ("nada a fazer no mundo" [21]), because he is "weary" (21) ("cansado" [21]) and "desperate" (21) ("desesperado" [21]) and can no longer bear the "routine of [his] {being} and, were it not for the constant novelty in writing, [he] {would} die symbolically each day" (21) ("rotina de [se] ser e se não fosse sempre a novidade que é escrever, [ele] morreria simbolicamente todos os dias" [21]). He writes because he "cannot stand repetition" (40) ("d[á-se] mal com a repetição" [41]), for repetition "{separates} [him] from potential novelties within [his] reach" (40) ("afasta-[o das suas] possíveis novidades" [41]). This is very close to what Lispector says in "Literature and Justice," where she indicates that she needs to be surprised in order to write and since justice is for her a very basic and obvious concern, she cannot really write about it, at least not explicitly.

Lispector's writing becomes then a therapeutic medium to appease the tedium she feels in her everyday life, a life that has become habitual, mechanical, and subdued by all kinds of social symbolical values. The *force majeure* and the "force of law," which draw our writer-narrator to write, can be seen as symbolizing the need she has to connect with her authentic and primary self, to reach the place where she can be whole and listen to her unconscious sides, the sides without name, without organized rational discourse or symbolical language, where the poetic (fluid) predominates. Writing allows our narrator to enter what Heidegger would call "dwelling." For Heidegger, the dwelling experienced through art (especially poetry) corresponds to entering into a real, total (whole), and authentic existence. It is precisely because "everyday language is a forgotten and therefore used-up poem, from which there hardly resounds a call any longer" (208) that Lispector needs to write continuously and in a poetic fashion. She writes because she cannot stand the "routine of [her] {being} and, were it not for the constant novelty in writing, [she] {would} die symbolically each day" (21) ("rotina de [se] ser e se não fosse sempre a novidade que é escrever, [ela] morreria simbolicamente todos os dias" [21]). She writes because she wants to regain the Heideggerian "call." In an article titled "Temporal Convergence: Poiesis and the Arts of Dwelling in Time," using a Heideggerian perspective, Elizabeth Anthony argues the importance and success of art in treating people with mental health issues. She writes, "Poiesis could . . . be described as the act of uncovering and responding to the call of our authentic Being, which we too often just scuff around, using-up the poem our daily life might be," and so "Poiesis in these terms in not just the making of an art product or performance, but a making of existence" (5). Undoubtedly, writing, being art, becomes "a making of existence" for the narrator-writer of *A hora* too. In *Correspondências* (Correspondências) Lispector admits being a "person with a sick soul" ("pessoa de alma doente") whose problems cannot be "understood by healthy people" ("compreendidos por pessoas . . . sãs"[75]), someone who is extremely sensitive, who feels too much, who feels the pain of others on her shoulders and a guilt about the misery affecting the world in general (71). This guilt, pain, responsibility, and extreme sensitivity towards others and otherness comes across quite well not only in *A hora* but also in "Literature and Justice" and *Água viva*. For example, in *A hora* the narrator says: "I must write about this girl from the northeast otherwise I shall choke. She accuses me and the only I can defend myself is is by writing about her" (17) ("Preciso falar dessa moça senão sufoco. Ela me acusa e o meio de me defender é escrever sobre ela" [17]); "But why should I feel guilty? Why should I try to relieve myself of the burden of not having done anything concrete to help the girl? (23) ("Mas porque me estou sentindo culpado? E procurando aliviar-me do peso de nada ter feito de concreto em benefício da moça" [23]). And the first subtitle of the novella, *The Blame is Mine* (*A culpa é minha*), further indicates that Lispector, being a fairly well-off middle-class woman, does indeed feel guilty and responsible for the poverty of Macabéa.

In *Água viva*, the female narrator also shows us a special sense of responsibility towards things other and the world in general; she feels that her job is to look after the flowers, the sea, the animals, and the people (55-56) so that they can live and remain themselves and not be merely an invention of the anthropomorphic mind who evaluates, measures, and classifies everything according to the human perception of reality and using a language (and consequently thought system) that has little to do with pure reality. As Wordsworth would put it, she is a poet and as such, possesses a special sensitivity which allows her to see into things that remain inaccessible (hidden) to others (254-57), for they have lost the "call" and have became prisoners of the everyday dead language in the Heideggerian sense. As a poet, Lispector possesses the powers to renew the world, to restore its freshness and access its truest essence by using a language that is loving, gentle, and liberating—the language of love, as Cixous would put it (*A Hora de Clarice* 129). In Zen, this extreme sensibility and pain experienced by Lispector could be attributed to the fact that she is an enlightened person. As Brazier puts it, "This ability to perceive all beings coming into and going out of existence continuously was one of the attributes acquired by the Buddha as part and parcel of his enlightenment. On the other hand what comes with this is a more generalized grief, a 'great grief'; aware of the universality of suffering, we deeply understand the words of the poet John Donne who bid us not send to know for whom the bell tolls since, in *every* case, it tolls for us" (243). If we add these symptoms and ways of being—all common in people who suffer from various mental health problems—to the fact that Lispector admits to taking tranquilizers (Lispector, *Correspondências* 311) to ease her feelings, we could suggest that Lispector suffered from at least moderate anxiety and depression. Thus, like others, as argued by Anthony in the aforementioned article, Lispector also uses her art in order to alleviate mental, psychological, and spiritual distresses. Art allows—or at least facilitates—humans to connect with their whole self, to integrate their personality so that they can then find psychological, emotional, and spiritual health and restore their life balance, a balance often disrupted by modern life with its emphasis on rationality and disregard for spirituality and irrational and unconscious epistemologies. Integration is used here in the Jungianian sense. Jung defends that all human sides and intelligences (conscious and unconscious—both collective and individual) must be listened to and fed so that humans can live a balanced, fulfilling life (*The Essential* 456-79). Australian Jungianian therapist, Maureen Roberts, makes extensive use of Jung's ideas relating to the integration of personality when treating patients with certain types of schizophrenia, depression, or other mental illnesses, whom she sees as having too much access to the unconscious world and as having lost their individual ego boundaries. The objective of this therapy is to find a balance by attempting to reestablish a more even access to both unconscious and conscious sides and to redefine (restore) proper personal and collective boundaries (see Roberts). The Jungianian integration described here is similar to what Heidegger and Anthony refer to as dwelling, that is, the entering of the being into a state of authentic or whole existence. This is also very close to the Zen holistic philosophy as well as to African epistemologies as discussed in chapter 1 (for the link between Zen Buddhism and the writing of Lispector see also Igor Rossini, *Zen e a Poética Auto-Reflexiva de Clarices Lispector*).

Through writing, the narrator-writer of *A hora* can leave the symbolic world temporarily and reach a zone where her body, instinct, intuition, and unconscious and spiritual sides can take the lead—a zone where reason and discourse are temporarily suspended, as it were. Through her writing, she can reestablish the wholeness necessary to attain a state of equilibrium, a state where all her sides (epistemologies) come together thus allowing her to be unbroken: "To think is an act. To feel is a fact. Put the two together—it is me who is writing what I am writing. God is the world. The truth is always some inner power without explanation. The more genuine part of my life is unrecognizable, extremely intimate and {has no single word that can that define it}." (11-12); "In writing this story, I shall yield to emotion . . . In no sense am I an intellectual, I write with my body" (16) ("Pensar é um ato. Sentir é um fato. Os dois juntos—sou eu que escrevo o que estou escrevendo. Deus é o mundo. Com esta história eu vou me sensibilizar . . . A verdade é sempre um contacto interior e inexplicável. A minha vida mais verdadeira é irreconhecível, extremamente interior e não tem uma só palavra que a signifique." [11]; "Eu não sou um intelectual, escrevo com o corpo" [16]). The nondiscursive and alogical epistemologies become the way of recapturing the "true" knowledge about the world and oneself, the knowledge that is not yet touched by language, discourse, and consequently all sociopolitical power structures and their multirepercussive oppressing mechanisms. These epistemologies allow Lispector to start afresh, at least in theory and temporarily. As Cixous puts it, Lispector allows for the rational intelligence to be replaced by the "nonintelligent" intelligences: "The sensation that precedes thought is nonintelligence. To understand it, an intelligence must be invented that is *água viva*, or living water itself" (*Reading* 58). Nonintelligence can be loosely defined as the type of knowledge that is not completely filtered through the rational mind, that comes from the unconscious, imagination, instinct, intuition, body, and spirit. This "nonintelligence" is remarkably close to Zen Buddhism principles and is the prerequisite to achieve the *satori* (sunyata, nirvana) (Susuki 163-68). The term *água viva* ("living water") used above by Cixous refers to Lispector's novel *Água viva* but also to the general approach Lispector takes toward language—one that sees conventional language as a corruptive agent that adulterates the authenticity of being and reality, thus the need to write poetically and using nonlinguistic media and ambivalent metaphors.

In the act of writing Lispector can experience the feeling of bliss or jouissance in the Cixoucian and Kristevan sense—and it is the continuous search for this jouissance that moves Lispector's pen. As she has said in an interview, "Each book I write is a painful and happy beginning. That capacity to renew myself completely as the time passes is what I call to live and to write" (qtd. in Gutierrez 4). Lispector's writing, described by Cixous as *écriture féminine,* is a way to reach the presymbolic world, the unnameable of the Kristevan (and also Platonic) chora, the mother's womb. Cixous had defined *écriture féminine* in the following terms: "It is impossible to define a feminine practice of writing [*écriture féminine*], and this is an impossibility that will remain, for this practice can never be theorized, enclosed, coded—which does not mean that it doesn't exist. But it will always surpass the discourse that regulates the phallocentric system: it does and will take place in areas other than those subordinated to philosophical-theoretical domination. It will be conceived of only by subjects who are breakers of automatisms, by peripheral figures that no authority can ever subjugate" (*Newly Born* 56). According to Cixous, *écriture féminine* is also not exclusive to women. Anyone can write in a *féminine* fashion as long as one allows the nonintelligences to be brought forward in one's writing. As seen in chapter 1, and given the characteristics of Mia Couto's writing, one could easily describe him as a male writer who could fit into this category of writing—and Coetzee too, as I discuss in chapter 4. It is in the unnameable that Lispector, the writer and narrator of *A hora,* finds her primal self, the self before the self, the place where divisions pertaining to gender, class, object/subject, matter/spirit, nature/nurture, mother/child (and so on) are eradicated and where she is able to find her authentic or whole self, a self that is undivided and uncorrupted by social-symbolical constraints. Writing allows Lispector to attain sublimation, the state where self-consciousness is temporally erased and where she can again "meet" the lost perfection of what in psychoanalysis is referred to as primary narcissism, or the life energy: "If I continue to write, it's because I have nothing more to accomplish in this world except to wait for death. Searching for the word in the darkness. Any little success invades me and puts me in full view of everyone. I long to wallow in the mud. I can scarcely control my need for self-abasement, my craving for licentiousness and debauchery. Sin tempts me, forbidden pleasures lure me. I want to be both pig and hen, then kill them and drink their blood. I think about Macabéa's vagina, minute, yet unexpectedly covered with a thick growth of black hairs—her vagina was the only vehement sign of her existence" (70) ("Se ainda escrevo é porque nada mais tenho a fazer no mundo enquanto espero a morte. A procura da palavra no escuro. O pequeno sucesso me invade e me põe no olho da rua. Eu queria chafurdar no lodo, minha necessidade de baixeza eu mal controlo, a necessidade da orgia e do pior gozo absoluto. O pecado me atrai, o que é proibido me fascina. Quero ser porco e galinha e depois matá-los e beber-lhes o sangue. Penso no sexo de Macabéa, miúdo mas inesperadamente coberto de grossos abundantes pêlos negros—seu sexo era a única marca veemente de sua existência" [70]). Here the narrator is being very libidinal. She is "sinking very low": she wants to be sexual and promiscuous to the extreme. She wants to become dirty, mix with mud, drink blood, and become a hen and a pig. In sum, she wants to reach (regain) what Kristeva would call the "abject":

> The "abject" is "our reaction (horror, vomit) to a threatened breakdown in meaning caused by the loss of the distinction between subject and object or between self and other. The primary example is the corpse (which traumatically reminds us of our own materiality); however, other items can elicit the same reaction: the open wound, shit, sewage, even a particularly immoral crime (e.g., Auschwitz). Kristeva posits that abjection in something that we must experience in our psychosexual development before entering into the mirror stage, that is, the establishment of such boundaries as self and other or human and animal. Kristeva also associates the abject with the maternal since the establishment of the boundary between self and other marks our movement out of the chora. (Felluga, "The Abject, abjection"; see also *Pouvoirs de l'horreur* and *The Kristeva Reader*)

Yet in truth Lispector cannot ever regain that abject or choric stage and so writing (art) functions as the symbolical (subliminal) medium to reach that primary stage. In other words, art functions as the ultimate sublimation: it is the only way Lispector finds to symbolically regain (access) her forever lost life energy, an energy (residue) that we all possess. Her writing fulfills, at least temporarily, that powerful yearning for the chora, the abject, or what could be referred to as the unbroken, distended, apersonal ego. As Mark Epstein explains in his book, entitled *Thoughts Without a Thinker: Psychotherapy From a Buddhist Perspective*,

> Our life energy, or *libido*, has as its original source the unencumbered union of infant and mother, which the psychoanalysts called primary narcissism. According to Freud, the ego originally includes everything, taking an entire mother-infant conglomeration as its own. Only later does the ego spin off an external world from itself, reducing itself to a "shrunken residue" of the much more pervasive whole that it once encompassed. Yet the paradise that predated the emergence of self-conscious desire continues to colour our perceptions of the way things are. . . . From an analytic perspective, all sublimation is really an attempt to transform these energies of ego libido and object libido into a "higher state or place of existence" where "something of . . . the original unity is in the process of being restored." Eerily echoing

> the Buddhist philosophies of medieval India, the analytic view contends that sublimation actually urges the individual toward reconciliation of the endless search for perfection. We are all haunted by the lost perfection of the ego that contained everything, and we measure ourselves and our loves against this standard. We search for a replica in external satisfactions, in food, comfort, sex, or success, but gradually learn, through the process of sublimation, that the best approximation of that lost feeling comes from creative acts that evoke states of being in which self-consciousness is temporarily relinquished. These are the states in which the artist, writer, scientist, or musician, like Freud's da Vinci, dissolves into the act of creation. (81-82)

Lispector does in fact characterize her writing as a way to attain what in Zen Buddhism would be referred to as sunyata, a state symbolizing the emptiness of thought, the suspension of discursive thinking, and the "seeing" (the arriving at ultimate knowledge) through the eye of the spirit—an eye that refuses dissection and reconnects with the "all is one," an eye that sees, thinks and knows outside of language and rational discursive rethorics. In the sense that the attainment of sunyata is characterized by an emptiness of symbolical discourses and the erasure between object and subject, individual consciousness and collective conscious, I and You and It, it in fact becomes very close to the concepts of the abject and choric realm as defined by Kristeva. For Lispector, writing actually functions as a meditative exercise that will allow her to experience and enter the spiritual nirvana; it is like a prayer:

> I am warming up before making a start, rubbing my hands together to summon up my courage. I can remember a time when I used to pray in order to kindle my sprit: movement is spirit. Prayer was a means of confronting myself in silence away from the gaze of others. As I prayed I {attained the hollow of the soul—and this hollowness} is everything that I can ever hope to possess. Apart from this, there is nothing. But emptiness, too, has its value and somehow resembles abundance. One way of obtaining is not to search, one way of possessing is not to ask; simply to believe that my inner silence is the solution to my—to my mystery. (14)

> Estou esquentando o corpo para iniciar, esfregando as mãos uma na outra para ter coragem. Agora me lembrei de que houve um tempo em que para me esquentar o espírito eu rezava: o movimento é espírito. A reza era um meio de mudamente e escondido de todos atingir-me a mim mesmo. Quando rezava conseguia o oco da alma—esse oco é o tudo que eu posso jamais ter. Mais do que isso nada. Mas o vazio tem o valor e a semelhança do pleno. Um meio de obter é não procurar, um meio de ter é o de não pedir e somente acreditar que o silêncio que eu creio em mim é resposta a meu-
> —a meu mistério. (14)

The narrator's attained "hollowness of the soul" is possible because she uses writing in a manner that is nonconventional, in which the intelligence of the nonintelligent can speak, a manner that is not "subordinated to philosophical-theoretical domination" and to "automatisms" (Cixous, *Newly Born* 56), a poetic manner, that is. In *Água viva,* the first person female narrator also says: "The true thought seems to have no author. And beatitude has that same characteristic. Beatitude starts at the moment when the act of thinking has been liberated from the form. Beatitude starts at the moment when the thinking-feeling has overcome the thinking need of the author—he no longer needs to think and is now near the greatness of the world" (*The Stream* 88) ("O verdadeiro pensamento parece sem autor. E a beatitude tem essa mesma marca. A beatitude começa no momento em que o ato de pensar liberou-se da necessidade da forma. A beatitude começa no momento em que o pensar-sentir ultrapassou a necessidade de pensar do autor—este não precisa mais pensar e encontra-se agora perto da grandeza do mundo" [*Água viva* 82]). It is when she stops thinking and being the author of her thoughts that she is able to achieve beatitude: the true nirvana state where the "personal I" can have a view of (enter) the vastness of the universe, a view of the "Great I." At this stage, she no longer resides in herself, in her limited and imprisoning form: she dwells. Interestingly enough, the passage above directly echoes the title of Epstein's book *Thoughts Without a Thinker: Psychotherapy from a Buddhist Perspective,* which is based on Pirandello's play, *Six Characters in Search of an Author.*

Just as the practitioners of Buddhism often use chants, or better yet, hums, which are often just sounds emitted with the lips closed, to meditate and ready themselves to reach the sunyata, our narrator tells us that she used to pray in silence, suggesting that she too uses the hum or the chant so that she can ready himself for the nothingness experience. In tantric Buddhism, hums are referred to as Mantras and described as "sacred sounds like Om, for example—[which are] transmitted from the master to his disciple at the time of initiation; when the disciple's mind is properly attuned, the inner vibrations of this word symbol together with its associations in the consciousness of the initiate are said to open his mind to higher dimensions" (Kapleau 346). Lispector also tells us that, in order to prepare herself for the writing experience, she needs to assume a specific physical posture: "I am warming up before making a start, rubbing my hands together to summon up my courage" (14) ("Estou esquentando o corpo para iniciar, esfregando as mãos uma na outra para ter coragem" [14]). This too is common in Buddhist practices when one is preparing oneself to enter meditation and achieve the sunyata. In tantric Buddhism these physical postures (gestures) are called Mudras: "These are physical gestures, especially symbolical hand movements, which are performed to help evoke certain parallel states of mind of Buddhas and Bodhisattvas" (Kapleau 346). All this suggests that our narrator is about to enter a meditative experience, to enter the "hollowness of the soul": it suggests that her writing is going to be a meditative chant itself, a hum (or poem) of sorts that will allow her to reach the nirvana possible through the emptiness of thought. The very fact that Mantras are utterances which have no disclosed (logical) meaning points to the importance of exiting language (discourse) to attain a spiritual realm, a realm that is more authentic and just, for it allows for discriminations inherent in all naming to be obliterated. If we take into account that poetry occupies a fundamental place in Buddhist practices precisely because language is approached from a viewpoint of being a mere "empty" (Omine 11; Brazier 12-13) symbol for that which is ultimately beyond our rational (and linguistic) grasp, the link between Lispector and Buddhism becomes quite clear. And so does the link between Lispector's worldviews, Buddhism, and African epistemologies, as explored in chapter 1.

The general incompetence of language

The fact that Lispector does not believe in the power of literature to change society and to portray the poor other accurately is tied to the way she perceives language in general. The writer distrusts the power of symbolic language and sees it not only as a medium which corrupts the "truth" of being and beings, but also as a system that alters, suppresses and oppresses that truth. Moreover, in a similar fashion to Lévinas and Irigaray, as discussed in chapter 2, Lispector seems to believe that there is a type of thought (way of being, feeling, and understanding ourselves and the world) that remains outside of language and rhetorical discourse, and which is less suppressing and allows for freedom and a constant renewal (and questioning) of social constructed categories pertaining to class, gender, and so on. This general disbelief in symbolic language (and discourse) and the belief that there is a more genuine "thought" that remains outside of language is present in all of Lispector's writing, and most intensely in *The Stream of Life*, which many critics have described as being the most metalinguistic work written by Lispector. In this work, we read:

> Writing is the way followed by someone who uses words like bait: a word fishing for what is not a word. When the nonword—the whatever's between the lines—bites the bait, something has been written. Once the between the lines has been hooked, you can throw the word away with relief. But there ends the analogy: the nonword, in biting the bait, incorporates it. What saves you, then, is to write absentmindedly. (14); In this dense jungle of words that wrap themselves thickly around what I feel and think and experience and that transform all that I am into something {that remains outside of myself}. I watch myself thinking. What I ask myself is this: who is it in me that remains outside even of thinking? (55); Each one of us is a symbol dealing with symbols—everything is a point of mere reference to the real . . . Reality has no synonyms. (66); {In the back of my thinking there resides the truth that is of the world. The illogicality of nature. What a silence. "God" is of such silence that it terrorizes me.} (71)
>
> Escrever é o modo de quem tem a palavra como isca: a palavra pescando o que não é palavra. Quando essa não-palavra—a entrelinha—morde a isca, alguma coisa se escreveu. Uma vez que se pescou a entrelinha, poder-se-ia com alívio jogar a palavra fora. Mais aí cessa a analogia: a não-palavra, ao morder a isca, incorporou-a. O que salva então é escrever distraidamente. (20); Nesta densa selva de palavras que envolvem espessamente o que sinto e penso e vivo e transformam tudo o que sou em alguma coisa que fica fora de mim. Fico me assistindo pensar. O que me pergunto é: quem em mim é que está fora até de pensar? (61-62); Cada um de nós é um símbolo que lida com símbolos—tudo ponto de apenas referência do real . . . mas a realidade não tem sinônimos. (73); No atrás do meu pensamento está a verdade que é a do mundo. A ilogicidade da natureza. Que silêncio. "Deus" é de um tal enorme silêncio que me aterroriza. (*Água viva* 78)

In *A hora* we can also find many examples of the Lispectorian distrust of symbolical language. As the narrator says, "The truth is always some inner power without explanation. The more genuine part of my life is unrecognizable, extremely intimate, and {has no word to define it}" (12) ("A verdade é sempre um contacto interior e inexplicável. A minha vida mais verdadeira é irreconhecível, extremamente interior e não tem uma só palavra que a signifique" [11]). Given the fact that Lispector's most truthful life (and self) is unrecognizable, extremely interior, and has no word to explain it, as she puts is, it then follows that the truth of the other, the truth of the Macabéa that Lispector is trying to grasp and portray through her writing, also remains unreachable. Thus it is not really a matter of not wanting to explain the other (or the self) but rather a matter of not possessing a language to do so, for language is only an imperfect translation of reality and often, too, a creation of an unreal and artificial reality. The novella starts like this: "Everything in the world began with a yes. One molecule said yes to another and life was born" (11) ("Tudo no mundo começou com um sim. Uma molécula disse sim a outra molécula e nasceu a vida" [11]). If one wanted to read this phrase at what I choose to call a traditional level, one could suggest that the very fact that Lispector has decided to write about Macabéa is an attempt on her part to understand and tell the reality of the poor other, an other who cannot speak for herself, an attempt to deal with the "social problem" in a more direct manner. Thus, the "everything started with a yes" could be seen as referring directly to the power of the word to tell the reality of Macabéa and give life (and importance) to her own being, a being who lacks a voice of her own and possesses no capacity to fight for herself or even be recognized as a full human being by the society surrounding her. The expression, "everything started with a yes" would then literally mean that by writing about Macabéa, the author is giving her a language and making her a real being, someone who leaves anonymity to enter the reality of the word and the human world. This reality is of high importance given the power generally attributed to communication through language, be it written or spoken. It is not only that society tends to view those who cannot speak and communicate "properly" (through standard language) as being less intelligent, it is also that written and spoken language is seen as a tool that only humans possess and often, too, as the only mechanism which allows humans to think, reason, and make abstractions. Thus, if one cannot use language, the tendency is to perceive that person as someone who is less human, less capable to think, less intelligent, in other words, more animal.

We could argue, then, that Lispector's narrative is an attempt to bring humanness to a person who has been ignored by society and by extension also an attempt to sensitize the Brazilian public (the rich and the poor, the oppressors and the oppressed) about the misery, poverty, inequality, and oppression regulating Brazilian society—a sensitization that would hopefully contribute to everyone's engagement in changing the oppressive reality. This view would very much appeal to the Brazilian self-proclaimed engaged writers who saw in their literary works a powerful fighting mechanism capable of accurately revealing, unmasking, and even ending or decreasing the oppression dominating their society. However, given the disbelief of

Authenticity of Being as the Politics of Agency in Lispector

Lispector in the power of the word to portray reality as it is, the "yes" of the commencement of the novella would actually seem to equate to a "no." The sentence "everything started with a yes" becomes "everything in the world ended with a yes." Lispector contests the logocentric idea that sees the logos (word) as the ultimate truth capable of explaining and revealing the world, others, and ourselves to ourselves. For Lispector, whenever language is used, the speaker and the listener are transported to a world of abstractions and absences, leading them farther and farther from reality: the world as it is ceases to exist and we are taken to a sort of imagined reality, a reality changed by the use of language. To the popular biblical phrase "In the beginning was the Word, and the Word was with God, and the Word was God," Lispector would answer, "In the beginning was the world, and the world was without God, and then man invented the word and became God." In other words, in the beginning the world was devoid of symbolical language (and concepts), then language was invented by humans, thus corrupting the authenticity of being and imprisoning humans in all kinds of discriminatory and oppressive categories. For the narrator of *A hora* "God is the world" (11) ("Deus é o mundo" [11]) and the world cannot be told accurately through language, for once we enter the linguistic system we "kill" the world and create a sort of mirage that will enclose us in all kinds of prisons, prisons made of words which then become concepts, and laws, and stories about what we are or ought to be. In the narrator's own words: "{Yes, but} remember that no matter what I write, my basic material is the word. So this story will consist of words that form phrases from which there emanates a secret meaning that exceeds both words and phrases" (14-15) ("Sim, mas não esquecer que para escrever não-importa-o-quê o meu material básico é a palavra. Assim é que esta história será feita de palavras que se agrupam em frases e desta se evola um sentido secreto que ultrapassa palavras e frases" [14]). The world in its naked reality becomes God; God is the word in its flesh, as it were, a "word" that is not discursive or rational and is apprehended by the subject only via the unintelligible. Thus, the real story of the world and its people relies in the "secret meaning that exceeds both words and phrases" (14-15) ("sentido secreto que ultrapassa palavras e frases" [14]). The truth of the characters (including the narrator, himself a character in the book) described in the story is beyond what is said in the words and phrases used by the storyteller. The truth remains in the prediscursive. When the narrator tells us that "God is the world," he is not necessarily saying that God invented and created the world and the word, as a traditional Christian might believe, but rather that the physical world around him is seen as being God itself: God is all the things that exist in their truest reality, things that are present and which we are able to feel, touch, hear, smell, and see. God is what we are able to experience with all our senses. One can feel and touch one's body, a stone, a tree, or a flower, and the reality that one gets from those acts (Lispector would actually call them facts) is God itself. God is the ultimate and most genuine way of being: it is the Word with a capital W, the word before the word, the world before the word. As Lispector puts it in *A hora*, "To think is an act. To feel is a fact." (11-12) ("Pensar é um acto. Sentir é um facto" [11]), meaning that facts become more important than thoughts (or acts), for the latter are always corrupt; they are abstractions. Thought, which is an act, is synonymous with spoken or written language and is therefore seen as a corruption of the authentic reality which is only accessible through instinct, feeling, touch, spiritual insight, and unconscious forces. In this sense Lispector, like Lévinas, Irigaray, and Saramago, is attempting to "drink" from phenomenological realities as much as possible so that she can erase or reconsider ready-made concepts that are responsible for much of human alienation and oppression.

The political agency of nonlinguistic narrative strategies

As Maureen Conley points out,

> Lispector's contact with the world is immediate: her language portrays the struggle that human beings engage in with their social milieus and with themselves . . . The will to encapsulate that world by writing it is [turned into an] immediate relation of language and sensation. Cixous accounts for this difference by forging the concept of *écriture féminine*, fraught with the existential and historical position of the female in a world that marginalizes the human subject, but that effectively redeems it through the way it offers anyone, male or female, a *living* relation with language and experience . . . Cixous, with Lispector strives toward a mode of reading, writing, and speaking nonexclusive differences so that the other is other without being thought of in merely negative or positional terms such as that of the nonself. Of course, by definition, language forces us to go through negativity, since the words replace things, but, following her work, the question that we can ask is exactly of how to go about inflecting that negativity. (*Reading With* 8,11)

Conley's views are echoed in the following passage from *A hora*, where Macabéa is described by the narrator as speaking a language that is almost inaccessible; she is someone whom the narrator cannot fully "tell" (understand, penetrate), someone who evades his understanding: "{She [Macabéa] spoke, yes, but she was extremely mute. Sometimes I am able to get a word out of her but she slips through my fingers} (*The Hour* 29) ("Ela [Macabéa] falava, sim, mas era extremamente muda. Uma palavra dela eu às vezes consigo mas ela me foge por entre os dedos" [*A hora* 29]). If conventional language and literature (in this case, à la Jorge Amado and his like) are unable to tell the truest reality of a person and in fact "hurt" that person by imprisoning her in a world of oppressive values and ideals—as Lispector suggests in *A hora* and many of her other works—is there a language and a literature better suited to be closer to the real? For Lispector there is, for if it is true that the author kills the language of convention and distrusts its capacity to tell the "true story," it is also true that she makes a point of telling the "truest story" possible in the process. She makes a point of inflecting the negativity inherent in all language, as Conley suggests above. On the one hand, Lispector deconstructs the old views on language and literature, such as those held by the writers of the *Regionalist Novel* who saw their literary writings and language as exact reflections of the Brazilian social reality and the Brazilian poor other. And on the other, she offers us another way of describing the reality of the other, a way that might be the best way of all, for it allows us to get closer to what can be described as the presocial or presymbolic reality and the authenticity of beings and being. *A hora* both deconstructs and constructs: it demolishes the old "building" (or at least it exposes the fragility of its structures) but it also erects another "building," one that allows us to get a better view of the world, ourselves, and others, a building where everyone is more at home, as Heidegger would say (190). It is through the use of silence, poetic language, images of music, and ambivalent metaphors that Lispector creates a narrative where the voice of the poor other and her otherness can in some ways be captured and yet respected.

Based on Cixous's definition of *écriture féminine*, Conley defines poetry as follows:

> Poetry is not understood as subversive, as a "revolution" in and of language, but as that which precludes strategies of capture and containment and that—contrary to philosophy—allows for otherness. Cixous's belief in the virtues of poetry in its largest sense is much opposed to the development of a certain prose common to modern technocracies, in which discourse favours the efficacy of clarity and the pragmatics of meaning and fills all the gaps and fissures for the purpose of appropriation. Poetry not in its Appollonian form but as a residue of Dionysian culture, insists on a necessary *part sauvage*. (Conley 6)

Contrary to conventional language, which is objective and tends to denote only one meaning, poetic language is subjective, multiperspectival, multivoiced and paradoxical. Conventional language (and conventional literature) is often more interested in communicating a message rather than questioning and going beyond itself or reaching what Owen Barfield has called "knowledge" in his book *Poetic Diction*:

> Although without the rational principle, neither truth nor knowledge could ever have been, but only Life itself, yet that principle alone cannot add one iota to knowledge. It can clear up obscurities, it can measure and enumerate with greater precision, it can preserve us in dignity and responsibility of our individual existences. But in no sense can it be said to *expand* consciousness. Only the poetic can do this: only poesy, pouring into language its creative intuitions, can preserve its living meaning and prevent it from crystallizing into a kind of algebra . . . In Platonic terms we should say that the rational principle can increase *understanding*, and it can increase *true opinion*, but it can never increase *knowledge*. And herein is revealed the levity of chanting with too indiscriminate praises the triumphal "progress" of our language from Europe to Cathay. (144)

Poetic language aims at attacking and destabilizing itself so that it can reach a truth that might lie outside language—reach that "knowledge" which Barfield speaks of. In poetic language, words acquire a fluid, unstable, and mutable nature, making it impossible to know exactly what they mean, or at the very least, known words are injected with new meanings, as Barfield also argues (111-51). In poetic language—and in all language, at least theoretically—the relationship between the signifier and the signified is altered: a cat might very well become a dog or a goat, for the names are recognized as being merely arbitrary signs and as such have no legitimate grounding, except the one stipulated by convention, which is often oppressive. As Cixous puts it, "Beware, my friend, of the signifier that takes you back to the authority of a signified" (*Newly Born* 319). And she adds that "what is most true is poetic . . . Oxymoronic writing: perhaps, but it's reality that is oxymoronic" (*Rootprints* 1, 19). Cixous's reasoning about language is similar to the Derridean deconstructionist theory of *différance* as explicated in *Of Grammatology* (10-18), which argues that meaning is a ceaseless process of present and absent differences and thus each signifier can never be pinpointed to a single signified but rather to several, a case also argued by Barfield (111-51). This infinite play of signifiers makes it impossible for any of us to ever fully possess what we say or write.

It is precisely in the multiplicity of possibilities that characterize poetic language that Lispector finds one way of inserting the most real voice of Macabéa. The fact that *A hora* has fourteen subtitles is the first sign that the novella is using poetic language as its main medium and playing with the multiplicity of meaning that is inherent to poetry. Even though the author has chosen only one title, we know that inside that title there are many other titles, many other stories, that is. Like Couto and Saramago's "stories," Lispector's story is full of mise en abymes, full of little Russian dolls. What Lispector writes is a story about a story about another story—an infinity of stories trying to catch the "real" story: the word before the word, Macabéa as flesh and bone, Macabéa unmediated by discourse. In a manner similar to the Derridean theory of *différance,* the Lispectorian meaning is always running away from or evading each of her used signifier titles. Each "center" or the meaning of each title "walks," it mutates to the "periphery" so that it can try and substantiate itself (take grasp), yet that never seems to happen. There is an incompleteness that always remains, demonstrating thus that Lispector knows that the true meaning is in the untold, that which resides outside language; the meaning is in the unsaid, in the silence of language. The true meaning can never be said, voiced, written.

The narrator of the novella tells us that the book that he is writing is "a question" (17) ("a pergunta" [17]), further suggesting that he has no possibility of fully knowing what he is saying in the story, no possibility of capturing the essence of Macabéa. He describes his writing as "{a humid haze}" ("uma névoa úmida" [16]) because the words used point not to what they mean but rather to what is beyond them. The words are fuzzy, "cloudy," unclear, and incapable of telling the true story. Words are like the tantric Buddhist Mantra: magic uterances that have no logical, defined meaning but which possess a sacred (spiritual) power capable of allowing its user to reach emptiness of thought (sunyata). Words are "humid" because they are fluid, mutable, unstable, and rich: they allow for "a word" beyond the word; they allow for the infinite playing-game between the signifier and the signified, and it is in this game that the essence of Macabéa can be visualized, envisaged, imagined. Our male narrator says he writes mainly because he has "captured the spirit of language and at times it is the form that constitutes the content" (17-18) ("capt[ou] o espírito da língua e assim às vezes forma é que faz o conteúdo" [18]). This spirit of the language refers to the capacity to see beyond words, or at least the capacity to see the poverty of words, especially conventional words (and narrative strategies); it refers to poetic language's mantric capacity to bring about wisdom and even a spiritual connection with the world. As Lispector puts it in *Água viva*, "Listen only superficially to what I am telling you and from the lack of meaning another meaning will emanate" ("Ouve apenas superficialmente o que te digo e da falta de sentido nascerá um sentido" [23]). The spirit of the word lies in the way our narrator uses that word, in the form of his narrative: in how he says it and not what he says. The "what" is actually inconsequential since one has no way of understanding logically (discursively) the content of the language being used, just like the tantric Buddhist mantra. In fact, on a grander level, Lispector's novella can be seen as what in Zen Buddhism is referred to as a koan. As illustrated by Philip Kapleau: "In Zen a koan is a formulation, in baffling language, pointing to ultimate Truth. Koans cannot be solved by recourse to a logical reasoning but only awakening a deeper level of the mind beyond the discursive intellect" (335-56). And as Suzuki postulates: "The *kõan* given to the uninitiated is intended to destroy the root of life . . . to make the calculating mind die . . . to root out the entire mind that has been at work since eternity, etc. This may sound murderous, but the ultimate intent is to go beyond the limits of intellection, and these limits can be crossed over only by exhausting oneself once for all, by using up the psychic powers at one's command. Logic then turns into psychology, intellection into conation and intuition. What could not be solved on the plane of consciousness is now transferred to the deeper recess of the mind" (295).

A hora is described by the narrator as being a painting, a photograph, a mere silence, a piece of music, a book without words, where the phenomenological reality of the characters should be seen, felt, and touched with all the senses, understood with all the nonintelligent intelligence rather than through the mind's eye:

> {In writing this I will sensitize myself. . . . I am not an intellectual}, I write with my body. . . . The words are sounds transfused with shadows that intersect unevenly, stalactites, woven lace, transposed organ music. I can scarcely invoke the words to describe this pattern, vibrant and rich, morbid and obscure, its counterpoint the deep bass of sorrow. *Allegro con brio*. I shall attempt to extract gold from charcoal. I know I am holding up the narrative and playing at ball without a ball. Is the fact an act? I swear that this book is composed without words. {It is a mute photograph.} This book is a silence. . . . {I write with bold and severe} strokes like a painter. {I shall deal with the facts} as if they were those impossible stones which I mentioned earlier. . . . Is it {really possible for actions to exceed words? But as I write—I shall give the real names to words}. Each thing is a word. And when there is no word, it must be invented. (16-17); (This story consists of nothing more than crude items of primary material that come to me directly before I even think of them. I know lots of things that I cannot express.) (69)

> Com esta história vou me sensibilizar. . . . Eu não sou um intelectual, escrevo com o corpo. . . . As palavras são sons transfundidos de sombras que

se entrecruzam desiguais, estalactites, renda, música transfigurada de órgão. Mal ouso clamar palavras a essa rede vibrante e rica, mórbida e obscura tendo como contratom o baixo grosso da dor. Alegro com brio. Tentarei tirar oiro do carvão. Sei que estou adiando a história e que brinco de bola em bola. O fato é um ato? Juro que este livro é feito sem palavras. É uma fotografia muda. Este livro é um silêncio. (16) Escrevo em traços vivos e ríspidos de pintura. Estarei lidando com fatos como se fossem as irremediáveis pedras de que falei. . . . Será mesmo que a ação ultrapassa a palavra? Mas que ao escrever—que o nome real seja dado às palavras. Cada coisa é uma palavra. E quando não se a tem, inventa-se-a. (17); (Esta história são apenas fatos não trabalhados de matéria prima e que me atingem direto antes de eu pensar. Sei muita coisa que não posso pensar.) (69)

The photograph and the painting can be seen: they are images rather than words, and it is as such that our narrator wants us to see his novella. In this sense the novella actually resembles what in tantric Buddhism is called a mandala: "This word has the meaning of 'circle,' 'assemblage,' 'picture.' There are various kinds of mandala, but the commonest in Esoteric [tantric] Buddhism are of two types: a composite picture graphically portraying different classes of demons, deities, Buddhas, and Boddisattvas (representing various powers, forces, and activities) within symbolic squares and circles, in the center of which is a figure of the Buddha Vairochana, the Great Illuminator; and a diagrammatic representation wherein certain sacred Sanskrit letters (called *bija*, or seeds) are substituted for figures" (Kapleau 346). It is also through music and silence that the narrator of *A hora* wants us to understand his message. Like the visual arts (painting and photography), silence and music also allow for the untold and the unsaid to be understood at an unconsciousand prediscursive level. It is only by doing this that our narrator is able to capture the spirit of the language and the facts in their most real sense, the facts uncontaminated by reality. The aim of the narrator is to contain (to exit or suspend) the imprisonment and used-up poem of everyday conventional language, to "get out" of that poem, so that the world of Macabéa can be reinvigorated and cleansed thus enabling her to get closer to the "Heideggerian call" and also exit the sociosymbolical categories that oppress her. The novella then becomes not a book with words, but a book that one can feel, see, touch, and hear—a book that speaks a language that tries to remain outside rationality. In this sense, the novella becomes the world, the facts rather than the acts, the facts "cleansed" of all rhetorical "garbage"—the facts that our narrator so much values: "I am becoming interested in facts: facts are solid stones. {There is no way to evade them. Facts are words told by the world}" (71) ("Estou me interessando terrivelmente por fatos: fatos são pedras duras. Não há como fugir. Fatos são palavras ditas pelo mundo" [71]). These facts are the things in themselves, the things our narrator is "touching" by writing a novella that resembles a painting, or a photograph, or a piece of music, or just pure silence. In this sense, the novella becomes performative; it becomes action, for it textually enacts what it preaches by recreating the physical phenomenological reality and emptying itself from conventional rhetorical and linguistic discourses. Lispector's novella then becomes a mise en abyme comparable to Couto's story, "A menina sem palavra." The fact that the novella is described as being a "thing" (1) ("coisa" [1]) further points to its phenomenologicality and intent to exit rhetorical discourse.

Macabéa is someone who does not master the language of the society she lives in. This inability to speak the "proper" language would generally be seen as a negative thing, as it prevents Macabéa from being integrated into her society and thus from fully benefiting from it. But this inability to speak and master society's language is in fact a blessing because it allows Macabéa to maintain the authenticity of her being and of being. Macabéa's language is limited and often irrational or incoherent. She speaks very little to others, has trouble initiating or maintaining an engaging conversation with her coworkers, friends, and boyfriend, and often just observes people, animals, or objects as if engaged in silent meditation. She is also unable to explain what she feels or thinks in a language that others can understand and fails to understand the meaning of words she hears on the radio, words such as "culture" ("cultura"), "mimicry" ("mimetismo") and "electronic" ("electrónico"), expressions in fact associated with urban life and the so-called sophistication and technological ways of the big city. Unlike Olímpico, who recognizes the importance of speaking well, often hiding his ignorance or inability to understand certain words, Macabéa does not care to hide her ignorance about the meaning of certain words. She is not socially adept (or aggressive enough) to understand the importance of pretending to know the meaning of difficult words. Contrary to Olímpico, she cannot mimic the life and the ways of the city and prefers to remain herself, a self where the "marks" of low social status are "profoundly imprinted upon," thus leaving her as an openly vulnerable target for oppression. Ironically, Macabéa does not even understand what the word "mimicry" means and therefore cannot conduct her life in a mimetic way to at least pretend to be someone else, which could make her less of a target for oppression.

By not knowing the language of the big city, Macabéa is also refusing the life and values associated with that big city, even if she is not consciously aware of it. The only way to maintain her innocence and her nonculpability is to remain "dumb" and alienated from her social milieu, one where oppression and the repressive pervasiveness of capitalism abound. The conversation between Olímpico and Macabéa in the park is a good example of Macabéa's total inadequacy in dealing with the life of the modern urban milieu of Rio de Janeiro. In this encounter between the two, no actual conversation can take place, for Macabéa cannot understand Olímpico's language, ambitions and aspirations—which are directly related to and dependant upon the notions of success and fulfillment regulating Brazilian society. While Olímpico seems to know very well who he is and what he wants from life, Macabéa cannot even speak about herself in a coherent manner or understand who she is at a rational level. She does not know "how to say" (48) and cannot put into words what she feels, thinks and believes in. The very fact that Macabéa is not aware of what is happening to her (or precisely because she is not aware) and is unable to speak society's language can be taken as indication that she is in touch with her unconscious self—a self that allows her to listen to nonsocial logics, nonsocial intelligences and knowledge. Macabéa's inability to know herself rationally and speak the language of the society which is eager to put her into a social category can in fact be seen as her ultimate resistance: the only way to maintain and reclaim her authentic self. When compared to Olímpico, who has internalized society's notions of success and wants to live accordingly, Macabéa is in fact portrayed as a freer individual:

He: Look, I'm going {because you are impossible!}
She: {I can't help it. I only know how to be impossible, nothing else. What do I do to become possible?}
He: You talk a load of rubbish. Try to talk about something {that you like}.
She: {I think I don't know how to say.}
He: You don't know what?
She: Eh?
He: Look, you are getting on my nerves. Let's just shut up. Agreed?
She: {Yes}, whatever you say.
He: {There is really no solution for you.} As for me, I've been called so many {times} that I've turned into myself. In the backwoods of Paraíba everybody has heard of Olímpico. And one day the whole world is going to be talking about me. (48)

Ele: Olhe, eu vou embora porque você é impossível!
Ela: É que só sei ser impossível, não sei mais nada. Que é que eu faço para ser possível?
Ele: Pare de falar que você só diz besteiras! Diga o que é do teu agrado.
Ela: Acho que não sei dizer.
Ele: Não sabe o quê?
Ela: Hei?
Ele: Olhe, até estou suspirando de agonia. Vamos não falar em nada, está bem?
Ela: Sim, está bem, como você quiser.
Ele: É, você não tem solução. Quanto a mim, de tanto me chamarem, eu virei eu. No sertão da Paraíba não há quem não saiba quem é Olímpico. E um dia todo o mundo vai saber de mim. (48-49)

Macabéa is described as being "impossible" by Olímpico precisely because of her way of being and speaking, a "way" that is noncompliant with or disregards society's ways. She is an outcast who cannot or does not want to follow the logic informing and regulating her society. Such behavior is very different from Olímpico's, for he knows what social success means and what to do to achieve it. In that sense then, Macabéa remains a virgin; she remains pure and innocent. She remains in the "between the lines" (14) referred to in *The Stream of Life* or in the "part sauvage" (Conley, Introduction 6). Olímpico, on the other hand, becomes the prostitute who is willing to do whatever it takes to succeed in the big capital: he "enters the lines" of society and all its oppressive and corrupted ways. As Olímpico says, Macabéa "has no solution" because she cannot internalize, follow, and thus accept society's guidelines for happiness and success. Indeed, there is no viable solution for Macabéa's self in the big city of Rio de Janeiro—a city that is highly technological and patriarchal, overly values rational knowledges, and is concerned mostly with material possessions.

Olímpico says he became himself after hearing people call his name time after time, which is to say that he accepts the name given to him by society and by extension, the values, language, and rules that guide, inform, and dictate to that same society, a society which exploits the majority of its people and imposes definitions of success based on capitalist alienating and unnatural principles. Olímpico does not question the identity others give him, an identity forged on the premises of same and other, with him being the other and the affluent habitants of Rio de Janeiro being the same. What he wants is to become the same, even if to attain that sameness he has to "kill" his own self. Like the bitch Ugolina in Saramago's novel and the women who support the oppressive patriarchal regime of Salazar, Olímpico "eats" (destroys) his own self to become the same: "the desirable clan of the south" (59) ("ambicionado clã do sul" [59]), the powerful and oppressive agent of capitalism. As Lispector puts it, "{he was destined to go up in the social ladder and join the world of the privileged. He was hungry to become other}" (65) ("seu destino era o de subir para um dia entrar no mundo dos outros. Ele tinha fome de ser outro" [65]). The very fact that Olímpico is born out of wedlock—as his last name Jesus indicates—suggests that he is indeed an other, a mistake, someone who has no legitimate right to exist, as it were. Yet, despite that he refuses to accept that anonymity (identity) given to him by an ultra-patriarchal society and craves to become the same.

Macabéa's own name is a strange one, one people have trouble understanding (recognizing) and which Olímpico finds hideous and "diseased":

If you don't mind my asking, what's your name?
Macabéa.
Maca—what?
Béa, she was forced to {complete}.
{Forgive me}, that sounds like the name of a disease, a skin disease.
I agree but it's the name my mother gave me because of a vow she made to Our Lady of {Good Death} if I should survive. For the first year of my life I was not called anything because I didn't have a name. I'd have preferred to go on being called nothing instead of having a name that nobody has ever heard of, {but I guess it worked out well}. (43)

E, se me permite, qual é mesmo sua graça?
Macabéa.
Maca, o quê?
Béa, foi ela obrigada a completar.
Me desculpe mas até parece doença, doença de pele.
Eu também acho esquisito mas minha mãe me botou ele por promessa a Nossa Senhora da Boa Morte se eu vingasse, até um ano de idade eu não era chamada porque não tinha nome, eu preferia continuar a nunca ser chamada em vez de ter um nome que ninguém tem mas parece que deu certo. (43)

The strangeness of Macabéa's name further reinforces the idea that she does not adhere to the rules and ideals that govern her society. Her name comes from the

Jewish name Maccabees, the name given to the Jewish Hasmonean family who in 168 BC began the revolt against Hellenism and Syrian rule and reigned over Palestine from 142 BC to 63 BC ("The Maccabees"). Among other things, the name has come to symbolize those who do not adhere to convention or who hide themselves. Macabéa remains on the periphery, in the place where the discursive qualities of the symbolical world become "dumb" or "blind"—where they cannot "see." She cannot understand and incorporate the symbolical nor can the latter understand her. The "center" actually loses its capacity to rule or oppress, for the "periphery" refuses to be understood. The fact that Macabéa had no name until the age of one further suggests that she does not belong to the sociosymbolic world, the world replete with discriminatory categories where people are defined in terms of same and other, good and bad, and so forth. Macabéa remains in the unnameable, in the presymbolic, close to the "wild heart." As we have seen, Lispector also makes a point of using the least number of adjectives and sophisticated words to describe Macabéa, which shows that she respects Macabéa's otherness and wants to keep her in the "between-the-lines." The overuse of words would "kill" the otherness of Macabéa, making her a mere copy of Lispector: a copy of the same. As Cixous points out in *A hora de Clarice Lispector,* Lispector is the perfect author, the one who loves, respects, and wants to keep the other alive, even if that entails not knowing that same other. Both Lispector and Cixous are closely following what Lévinas refers to as the ethical relation towards the other (*Totality and Infinity* 194-214). Lispector is the type of writer our society needs, someone who is able to write without committing extreme authorial hubris and without annihilating the voice of the other completely: "Who possesses the dignity to be Macabéa's author? This 'book' murmurs to us: don't the beings who live in a written work have the right to have *the author they need*? Macabéa needs a very special author. It is for the love of Macabéa that Clarice Lispector will create the necessary author. *The Hour of the Star* . . . is a little great book that loves and knows nothing, not even its own name, in other words, not even its own title" (Cixous, *A Hora de Clarice* 129) ("Quem é capaz de ser digno de ser o autor de Macabéa? Esse 'livro' nos cochicha: os seres que vivem numa obra não têm direito ao autor *de que precisam?* Macabéa precisa de um autor muito especial. É por amor a Macabéa que Clarice Lispector vai criar o autor necessário. *A Hora da Estrela* . . . é um pequeno grande livro que ama e não sabe nada, nem mesmo seu nome. Quero dizer: nem mesmo seu título"). The "necessary author" as Cixous puts it, is very different from the conventional authors who tend to write their characters in ways that are often too arrogant, ways that do not leave space for that other to appear as he or she might be. Amado and the other Brazilian regionalist writers would be examples of such authors, who claim to tell reality as it is; and yet might just be fabricating innumerable others, others who reflect their social visions, values and perceptions: others who are really the same as them. What characters need is an ethical writer, one that sees with tenderness and respect and speaks about the other through nonlinguistic media or through poetry—media which allow us to read "between-the-lines." Lispector's intention is not fully to understand the reality of the other but merely to

Authenticity of Being as the Politics of Agency in Lispector

have brief glimpses of that other, glimpses that seem to have a spiritual dimension rather than an intelligible one, even though the spiritual seems to be based on physical or sensual apprehensions:

> How do I know all that is about to follow if it is unfamiliar and something that I have never experienced? In a street of Rio de Janeiro I caught {in the air} a glimpse of perdition on the face of a girl from the northeast. {Not to mention} that I myself was raised as a child in the northeast. Besides I know about certain things simply by living. Anyone who lives, knows, even without knowing that he or she knows. (12); {The definable is tiring me a bit. I prefer the truth that exists in the premonition.} (29); I am amazed at my own perception of the truth. Can it be that it's my painful task to perceive in the flesh truths that no one wants to face? If I know almost everything about Macabéa, it's because I once caught a glimpse {of the blank stare of a girl from the northeast with a sallow complexion. That glimpse revealed everything about her}. As for the youth from Paraíba [Olímpico], {I surely must have had photographed his face mentally—and when one pays an attention that is spontaneous and virgin of preconceptions, when one pays attention, the face reveals almost everything}. (56-57)

> Como é que sei de tudo o que vai se seguir e que ainda o desconheço, já que nunca o vivi? É que numa rua do Rio de Janeiro peguei no ar de relance o sentimento de perdição no rosto de uma moça nordestina. Sem falar que eu em menino me criei no Nordeste. Também sei de coisas por estar vivendo. Quem vive sabe, mesmo sem saber que sabe. (12); O definível está me cansando um pouco. Prefiro a verdade que há no prenúncio. (29); Fico abismado por saber tanto a verdade. Será que o meu ofício doloroso é o de adivinhar na carne a verdade que ninguém quer enxergar? Se sei quase tudo de Macabéa é que já peguei uma vez de relance o olhar de uma nordestina amarelada. Esse relance me deu ela de corpo inteiro. Quanto ao paraíbano [Olímpico], na certa devo ter-lhe fotografado mentalmente a cara—e quando se presta atenção espontânea e virgem de imposições, quando se presta atenção a cara diz quase tudo. (57)

The narrator knows something about Macabéa, something that is light, feathery, something that he caught in the air while having a brief glimpse at her in the streets of Rio de Janeiro. He also says he knows Macabéa at some level because he (like Lispector herself) lived in the northeast. Furthermore, his own living allows him to know things, even if only unconsciously. The "living" mentioned here seems to have very physical dimensions: our narrator lives and feels with his body and it is because of that that he is able to capture the essence of Macabéa, an essence that resides in the latter's body. It is the life of the narrator's body that allows him to capture the life of the other's body, but only slightly, in a manner that refuses the totality of the discursive and rational discourse and allows for the "infinity" of the other. Moreover, the narrator tells us that he caught a glimpse in the air about Macabéa's identity and feelings. This glimpse is equivalent to the Lévinasian concept of face which favors spiritual dimensions and apprehensions of life even if the body and the physical in general constitute the first site (and sight) of perception. Put differently, even though the physical image of the other (Macabéa) is the first thing the narrator sees, that physical image does not permit the observing subject to have a complete understanding of that other. What the narrator sees is only a small part of that other, for the totality of that other is unreachable to him in logical and discursive terms and remains in the realm of the infinitum.

In a similar manner, the narrator can "sort of know" (or almost know) Olímpico because he took a mental photograph of him. The photograph refers to the memory of the sensuality (of the senses) imprinted in the spirit, a memory that is different from the intelligible (rational) understanding, which would be based on a mental and discursive understating of that same other. The mental photograph then refers to the primacy of the senses (vision) over the intellect and it is this primacy that leads to the spiritual apprehension of the other. The spiritual is thus mostly rooted in the sensual and prediscursive. The spiritual is that "spontaneous and virgin attention," an attention bare of preconceptions, an attention not mediated by discourse, one that allows a "clean" stare. This would be the equivalent of what in Buddhism is referred to as "bare attention." As Mark Epstein writes, "Common to all schools of thought, from Sri Lanka to Tibet, the unifying theme of the Buddhist approach is this remarkable imperative: 'Pay attention, moment by moment, to exactly what you are experiencing, right now, separating out your reactions from the raw sensory events.' This is what is meant by bare attention: just the *bare* facts, an *exact* registering, allowing things to speak for themselves as if seen for the first time, distinguishing any reactions from the core event. . . . Bare attention is impartial, nonjudgmental, and open. It is also deeply interested, like a child with a new toy." (110-18)

Despite the fact that Macabéa cannot voice what pleases her to Olímpico or other people, we know that she experiences moments of extreme pleasure and existential fulfillment. For example, she enjoys dancing alone during her day off when she has enough space in the room that she shares with the four Marias; she enounters a kind of cosmic love through the simple act of feeling the presence of a very large tree; she experiences erotic pleasure in her dreams as she discovers her sexuality; she emits cries of happiness and feels a certain sadness and nostalgia (a "saudade") when listening to Caruso's *Una furtiva lacrima*, the rooster's crow in the morning, and the awakening noises of Acre street; she enjoys the clock sounds of Rádio Relógio that she frequently listens to, and she adores guava with cheese. Furthermore, she takes great satisfaction in going to the marina, where she stares languidly at the merchant sea men and cargo ships, while also listening to and savoring the departing and arrival whistles of the latter:

> The {filthy} docks made the girl yearn for the future. (What's happening? It's as if I were listening to {happy tunes} being played on the piano—a sign perhaps that the girl will have a brilliant future? I am consoled by this possibility and will do everything in my power to make it come to pass. . . . From time to time, the girl was lucky enough to hear a cockerel {sing life and then she would remember the backwoods of Alagoas with nostalgia}. Where could there be room for a cockerel to crow in that warren of warehouses storing goods for export and import? . . . Acre Street for living, Lavradio Street for working, the docks for excursions on Sunday. Now and

then the lingering sound of a cargo ship's signal that strangely {caused her to feel a tightening sensation in her heart}, and in between each signal, the consoling though somewhat melancholic cries of the cockerel. The cockerel's song came from the never-never land. It came from the infinite right up to her bedside, offering her gratitude. (30-31); *Una furtiva lacrima* had been the only really very beautiful thing in Macabéa's life. Drying up her own tears she tried to sing what she had heard but her voice was as rough and tuneless as her own body. When she heard her own voice, she began to weep. She was weeping for the first time and had never imagined that there was so much water in her eyes. She wept and blew her nose, no longer knowing why she was weeping. She wasn't weeping because of the way she lived: for, never having known any other way of life, she accepted the fact that her life was just "so." I also believe that she was weeping because through music she could perhaps perceive that there existed other ways of feeling; that there were more delicate forms of existence which even possessed a certain spiritual refinement. (50-51); One day Macabéa enjoyed a moment of ecstasy. It happened in front of a tree that was so enormous that she could never put her arms around its trunk. Yet despite her ecstasy, she did not inhabit with God. She prayed with total indifference. Yes. Yet that mysterious God of others sometimes bestowed on her a state of grace. Bliss, bliss, bliss. Her soul taking flight. She had also seen the flying saucer. She had tried to confide in Glória but found no way of doing so, for she didn't know how to express herself and what was there to confide, anyway? The atmosphere? One doesn't {confide all, for all is a hollow void}. Sometimes, grace {would come to her} as she sat at her desk in the office. Then she would go to the washroom in order to be alone. {Standing and smiling until it passed it seems that that God was very merciful with her: he gave her what he took from her. Standing and thinking about nothing, her eyes soft.} (63)

O cais imundo dava-lhe saudade do futuro. (O que é que há? Pois estou como que ouvindo acordes de piano alegre—será isto o símbolo de que a vida da moça iria ter um futuro esplendoroso? Estou contente com essa possibilidade e farei tudo para que esta se torne real.) . . . Uma vez por outra tinha a sorte de ouvir de madrugada um galo cantar a vida e ela se lembrava nostálgica do sertão. Onde caberia um galo a cocoricar naquelas paragens ressequidas de artigos por atacado de exportação e importação? . . . Rua do Acre para morar, rua do Lavradio para trabalhar, cais do porto para ir espiar no domingo, um ou outro prolongado apito de navio cargueiro que não se sabe por que dava aperto no coração, um ou outro delicioso embora um pouco doloroso cantar do galo. Era do nunca que vinha o cantar do galo. Vinha do infinito até a sua cama, dando-lhe gratidão. (30-31); *Una furtiva lacrima* fora a única coisa belíssima na sua vida. Enxugando as próprias lágrimas tentou cantar o que ouvira. Mas a sua voz era crua e tão desafinada como ela mesma era. Quando ouviu começara a chorar. Era a primeira vez que chorava, não sabia que tinha tanta água nos olhos. Chorava, assoava o nariz sem saber mais por que chorava. Não chorava por causa da vida que levava: porque, não tendo conhecido outros modos de viver, aceitara que com ela era "assim." Mas também creio que chorava porque, através da música, adivinhava talvez que havia outros modos de sentir, havia existências mais delicadas e até com um certo luxo da alma. (51); Um dia teve um êxtase. Foi diante de uma árvore tão grande que no tronco ela nunca poderia abraçá-la. Mas apesar do êxtase ela não morava com Deus. Rezava indiferentemente. Sim. Mas o misterioso Deus dos outros lhe dava às vezes um estado de graça. Feliz, feliz, feliz. Ela de alma voado. E também vira o disco voador. Tentara contar a Glória mas não tivera jeito, não sabia falar e mesmo conta o quê? O ar? Não se conta tudo porque o tudo é um oco nada. Às vezes a graça a pegava em pleno escritório. Então ela ia ao banheiro para ficar sozinha. De pé sorrindo até passar (parece que esse Deus era muito misericordioso com ela: dava-lhe o que lhe tirava). Em pé pensando em nada, os olhos moles. (63)

All these pleasures and the feelings experienced through them are in one way or another Macabéa's ways of speaking through what can be described as a nonsocial or nonrational language, ways of speaking through and with her unconscious, psychic, and spiritual forces. The tree metaphor is a perfect example of the experiencing of the Zen Buddhist sunyata or satori state. Macabéa feels the immensity of the tree in her even though she cannot physically hug the tree. In its immensity, the tree becomes the universe as a whole, the universe whose force Macabéa can now feel through her connection with the tree. This connection becomes spiritual and this is the reason we are told Macabéa experiences a state of bliss, a state of grace, her soul taking flight; she enters the Buddhist "Great" I referred to by Iisuka (119). We are also told that she sees a flying saucer as if she herself were observing her soul flying through the universe. Her soul is no longer imprisoned in the finitude of her frail body; it is now transparent, hollow and formless, just like air. Once again, Macabéa is experiencing the emptiness of thought, the nirvanic sunyata, the satori, the "Great I." As Suzuki says, "the *satori* is nothing other than emptiness, which is, after all, no-emptiness. [This] reality is beyond intellection, and that which lies beyond the intellection we call emptiness" (qtd. in Roy 135). This experience resides outside the grasp of the form of discursive language and thought and so Macabéa possesses no way of recounting it to Glória: "One doesn't {confide all, for all is a hollow void}" (63) ("Não se conta tudo porque o tudo é um oco nada" [63]). Here Macabéa "cannot tell" not because she is not good with words but because she knows words cannot express the blissfull "hollow void" that she has experienced. In this implied metaphor of the sunyata, Macabéa is able to transcend her individuality and erase distinctions of subject and object, thus overcoming all discriminations, to become part of the larger cosmos, part of the "all is one"—just like the character Joana in Lispector's other novel *Perto do Coração Selvagem*. In the sunyata, Macabéa evades all suppressions and restrictions of modern life with its habitual and mundane acts which often rob us of the "sanctity" and whole of life. Macabéa does not need to be a socially accepted member of Rio de Janeiro's urban society to feel happy and experience the ultimate existential ecstasy. In fact, it seems that she is able to reach a more authentic state of being precisely because she remains outside that oppressive discursive society, a society all against her, where the categories of same and other, superior and inferior, abound and where the possession of material things is seen as the best way to achieve happiness—contrary to Zen Buddhism where detachment from material things (nongreediness and noncraving) is a requirement to attain enlightenment (Iisuka 21-23; Epstein 59-61). In *Esboços Não Acabados e Vacilantes: Despersonalização e Experiência Subjectiva na Obra de Clarice Lispector*, Rafaela Teixeira Zorzanelli also argues that Lispector often uses the strategy of the subjective experience in order to arrive at depersonalization, to attain the stage of prethinking and awareness that allows the subject to see anew without the societal lens constraining paradigms and language.

Like the large tree, the docks also exert a great power over Macabéa precisely because they symbolize a place of possibilities, the locale where all categories dividing the world and classifying people are erased (or suspended) and the "all is one" of Zen is attained symbolically. The docks are a place where everything is possible, a place which all the ships leave and return to; a place from which Brazilian goods are taken out to the rest of the world and also the place which brings back the world's goods to Brazilians. In other words, it is the site where world meets world, where one becomes all and all becomes one, in the Zen sense—the site that symbolizes the whole, the primal, the unnameable, the undifferentiated. This is why the docks are referred to as being "filthy" ("imundo"), very directly echoing Kristeva's abject, which she also refers to as "l'immonde" and "l'impropre" (*Pouvoirs* 10). This adjective can be read in two ways here: "filthy" and "nonworld." Both readings, however, have very similar meanings: "filthy" suggests that which is not yet cleaned (the muddy), organized and discernable to the eye. "Nonworld" suggests that which is not yet made and created, the vast amorphous mass before the creation of the world. Either way, the ultimate symbolism of the word is the same: the existence of a presymbolic world, a world devoid of discriminatory divisions and thus a world that contains all the possibilities, all the elements of life, and for that reason also all the potentiality of life, of change, transformation, and becoming. This reading of the docks also permits the envisaging of a better and more just Brazilian society, different from the current one, which is riddled with discrimination, materialism, and inhumanity, and which is oppressing Macabéa. This envisaging (imagining) is directly hinted at by the narrator of the novella: "What's happening? It's as if I were listening to {happy tunes} being played on the piano—a sign perhaps that the girl will have a brilliant future? I am consoled by this possibility and will do everything in my power to make {it a reality} (30) ("O que é que há? Pois estou como que ouvindo acordes de piano alegre—será isto o símbolo de que a vida da moça iria ter um futuro esplendoroso? Estou contente com essa possibilidade e farei tudo para que esta se torne real" [30]). It might be precisely the need (even if only at the unconscious level) to live a more fulfilled and repression-free life and the feeling or intuition that a better society might exist (or be envisaged) elsewhere that attracts Macabéa to the docks, a society that does not have rigid definitions of beauty and success and which accepts the other as the other in his or her difference, without wanting to make him or her into a same. After all, the docks are the site that brings "otherness" into itself and which also takes "otherness" away—away to other selves. Thus, the yearning that Macabéa feels when contemplating the docks, that "nostalgia for the future," can indicate both her need to regain her primal (prehuman) self and all it entails and also the yearning to be reborn in a distant more equitable and just society where she would be able to benefit socially and culturally—to be fully integrated, that is. A more pessimistic reading of the docks could indicate the reverse. Being the place where ships bring wealth and take it away, the docks also represent the capitalist and imperialist system at large, the "filthy" system oppressing Macabéa.

The rooster's crow, the whistles of the ships at the docks, and Caruso's song also cause Macabéa to feel "nostalgia" ("saudade"); they cause her to cry and feel "a tightening sensation in her heart" (30) ("um aperto no coração" [30]), to feel both joy and sadness, that is. Why do these sounds have the power to touch Macabéa so deeply? The concept of *saudade* involves a yearning for something or someone (a time, a place, a person, a lost state of being or feeling). Feeling saudade also means that one is experiencing contradictory feelings of happiness and sadness, for even though one is yearning for the lost, one is also greatly enjoying the present state of remembrance, in other words, the act of remembrance itself. Whithin the Portuguese culture, this feeling of saudade is often associated with and expressed through *fado* music. But this feeling is common to many societies. It can be argued that Macabéa feels saudade when hearing these sounds because they constitute a presymbolic language which reminds Macabéa of her presocial self, of the completeness and wholeness she had experienced when in her primal state. These three sounds could in fact be compared to *fado* music and to the language spoken by the little girl in Couto's story, in the sense that they all seem to represent a lost language and the loss of a certain state of being, feeling and understanding the world, which has spiritual dimensions and evades rational epistemologies. The sounds symbolize a way of knowing that stands above (and outside) of the rational eye: a way of "overstanding," echoing the Rastafarian framework as discussed in chapter one. Through these sounds, Macabéa is able to exit the death of everyday language in the Heideggerian sense and all its inherent compartmentalization of time, memory, body, spirit, and so on, and thus get closer to her authentic self.

We can also suggest that the sounds of the ships and the cock's crow are symbols of pure and instinctual cries of emotion, cries of the only authentic and very first language human primitives possessed—a language which consisted merely of sounds emitted by humans when they experienced emotional or physical pain. This language theory, called "interjectional theory" was first forged by Democritus (see Cassirer 109-36). This primary language was not yet linked to rational thought, since language is considered by many to be the mother of all—or at least advanced—rational thought. Within this context, then, it makes sense to suggest that the sounds heard and deeply felt by Macabéa remind her of her authentic primary self, the self which was not yet filtered through language symbolism and which was in some ways more real, less corrupt, less abstract, less alienated and alienating. The sounds can evoke saudade in Macabéa, sadness and happiness, that is, because they remind her, even if only unconsciously, that she has lost something—something that made her a more authentic being. Her cry then becomes a cry for a "lost adoration," and this is why

Authenticity of Being as the Politics of Agency in Lispector

it evokes both sadness and happiness. In other words, the remembrance of what is being evoked by the sounds is a good remembrance but also a sad one, for Macabéa is now far away from that primary prelanguage, far from the state experienced prior to the invention of the symbolic language—far from the prehuman state, if we take as valid the idea that symbolic language is what makes us human.

The narrator also tells us that what he is writing is not exactly (or not only) narrative, but rather a "scream" (13) ("grito" [13]), further suggesting that Macabéa's speech is close to a language of pure emotion, instinct, and irrationality: "{This} is not simply a narrative, but above all primary life that breathes, breathes, breathes. {Porous material. I shall one day live here the life of a molecule with its potential explosion of atoms. What I am writing is something more than invention; it is my duty to relate this girl's life among thousands of others like her. It is my duty, to reveal her existence, even if it has little art}. For one has the right {to scream. So, I am screaming. A pure scream that begs no charity} (13-14) ("Não se trata apenas de narrativa, é antes de tudo vida primária que respira, respira, respira. Material poroso, um dia viverei aqui a vida de uma molécula com seu estrondo possível de átomos. O que escrevo é mais do que invenção, é minha obrigação contar sobre essa moça entre milhares delas. É dever meu, nem que seja de pouca arte, o de revelar--lhe a vida. Porque há o direito ao grito. Então eu grito. Grito puro e sem pedir esmola" [13]). Through the scream, the narrator allows Macabéa's authenticity to be recaptured: screaming is all he can do, for screaming is the only way to reclaim the Maccabean primary and presymbolic language. What the narrator writes is "more than invention" (13) ("mais do que invenção" [13]) because it tries to capture the authentic in Macabéa. Moreover, what he writes has "little art" precisely because it tries to reestablish the Democritian language of interjection, that language before social (rational) symbolism. Thus, Lispector's art is to capture the nonart, that which is instinctual, primal, and emotional: the wild.

Macabéa is described as follows: "{I forgot to say how alarming it was to observe} how the breath of life surged within Macabéa's parched body; expansive and almost unlimited, and as abundant as the breath of a pregnant woman, impregnated by herself, by parthenogenesis: {she experienced schizoid dreams in which she saw immense antediluvian animals, as if she had lived in the most remote age of this bloody land}" (59-60) ("Esqueci de dizer que era realmente de se espantar que para corpo quase murcho de Macabéa tão vasto fosse o seu sopro de vida quase ilimitado e tão rico como o de uma donzela grávida, engravidada por si mesma, por partenogênese: tinha sonhos esquizóides nos quais apareciam gigantescos animais antediluvianos comos se ela tivesse vivido em épocas as mais remotas desta terra sangrenta" (60). By describing Macabéa as being someone who has schizoid dreams and is closer to the epoch of the gigantic antediluvian animals, our narrator is telling us that she is very much in tune with her preconscious forces. The antediluvian animals appearing in her dreams are indicative that Macabéa is in touch with her collective unconscious, with her psychic and spiritual dimensions. These animals can in fact be equated with Jung's collective archetypes (Jung, *The Essential* 59-69). And in Zen Buddhism these would be the psychic remembrances Macabéa possesses of previous lives, which can be linked to reincarnation. Generally speaking, Buddhism defends that people are bound to reincarnation (enter the wheel of life: the continuous pain of birth and death) until they reach the ultimate nirvana (enlightenment, literally meaning "blowing out" of existence). When we reach the ultimate nirvana, we are liberated from the wheel of life (the cycle of reincarnation). This does not mean that we cease to exist, but rather that we exist in a dissolved, spiritual manner, our energy dissolved in the cosmic void. Reincarnation also entails the remembrance of past lives even if only at an unconscious level (see Venerable Thera, "Rebirth"; Epstein, *Thoughts Without a Thinker* 75-88; Suzuki, *The Essentials of Buddhism* 327-83). Macabéa is described as being able to "impregnate herself," further indication that she is in touch with her psychic and spiritual aspects. Despite her frail body, she is described as possessing "an almost unlimited breath of life," precisely because her identity does not reside in her body alone. Her body is only a small part of her "entire self," which has various physical, psychic, spiritual, cosmic, and mystical dimensions. This entire self is the "Greater I" she is able to access during her sunyata experiences.

It is also to maintain Macabéa's innocence and authenticity that Lispector must kill her at the end of the novella. Had Macabéa stayed alive to live the prophecies of the fortune teller who promised her a rich blond gringo husband driving a Mercedes, love, and happiness, she would have fallen into the trap of what society considers to be success and fulfillment, thus losing her innocence and her "higher" fulfillment. Moreover, given the impossibility of the realization of those prophecies, Macabéa would be condemned to be very unhappy in her life, since she had been told what "real" happiness means and entails:

> this foreigner is apparently called Hans, and he is the man whom you will marry! He has lots of money, but then all foreigners are rich. Unless I'm mistaken and I never make mistakes, he is going to show you a great deal of affection: and you, my poor little orphan, you will be dressed in satin and velvet, and you will even be presented with a fur coat! Macabéa began (bang) to tremble all over, for there is a painful side to a surfeit of happiness. The only answer she could think of:—I don't need a fur coat {for the climate of Rio. . . . —Well, you'll have it just to look coquette}. There's nothing like a fur coat to make a girl look chic. It's a long time since I've read such good cards. I'm always frank with my clients. . . . {And now} I'm going to give you a charm that you must wear tucked into the bra and against your skin, for you have no bust, poor thing, but you'll start to fill out. {Until you put on a little weight, stuff your bra with cotton-wool to give the impression that you've got some shape. . . . Macabéa felt drunk and did not know what she was thinking}: it was as if someone had delivered a sharp blow to that head of lank hair. Macabéa felt totally confused as if some great misfortune had befallen her. Most of all, she was experiencing for the first time what other people referred to as passion: she was passionately in love with Hans. Madame Carlota had guessed everything and Macabéa was horrified. Only now did she recognize that her life had been miserable. She felt like weeping as she perceived the other side. For as I've already stated, until

that moment, Macabéa had thought of herself as being happy. (77-78); Her life {was already} transformed. Transformed, moreover, by words—since the time of Moses the word had been acknowledged as being divine. Even when it came to crossing the street, Macabéa was already a new person. A person impregnated with a future. She felt within a hope more fierce than any anguish she had ever known. If she was no longer herself, this signified a loss that counted as gain. Just as there was sentence of death, the fortune-teller had decreed the sentence of life. Everything {suddenly became big and big, and so abundant} that, Macabéa felt like weeping. But she didn't weep: her eyes glistened like the dying sun. (79)

esse estrangeiro parece se chamar Hans, e é ele quem se vai casar com você! Ele tem muito dinheiro, todos os gringos são ricos. Ele vai lhe dar muito amor e você, minha enjeitadinha, você vai se vestir com veludo e cetim e até casaco de pele vai ganhar! Macabéa começou (explosão) a tremelicar toda por causa do lado penoso que há na excessiva felicidade. Só lhe ocorreu dizer:—Mas casaco de pele não se precisa no calor do Rio. . . . —Pois vai ter só para enfeitar. Faz tempo que não boto cartas tão boas. E sou sempre sincera. . . . E agora vou lhe dar um feitiço que você deve guardar dentro do sutiã que quase não tem seio, coitada, bem em contacto com a pele. Você não tem busto mas vai engordar e vai ganhar corpo. Enquanto você não engordar, ponha dentro do sutiã chumaços de algodão para fingir que tem. . . . Estava bêbada, não sabia o que pensava, parecia que lhe tinham dado um forte cascudo na cabeça de ralos cabelos, sentia-se tão desorientada como se lhe tivesse acontecido uma infelicidade. Sobretudo estava conhecendo pela primeira vez o que os outros chamavam de paixão: estava apaixonada por Hans. . . . Macabéa estava espantada. Só então vira que sua vida era uma miséria. Teve vontade de chorar ao ver o seu lado oposto, ela que, como eu disse, até se julgava feliz . . . sua vida já estava mudada. E mudada por palavras—desde Moisés se sabe que a palavra é divina. Até para atravessar a rua ela já era outra pessoa. Uma pessoa grávida de futuro. Sentia em si uma esperança tão violenta como jamais sentira tamanho desespero. Se ela não era mais ela mesma, isso significava uma perda que valia por um ganho. Assim como havia sentença de morte a cartomante lhe deu sentença de vida. Tudo de repente era muito e muito e tão amplo que ela sentiu vontade de chorar. Mas não chorou: seus olhos faiscavam como o sol que morria. (77-79)

Macabéa had never felt she was unhappy before she heard Madame Carlota's story. The predictions of the fortune-teller are all based on what society sees fit and appropriate for a young woman: romantic love where the husband appears as the multifaceted provider, the person who can give Macabéa the love and protection she "must" need as a woman and buy her all sorts of material things. The fortune-teller focuses on the appearance of Macabéa a great deal, stressing the clothes Macabéa will gain with her marriage (i.e., the fur coat, the velour and satin dress), thus implying that the marriage is the story she as a young woman should want to enter: the story that will make her happy and complete. The marriage to the rich gringo is the fairytale engendered by a society that sees women as incomplete beings without the presence of the masculine Other (the same, the complete being) and sees marriage as the institution that will bring great happiness to both sexes. Moreover, Madame Carlota also gives advice to Macabéa on how to become more attractive: she tells her to put "a charm" ("um feitiço") (a piece of cotton wool) inside her brassiere to make her breasts seem fuller until she gains more weight and to use Aristolino soap so that her hair can grow stronger and nicer. The message here is that in order for a woman to get married and find a man who will want her, she must fit into a certain type of ideal womanhood and femininity: she needs to modify her body and appearance to give the man what he apparently wants. In other words, women must "kill" themselves in order to be accepted by men. They must become the coquettes referred to by Irigaray (see chapter 2) and the others of the same who must prostitute themselves in order to follow the feminine ideal engendered in a patriarchal society. They are the Ugolinas of Saramago's novel *O ano* as illustrated in chapter 2.

Having been a prostitute and a brothel co-owner, Madame Carlota understands men very well: she knows women must be coquettes and pay extreme attention to their physical appearance in order to satisfy men's sexual desires and fantasies. She is thus the perfect person to tell Macabéa what to do to get a husband. But Macabéa is too innocent and authentic to be a prostitute in any sense, and this is why Lispector must kill her at the end. Her death is her only viable salvation from society's many prisons or stories: salvation from the ideal fairytale, with all its romantic and patriarchal notions of love, salvation from the capitalist system which sees material goods as the climax of success, and salvation from a world where the other has no room to be and can only live under the shadow of the same.

The words pronounced by the fortune-teller are corrupted words, for they reflect all kinds of social evils: unfair and discriminatory classifications of people, unrealistic conceptions of happiness, and materialistic possessions to an extreme, mirroring the absurdity of the capitalist system which favors only a minute number people and exploits the vast majority. The very fact that Macabéa is told that she will gain a fur coat with her marriage to the gringo is a direct reflection of the waste of resources that takes place within the capitalist system, for as Macabéa rightly and ironically points out, she does not need a fur coat for the climate of Rio de Janeiro. Within such a system, people acquire possessions they do not need, while others die from hunger everyday. The words pronounced by Madame Carlota symbolize all the stories society has written (fabricated) in the name of happiness and advancement but which have caused great human alienation and thus ought to be ignored, demolished, or at the very least, questioned and rewritten. These words are not sacred or divine, as Lispector ironically suggests when comparing them with Moses's words. On the contrary, they are unsacred, untruthful, and alienating and must therefore be deconstructed or proven wrong. Again Lispector is undermining the power of language and implying that language can actually cause a lot of harm to humans: it can "give" them a life that has nothing to do with their most intimate (authentic) being or yearnings. It is not just that language does not tell reality as it is, it is also that language can change, corrupt, and invent reality: "Everything {suddenly became big and big, and so abundant} that, Macabéa felt like weeping" (79) ("Tudo de repente era muito e muito e tão amplo que ela sentiu vontade de chorar" [79]). This reality invented by words is inauthentic and alienating because with language comes (rational) thought and with rational thought comes abstraction and the construction of an entire system of values, many of which are oppressive, thus making us slaves of our own inventions. This is why Lispector tells us that Macabéa feels drunk and disoriented with the predictions of the fortune-teller, implying that Macabéa is not happy in the "real" sense, but rather just numbed by the power of language. For the first time, she feels utterly lost and confused, for she has been tricked by language and all its "fabulous stories" about love, success and happiness. When Lispector writes, "Just as there was sentence of death, the fortune-teller had decreed the sentence of life" (79) ("como havia sentença de morte a cartomante lhe deu sentença de vida" [70]), she actually means the opposite. Put differently, the words of the fortune-teller constitute a death sentence for Macabéa and not a life sentence, since living out the predictions of Madame Carlota would equate to falling prey to social corruption and unrealistic conceptions of happiness and success; it would equate to the annihilation of the Macabéan authentic self.

Macabéa's death is described as a highly spiritual act. Spirituality appears here as an act that has sexual (sensual) undertones, for it represents a release, a release from life and suffering and a merging with the "Great I." Death represents the ultimate freedom for Macabéa's body and her entrance into the spiritual realm; it represents freedom from a society which was annihilating her, freedom from the stories that society wanted her to live out:

> As she lay there, she felt {a supreme happiness}, for she had been born for death's embrace. Death, which is my favorite character in this story. Was Macabéa about to bid herself goodbye? I don't believe she was going to die, for she has so much to live. There was even a suggestion of sensuality in the way she lay there huddled up. Or is this because the {predeath} represents some intense sensual longing? . . . A sensation as pleasurable, tender, horrifying, chilling, and penetrating as love. Could this be the grace you call God? Yes? Were she about to die, she would pass from a virgin to a woman. No this wasn't death. Death is not what I want for this girl: a mere collision that amounted to nothing serious. . . . Macabéa had perceived the almost painful and vertiginous moment of overwhelming love. {Yes, the painful and so difficult reflowering} that she enacted with her body and the other thing you call a soul and I call—what? At that instant, Macabéa came out with a phrase that no one among the onlookers could understand. She said in clear, distinct voice:—As for the future. {Did she yearn for a future?} I hear the ancient music of words upon words. Yes, it is so. At this very moment Macabéa {felt a deep nausea in the pit of her stomach and almost vomited. She felt like vomiting something that was not matter, something luminous}. Star with a thousand pointed rays. . . . And then—then suddenly the anguished cry of a seagull, suddenly the voracious eagle soaring on high with the tender lamb in its beak, the sleek cat mangling vermin, life devouring life. (83-84); Death is an encounter with the self. Laid out and dead, Macabéa looked as imposing as a dead stallion. The best thing is still the following: not to die, for to die is not enough. {It does not complete me, me who needs so much.} (85)

> Então—ali deitada—teve uma felicidade suprema, pois ela nascera para o abraço da morte. A morte que é nesta história o meu personagem predileto. Iria ela dar adeus a si mesma? Acho que não vai morrer porque tem tanta vontade em viver. E havia certa sensualidade no modo como se encolhera. Ou é porque a pré-morte se parece com a intensa ânsia sensual. . ... Um gosto suave, arrepiante, gélido e agudo como no amor. Seria esta a graça a que vós chamais de Deus? Sim? Se iria morrer, na morte passava de virgem a mulher. Não, não era morte pois que não a quero para a moça: só um atropelamento que não significava sequer desastre . . . Intuíra o instante quase dolorido e esfuziante do desmaio do amor. Sim, doloroso reflorescimento tão difícil que ela empregava nele o corpo e a outra coisa que vós chamais de alma e que eu chamo—o quê? Aí Macabéa disse uma frase que nenhum dos transeuntes entendeu. Disse bem pronunciado e claro:—Quanto ao futuro. Terá tido ela saudade do futuro? Ouço a música antiga de palavras e palavras, sim, é assim. Nesta hora exata Macabéa sente um fundo enjôo de estômago e quase vomitou, queria vomitar o que não é corpo, vomitar algo luminoso. Estrela em mil pontas . . . E então—então o súbito grito esterorado de uma gaivota, de repente a águia voraz erguendo para os altos ares a ovelha tenra, o macio gato estralhaçando um rato sujo e qualquer, a vida come a vida. (84-85); A morte é um encontro consigo. Deitada, morta, era tão grande como um cavalo morto. O melhor negócio é ainda o seguinte: não morrer, pois morrer é insuficiente, não me completa, eu que tanto preciso. (86)

Death allows Macabéa to become anonymous again and it is in that anonymity that she achieves ultimate freedom. Anonymity allows her to rejoin the life cycle by becoming undifferentiated organic matter. She becomes the dirt, the abject, the chora in the Kristevan sense and also the air and the light that permeate the universe:

> She is finally free of herself and of me. Do not be frightened. Death is instantaneous and passes in a flash. I know, for I have just died with the girl. {Forgive me that death. It was unavoidable. If you have kissed the wall, you can accept anything. But suddenly I make one last gesture of rebellion and start to howl: the slaughter of doves! To live is a luxury. Suddenly it's all over. Macabéa is dead: the bells were ringing without making any sound.} I now understand this story, {this story is the imminence that lives in those bells, almost, almost pealing. The greatness lies in every human being}. Silence. Should God descend on earth one day there would be a great silence. The silence is such, that thought no longer thinks. Was the ending of my story as grand as you expected? Dying, Macabéa became air. Vigorous air? I cannot say. She died instantaneously . . . At heart, Macabéa {had been no more than a small music box out of tune}. I ask you:—What is the weight of light? (85-86)

> Ela estava em fim livre de si e de nós. Não vos assusteis, morrer é um instante, passa logo, eu sei porque acabo de morrer com a moça. Desculpai-me essa morte. É que não pude evitá-la, a gente aceita tudo porque já beijou a parede. Mas eis que de repente sinto o meu último esgar de revolta e uivo: o morticínio dos pombos!!! Viver é um luxo. Pronto, passou. Morta, os sinos badalavam mas sem que seus bronzes lhes dessem som. E agora entendo essa história. Ela é a iminência que há nos sinos que quase-quase badalam.

> A grandeza é de cada um. Silêncio. Se um dia Deus vier à terra haverá silêncio grande. O silêncio é tal que nem o pensamento pensa. O final foi bastante grandíloquente para a vossa necessidade? Morrendo ela virou ar. Ar enérgico? Não sei. Morreu em um instante... No fundo não passara de uma caixinha de música meio desafinada. E eu vos pergunto:—Qual é o peso da luz? (86-87)

Lispector suggests here that in her death, Macabéa might turn into energetic air. This suggestion has several implications and can thus be read at different levels. Apart from implying that Macabéa reenters her primal self and the logic and language that characterize that self, we can also say that by entering the anonymity granted by death, Macabéa becomes the symbol of all life potential. In other words, she reenters the Platonic and Kristevan chora and becomes "the nurse of all becoming and change," to use Plato's own words again. What this implies is that in a distant and more just society, this becoming and change would symbolize the full realization and acceptance of others like Macabéa, others who could maintain their otherness and yet be fully accepted. Moreover, in a similar fashion to the metaphor of the docks and as discussed earlier, the metaphors of the ending seem to possess various Zen Buddhist connotations. For one, her death can be interpreted as symbolizing her reentrance into the cycle of life. As the narrator puts it, "No this wasn't death. Death is not what I want for this girl: a mere collision that amounted to nothing serious" (82) ("Não, não era morte pois que não a quero para a moça: só um atropelamento que não significava sequer desastre" [84]). The use of the word "collision" here implies that her body is being changed (altered) when it is stricken by another, yet that which constitutes her self will not necessarily die—her body collides with others and otherness (other bodies) in the violent incident that is her death, it disintegrates only to become other things or beings; it merges with the chora, with the dirt where all potential of life resides and from where it will reemerge as something or someone else. In his discussion of Zen Buddhism, Brazier writes,

> In this universe nothing is ever lost, but everything changes. Loss is really transformation. Things seem to disappear, like the sticks in the fire, but "sticks" is actually just a concept in our minds for a particular stage in the evolution of earth becoming plant becoming branches firewood becoming ash becoming earth. It is for this reason that virtually all funerary rites in different cultures include references to renewal and growth. We designate a particular stage in this ongoing process "sticks" for our own convenience. Because of this there arises the illusion of a world full of "things" when what really confronts us is a world of process—flow. "Loss" brings us back to this reality. (238)

The silence achieved with Macabéa's death symbolizes the emptiness of thought, the reaching of the ultimate sunyata state. As Lispector says, "Should God descend on earth one day there would be a great silence" (85) ("Se um dia Deus vier à terra haverá grande silêncio" [86]). This state, which is the ultimate state of fulfillment in Buddhism, is the state in which Macabéa seemed to have lived most of her life, since she did not master, accept, and follow the language and ideals of her society, which were based on discrimination of all sorts and thus contrary to Buddhism. Throughout the novella, Macabéa is in fact often portrayed as the character living in the highest state of spiritual fulfillment. This is why Lispector expresses her sadness and revolt with Macabéa's death: "But suddenly I make one last gesture of rebellion and start to howl: the slaughter of doves!" (85) ("sinto o meu último esgar de revolta e uivo: o morticínio dos pombos!" [86]). Macabéa was a "dove," a being who had reached the sunyata stage while alive, who had become divine and highly spiritual and yet she was killed by the "noise" (stories) of society. In that sense, the novella has a very didactic message: Brazilian society must become more like Macabéa and when that happens, "God will come to earth" (85). Here God can be seen as representing not the monotheistic figure of the Christian God, but rather the acquirement of the sunyata stage, the reaching of nirvana that comes from true enlightenment. This stage would also entail the erasure of the individual self and the entering into what could loosely be described as the collective consciousness, the distended ego, or the "one is all"—a state of self-effacement and obliteration when humans feel part of each other and otherness, part of the "greater I."

The entrance into this "greater I" is clearly illustrated by the fact that Macabéa is described by Lispector as an entity who becomes light and air and by the fact that her death is described as "an encounter with the self" (86) ("um encontro consigo" [85]). The "self" referred to here is the Greater Self, the magnificent void where the individual "I" loses solitude and enters the collectivity of feeling and being, so to say, and in so doing enlightenment (nirvana) is attained. Macabéa is also said to want to vomit that which is not body, that which is luminous (85) and referred to as "Star with a thousand pointed rays" (86) ("Estrela em mil pontas" [85]). Here there is a direct suggestion that Macabéa will become a star, meaning that she has attained sunyata or satori (nirvana) on her last life and thus will be liberated from the painful world of reincarnation, from the wheel of life as defined in Buddhism: her energy will be released into the cosmic and formless void, she will be light and air. The novella then literally becomes a work about "the hour of the star"—the achievement of the "Ultimate Way" (Iisuka 20). In addition, a Buddhist reading of the novel, with its emphasis on the importance of moving from individual consciousness to collective consciousness (awareness) also possesses very direct social implications. It suggests that we must stop behaving like separate, self-sufficient, and selfish entities who do not care about the other—that other who is often destroyed, incorporated into the same, and forgotten, that other who goes hungry; it emphasizes the importance of creating a society that is communal and relational where the "other" is part of the "I" and where all work to achieve a society free of exploitation. In that sense, Buddhist principles are close to the Lévinasian ethics. As a whole, and with all its emphasis on poetic language, emptiness of thought and the refusal or questioning of rhetorical discourses, the novella does in fact become very much like a meditation exercise, an enlightenment Zen experience; it becomes the silence, the emptiness of thought (mind), the word without words, the nothingness that allows one to experience the nirvana of the sunyata; it becomes the God who has now descended on earth, as

Lispector would put it. As the narrator says at the beginning of the novel, "for what can one do except meditate in order to plunge into that total void which can only be attained through meditation. . . . I meditate without words {and about nothing. What complicates} my existence is writing" (9-10) ("que é que se há de fazer senão meditar para cair naquele vazio pelo que só se atinge com a meditação . . . Eu medito sem palavras e sobre o nada. O que me atrapalha a vida é escrever" [9-10]).

The fact that the novel possesses a highly spiritual Buddhist character does not mean that Lispector is suggesting one must exit the mundane, the phenomenological, the here and the now. For, as we have shown, Lispector (like Saramago) bases her philosophy of life in the physical world and gives primary importance to the present and to the immediate. It is the immediacy of life and the knowledge that comes from things (rather than thoughts) that Lispector values, for the former permit us to exit, or at least question, all intellectualisms, all rhetoric. This message about the importance of the immediacy of life and the importance of the phenomenological world is reiterated at the very end of the novel: "And now—now it only remains for me to light a cigarette and go home. Dear God, only now am I remembering that people die. Does that include me? Don't forget, in the meantime, that this is the season for strawberries. Yes" (86) ("E agora—agora só me resta acender um cigarro e ir para casa. Meu Deus, só agora me lembrei que a gente morre. Mas—mas eu também? Não esquecer que por enquanto é tempo de morangos. Sim" [87]). Here the narrator acts as if he is in fact waking up from some intellectual reverie of sorts, and he is, for he now realizes he has been immersed in the world of language and rhetoric and is thus reminding himself and us that that world is not as good or authentic as the one in front of us: not good as the red color of the ripe strawberries which are just waiting to be tasted by us, so that we can enjoy (and know) how the world really feels, tastes, and speaks to us—we can feel the primary language of life, the language before language.

The present is a time that must be enjoyed in its raw, undiscursive quality, just like Macabéa must be perceived by us readers and by the Brazilian society in question, so that she does not become a prisoner of all our "stories." This concentration on the present and the phenomenological is also a fundamental trait of Buddhism. The mind's capacity to attain emptiness (and nirvana) is in fact dependent upon our capacity to concentrate on the present and on a specific object, and then move to the larger cosmic order and to the bareness of thought and the spiritual connection that it brings us (Epstein, *Thoughts Without* 139-51). What this also entails is an awareness of and concentration on the immediate sociohistorical context, which consequently places importance on the need for the individual to work with and within the society at hand so that justice and peace can be achieved. As Roy puts it, "Far from being a mere psychological concentration that would exclude all forms of consciousness-of, this void [the emptiness or nothingness] integrates all components of our finitude. It embraces history as well as the cosmos. It is the Self that takes up all that is valid in the self, purifies it, and energizes it" (186). Or in the words of Suzuki, "The unattainability of *nirvana* comes from seeking it on the other shore of becoming as if it were something beyond time or birth-and-death (*samsara*). *Nirvana* is *samsara* and *samsara* is *nirvana*. Therefore, eternity, *nirvana*, is to be grasped where time, *samsara*, moves on" (359). Thus, Lispector's ultimate message (like that of Saramago) is not one of evasion but rather one of engagement in one's society. The spiritual (mystical consciousness) resides in the finite, not in the infinite, and thus it is in this finite universe (or neighborhood, as Lévinas would say) of ours that we must make encounter with the nirvanic light. In other words, what we must do is behave less like Ricardo Reis and more like Saramago's Lídia, more like Macabéa, and as I will soon demonstrate, also more like Coetzee's Michael K.

Chapter Four

Authenticity in Coetzee's *Life and Times of Michael K*

The provisional language of Coetzee

This is how John Maxwell Coetzee describes himself in *Doubling the Point: Essays and Interviews*—a mixture of literary critical essays written over a period of approximately twenty years (1970-1989) and personal interviews given to David Attwell between 1989 and 1991:

> I say: he is trying to find a capsule in which he can live, a capsule in which he need not breathe the air of the world. (392-93); So as a student he moves on the fringes of the left without being part of the left. Sympathetic to the human concerns of the left, he is alienated, when the crunch comes, by its language—by all political language, in fact. As far back as he can see he has been ill at ease with language that lays down the law, that is not provisional, that does not as one of its habitual motions glance back skeptically at its premises. Masses of people wake in him something close to panic. He cannot or will not, cannot and will not, join, shout, sing: his throat tenses up, he revolts. (394)

Coetzee is known for being a private man, someone who often avoids the public eye and is evasive in his answers to almost everything, perhaps because as he says, he distrusts language and all its rhetorical entrapments, "language that lays down the law, that is not provisional" (394), and also perhaps because he wants to "find a capsule in which he need not breathe the air of the world" (393). This capsule would be a place where Coetzee can find the space to be himself, a space not yet touched by historical and societal pressures, or rather "nightmares," as Stephen Dedalus would put it in Joyce's *Ulysses*: a capsule where he can "imagine the unimaginable" (68). It is precisely this space that Coetzee tries to rescue (or better yet imagine) as a writer— the space prior to the "language that lays down the law" so that he and his characters might have the chance to exist in what Lispector calls "the between the lines." He is in this sense very much like Lispector, for both are trying to find the authenticity of being, the site where the soul and the integrity of the self can have space to flourish and where language and discourse are not the lingua that truly speak.

Coetzee has been often accused of being too metaphysical, too removed from his country's immediate concerns and not able to offer much valuable contribution to the immense sociopolitical problems of a country like South Africa, a country where institutionalized racism has found the nest to grow to an outrageous climax. South Africa is a country where the ugliest ideas the human mind is capable of conceiving have been able to take shape, a country where people of different colors have been associated with different worth, and where laws have been manufactured to enforce, endorse, and justify such difference. It is a country which, during apartheid, enforced laws prohibiting marriages and sexual relations between whites and nonwhites; laws forcing nonwhites to live in specified zones; laws where schools, restaurants, buses and buildings were permitted to "wear" the sinister signs "Europeans Only" and "Non-Europeans Only" for way too long; laws that made it necessary for nonwhites to acquire passes to circulate in their own country; laws where nonwhites were often removed by force from their places and put in the right "zone"; laws where land could not be bought or leased by blacks from whites except in reserves; laws forcing all black people to become citizens of a designated territory and denied South African citizenship, and so on (Maylam 143-204). Law after law after law; Act after Act after Act so that people could "enter" the law and become prisoners of what has been perceived as one of the most calculating and Machiavellian political systems of recent history, a system so repellent that it made Nelson Mandela endure nearly three decades of his life in prison.

When compared to the Mandelian example of sacrifice for South Africa, Coetzee's fiction might appear to be less grand, less political, less deserving of applause. To be seen as an apolitical writer, as one who does not sufficiently or directly attack, address, and undermine the abhorrent apartheid system of South Africa might indeed be an unforgivable sin—especially for those who, like Amado, see the writer as a powerful political interventionist, as someone who cannot, and should not, be afforded the privilege of separating himself or herself from the urgency of sociopolitical struggles. And indeed, just as with Lispector, many writers and critics have voiced their unfavorable opinions about Coetzee's fiction. For example, Nadine Gordimer, one of the most important contemporary South African writers, who has tended to address the South African "problem" in a rather overt way in her novels, has stated the following in an article entitled "The Idea of Gardening: *Life and Times of Michael K* by J.M. Coetzee":

> Yet the unique and controversial aspect of this work is that while it is implicitly and highly political, Coetzee's heroes are those who ignore history, not make it. This is clear not only in the person of Michael K, but in other characters, for example the white doctor and nurse in the "rehabilitation" camp, who are "living in suspension," although for the woman, washing sheets, time is still as full with tasks as it has ever been, and for the doctor it is a state of being "alive but not alive," while for both "history hesitated over what course it should take." No one is this novel has any sense of taking part in determining that course; no one is shown to believe he knows what that course should be. The sense is of the ultimate malaise: of destruction. Not

even the oppressor really believes in what he is doing, anymore, let alone the revolutionary. . . . And so J.M. Coetzee has written a marvelous work that leaves nothing unsaid—and could not be better said—about what human beings do to fellow human beings in South Africa; but he does not recognize what the victims, seeing themselves as victims no longer, have done, are doing, and believe they must do themselves. Does this prevent his from being a great novel? My instinct is to say a vehement "No." But the organicism that Georg Lukács defines as the integral relation between private and social destiny is distorted here more than is allowed for by the subjectivity that is in every writer. The exclusion is a central one that may eat out at the heart of the work's unity of art and life. ("The Idea" 142-43)

Gordimer's critique of Coetzee's points directly to the fact that Coetzee fails to link the social with the individual in a way she finds satisfying, to uncover the structures that are at the base of personal oppression, that is, as the realist tradition à la Lukács would demand—a tradition Gordimer favors. As Lukács notes "every action, thought and emotion of human beings is inseparably bound up with the struggles of the community, i.e., with politics; whether the humans themselves are conscious of this, unconscious of it or even trying to escape from it, objectively their actions, thoughts and emotions nevertheless spring from and run into politics" (5).

Tony Morphet has also indicated how difficult it was to understand Coetzee's fiction when it first came out, and relate it to the urgent South African sociopolitical concerns. In his article, "Reading Coetzee in South Africa," he writes, "It was difficult to see just how Coetzee's work fit in with and contributed to the understanding of the special historical crisis that seemed so overwhelming. So we found ourselves alongside Michael K's 'doctor' struggling with illusive meanings. Part of our difficulty came when we realized that the fictions were playing 'games'; some obvious, others not. The game seemed to be somehow at our expense—at the expense of our understanding of and engagement in the seriousness of our historical situation" (15). To critiques like these Coetzee answers: "I would like to think that today the novel is after a bigger game than [the critical realist type]" (qtd. in Hewson149), and "in Africa the only address one can imagine is a brutally direct one, a sort of pure, unmediated representation; what short-circuits the imagination, what forces one's face into the thing itself, is what I am here calling history. 'The only address one can imagine'—an admission of defeat. *Therefore,* the task becomes imagining this unimaginable, imagining a form of address that permits the play of *writing* to start taking place" (*Doubling* 68). Or still—and we go back to his description of himself as given above: "[I am] trying to find a capsule in which [I] can live, a capsule in which [I] need not breathe the air of the world . . . As far back as [I] can see [I have] been ill at ease with language that lays down the law, that is not provisional, that does not as one of its habitual motions glance back skeptically at its premises" (*Doubling* 393-94). It is precisely this "provisional language," this "play of writing," the exiting of discourse in all the pervasive (and oppressive) forms that such writing entails, and the finding of a capsule from which to imagine the world and the oppressed other that Coetzee is aiming at in *Life and Times of Michael K*.

The provisional language and narratorial techniques that Coetzee uses in *Michael K* have been addressed in a rather novel way by Mike Marais in his book, *The Secretary of the Invisible: The Idea of Hospitality in the Fiction of J.M. Coetzee*. It is worth nothing some of Marais's arguments here. Using theories by Walter Benjamin, Theodor Adorno, Maurice Blanchot, and others, Marais intelligently argues that *Michael K* (along *Foe*) is a novel that remains and should remain unread, unfinished, unborn, a work that possesses an aesthetic autonomy, and which "relies on the auratic potential of art, its ability to gesture beyond its 'giveness,' its location in the cultural episteme, to achieve this end" (Marais 86). Because of these traits, the novel forges a relationship between reader, writer, text, and meaning that can be socially beneficial. Both the reader and the writer are forced to attain mimesis with the character and in that process accept, be, and feel the other: "I would argue that Coetzee . . . does try to use the other to alter the social domain. His entire notion of aesthetic autonomy is premised on a relationship that comes into being in reading, one that will then affect the reader's social relations. This writer's intention is that the reader should assume the burden of responsibility for the other and that this, in turn will alter his or her relations in society" (Marais 92). Perhaps it is this burden of responsibility that made me cry when I first read this novel. Had I entered a sublime realm of otherness and potentiality? Perhaps my emotional reaction was related to the fact that I understood the aura, the ineffable aspect of the book; I understood the possibility of what may lie beyond our typically rational and utilitarian way of looking at the world and its people, of reading novels with preset goals of wanting to understand them, to master them, to incorporate them in our set and mundane episteme of understanding that has forgotten how to unname and untame. Perhaps it was my intrinsic desire to connect with this other and otherness of the novel, embodied by the ways of Michael, and permitted by the ways of the author, that made me cry. It was a cry of yearning, of mourning for this other and his otherness, and joy too—the joy of discovering that someone else (the author) feels that way, has that need to see beyond what we have here and now and thus has created a novel like this. Then, I suppose, we could say that I had experienced mimesis in the sense discussed by Marais and mentioned above.

In her article, "Disrupting Inauthentic Readings: Coetzee's Strategies," basing her stance on positions taken by Derek Attridge and other critics of literature, such as Susan Sontag and Wolfgang Iser, Kathy Iddiols also makes important points about the importance of reading *Michael K* and other of Coetzee's novels authentically, by allowing them to speak their truth, their message rather than fall into the too common tendency of interpreting them through the lens of existing theories of narration. As she implies, this tendency will put literary theory above the novel thus preventing the novel to exist and speak its sui generis message:

> I [suggest] that inauthentic readings occur when more weight or authority is given to a secondary opinion, reading or response than to the primary text itself. With this in mind, then, I suggest that an authentic reading seeks to give its attention back to the text with all its originality and distinctiveness.

This type of response also demands that readers allow the original texts to speak for themselves, and do not appropriate them through singular or overpowering interpretations or readings. Authentic readings recognize that it is not possible to consider, theorize, review or even notice and understand all the individual elements that make up a text, and the reader is therefore not equipped or qualified to speak over it. This authentic type of response would seek to prevent inauthentic readings and interpretations [from] being heard at the expense of the original text.... This type of authentic response is necessary to preserve the potential and the power of a text, allowing it to survive, unimpeded and unlimited. (188-89)

Unclear narration and the ignorance of the narrators

The novel is divided in three sections. In each of these sections the attempts to tell K's story are constantly undermined by the incapacity of the two narrators, their inability to truly "reach" Michael K, that is. The first and last sections are narrated by a third-person narrator. This narrator, although omniscient, does not seem to know a lot about his main character, Michael K. Coetzee has in fact referred to this narrator as one who has limited omniscience: "There is a—if I can use an oxymoron—a limited omniscient point of view operating in part 1 of that book. That is to say, there is someone who is telling the story about Michael K, who looks like an omniscient narrator, but he doesn't actually tell you very much. And . . . there is no guarantee that he knows very much" (qtd. in Penner 94). In *J.M. Coetzee*, Head has stated that "the presentation of events, and the notion of K's development, are features which indicate a lingering realism in the novel, an effort to convey elements of typical historical action alongside the developing personal engagement of an individual in history" (98) and how the realism à la Lukács is questioned, so that the novel ends up making use of a "revitalized realism" (98). Penner has pointed out that the narrator of the novel "conveys Michael's cognition through visual imagery" (94). He cites the following passage from the novel as an example of this: "He saw, not the back notes spread on the quilt, but in his mind's eye a whitewashed cottage in the broad veld with smoke curling from its chimney, and standing in the front door his mother, smiling and well" (11). The use of this type of visual imagery (an ambivalent metaphor or capsule), very common throughout the novel, serves to minimize the narrator's voice in the novel. It allows the narrator to describe Michael K in a detached fashion, leaving the latter's identity barely touched by his text (his story) and interpretation open to the reader, thus creating the possibility for ambivalent (uncertain) readings of the protagonist's identity. Unlike what Penner suggests (94), this narrative strategy does not contribute to the portrayal of K as someone who possesses a primal innocence, which might be perceived as comic stupidity by the reader—at least the informed and ethical reader. On the contrary, it seems that this type of narrative strategy is used by the narrator to indicate both his ignorance about the true identity of K and his inability to reach K's epistemological view of the world (in the passage cited above, specifically, his thoughts about and perception of his mother, money, land possession). This will in turn create a sense of doubt and questioning in the reader: in the presence of only ambivalent metaphors, the reader, who might be used to thinking (and reading) in black and white terms, in terms of sameness and otherness, that is, might now reconsider his or her understanding and cognition of the other, be barred from the other's world and lose any stable ground for comparison.

Section two of the novel is narrated by the medical officer, who is obsessed with extracting the truth out of Michael K, obsessed with making K speak and yield his story, so that he can understand him. As illustrated by Derek Wright: "In *Michael K* . . . the black protagonist's thoughts, in the fashion of realistic fiction are laid open to us as if of their own accord, although in fact by the white author who then has to resort to internal stratagems within the novel's realistic frame, such as making the white doctor unable to prize open K's mouth . . . The reflexive metafiction of *Foe* is the logical next stage on from this, totally abandoning the token psychological realism of *Michael K* and, with it, the attempt to write from a non-white perspective . . . *Michael K* marks the end of a phase in Coetzee's writing: realism has gone to ground, the imperial text to earth" (qtd. in Head 99). And Teresa Dovey argues that section 2 of *Michael K* in fact "functions as a *mise-en-abîme* device, with the [Kenilworth] camp representing the structure of the narrative as a whole, and the unnamed medical officer, who takes on the task of 'absent' narrator of Sections I and III, representing the writer." She links "K's refusal to eat camp food" with "Coetzee's attempt to speak without being spoken, to represent the self of enunciation without this self being usurped by the subject of utterance" (*The Novels* 298). Dovey further qualifies the novel as making wide use of free indirect speech "which combines the voice of narrator and character," thus making the origin and validity of the written dubious (*The Novels* 282). I would stretch Dovey's concept and application of mise en abyme and say that such technique is present throughout the novel at many levels and is fundamental to demonstrate Coetzee's interest in pointing to the undisclosed nature of Michael K. In other words, if we take into account that a mise en abyme is a story inside a story inside a story (one thing standing for another) we can then say that Coetzee's abundant use of ambivalent metaphors in the novel, which I will discuss later, also function as mise en abymes. These mise en abymes serve to maintain the sacredness of K's self, his otherness in the infinitum, as Lévinas might say. K then becomes a "wonder" for us, one we keep "wondering" about but never get to fully understand. In that sense he becomes a Russian doll inside the Russian doll inside the Russian doll . . . in a manner similar to what happens in Couto's stories as discussed in chapter 1. (See also Dominic Head, *The Cambridge Introduction to J.M. Coetzee* (55-61) and Gillian Doodley, *J. M. Coetzee and the Power of Narrative*, for an account of the various narrative strategies used by Coetzee to make K a forever illusive figure.)

Aiming at discursive liberation or the exit of "white writing"

The inability of Coetzee's narrators to tell the story of the oppressed other of color has a very specific objective in *Michael K* and should be seen as an ethical move on the part of the narrator-implied author: to reach the other in nonoppressive ways, to liberate that other from European discourse, to liberate the other from "white writing." Coetzee defines white writing as writing not "by people with white skins but about European ideas writing themselves out in Africa" (*Doubling* 338-89). As Penner illustrates, "If Coetzee does not provide political solutions or a direct call to action to resolve South Africa's enormous problems, it is because he is striking at a more fundamental problem: the psychological, philosophical, and linguistic bases of the colonial dilemma (*Countries of the Mind* xiv). Along the same lines, Dovey argues that Coetzee's ambivalence and difficulty in writing about the other in the complex, divided, and highly racialized South African society has to do with the fact that he his a member of the white colonizing "race":

> What is the "correct" mode for a society which, self-divided, swings uneasily from the Geneva of Calvin to the Manchester of 1830 to the Los Angeles of today, in search of an identity it may never find? This question is a telling one, articulating as it does Coetzee's awareness of the inevitable imbrication of South African novelistic discourse in a set of conflicting international discourses, and the acute sense of a divided self seeking an identity which informs all of his novels to date. This preoccupation with identity cannot be written off as a modernistic obsession with problems of consciousness, nor can it be dismissed as simply another of postmodernism's self-reflexive gestures, serving to endorse the endless deferral of meaning, and, ultimately, a position of extreme relativity. Rather, it arises out of Coetzee's particular historical situation: that of being a white writer in South Africa in the last quarter of the twentieth century, of being a member of the colonizing race in a complex situation which demonstrates features of colonialism, postmodernism and neocolonialism. ("Writing" 18)

Coetzee is aware of the unjust, unethical, and Eurocentric ways in which the European colonizers, with the aid of European travel writers, scientists, ethnographers, and anthropologists have classified the Africans (see "Idleness in South Africa" in *White Writing*). What Coetzee tries to avoid in his writing, to the extent that he can, is the reproduction of the European discourse, which has a long history of swallowing difference into sameness. He tries to escape the reproduction of the type of writing in which the African is equated with a noncultured and noncivilized people, characterized by bestiality, idleness, amorality, lawlessness, atheism, and inferiority. He tries to avoid the type of writing in which the African is only thought of in terms of negative positionality: that which is "non-European," as the very wording in the apartheid sign is indeed an example of; the type of writing in which the European is the only one who is considered a full subject, a full human being to whom all the other beings ought to be compared; the type of writing where the European subject and his or her cultural framework is the universal standard (the model) in relation to which all the others ought to be measured against. As Coetzee writes,

> In the early records one finds a repertoire of remarkable facts about the Hottentots repeated again and again: their implosives ("turkey-gobbling"), their eating of unwashed intestines, their use of animal fat to smear their

bodies, their habit of wrapping dried entrails around their necks, peculiarities of the pudenda of their women, their inability to conceive of God, their incorrigible indolence. Though many of these items are merely copied from one book to another, we must believe that in some cases they were rediscovered or confirmed at first hand. They constitute some of the more obvious *differences* between the Hottentots and the west European, or at least the West European as he imagined himself to be. Yet while they are certainly differences, these items are perceived and conceived within a framework of *sameness*, a framework that derives from the generally accepted theses enunciated at the opening of the extract from Hondius above: that although the Hottentots may seem to be no more than beasts, they are in fact men. Hottentot society being a human society, it must be amenable to description within a framework common to all societies. They will be the universals, while particular observations inserted in the various slots will constitute the differentia that mark particular societies. (*White* 13)

An exploration into the impenetrable "capsules" of Michael K

When asked to comment about Michael K, Coetzee evades giving a straight answer; he refuses to take a position of narratorial (and authorial) authority and knowledge:

> You ask me to comment on *Michael K*. When I listen to novelists talking about their books, I often have the sense that they are producing for the interviewer a patter that has little to do with the book they intimately know. I might even call their response alienated, alienated as a more or less baffled, more or less self-protective measure. I am as capable as the next man of producing an alienated response. But I would feel less of a sell out if I said something like the following: I decline, if only because to do so is in my best interest, to take up a position of authority in relation to *Michael K*. What *Michael K* says, if it says anything, about asserting the freedom of textuality, however meager and marginal that freedom may be, against history (history, as you say, as a society's collective self-interpretation of its own coming-into-being) stands by itself against anything I might say about what it says. What I say is marginal to the book, not because I as author and authority so proclaim, but on the contrary because it would be said from a position peripheral, posterior to the forever unreclaimable position from which the work was written. (*Doubling* 205-56)

Just as Coetzee is "trying to find a capsule in which he can live, a capsule in which he need not breathe the air of the world" (*Doubling* 394), he also tries to find capsules in which Michael K can live, capsules from which he can envisage Michael K, without possessing or clearly defining him. These capsules are what I call ambivalent metaphors. Much has already been said about what are perhaps the main, and in some cases obvious metaphors or capsules (often referred to as allegories by critics) of *Michael K*. For example, using a Foucauldian perspective, Dominic Head has associated the camps (literal and symbolical) of the novel, including the hospitals, the schools, and disciplinary institutions, with the power and tyranny of all institutions, institutions which in this case oppress the individual in the name of democracy, order, and civilization, creating rules and laws that foster the illusion of freedom, when in reality they are used to "incarcerate" people in multiple ways (Head, *J.M. Coetzee* 103-34) and serve to justify (and make "legal") the racist system of apartheid, which is fundamentally unhumane and unethical. (See also Heider's article, "The Timeless Ecstasy of Michael K," in *Black/White Writing* and Timothy Strode's dissertation *The Ethics of Exile: Levinas, Colonialism and the Fictional Forms of Charles Brockden Brown and J.M. Coetzee*). I would add that in the novel, the institutions actually function as a sort of mise en abyme, a story about the "real" story of Michael K, the man whom the institutions try to tame and engulf in their bureaucratic and universal utilitarian rationalist frame. These camps or institutions are the "beasts" we need to unveil, to deconstruct in order to get closer to Michael K. By deconstructing the "camps," by seeing beyond its laws, we are refusing and refuting their legitimate right to exist and impose themselves onto people and therefore "seeing" into the truer nature of our hero Michael K, seeing beyond the laws that have tamed and imprisoned him, seeing with the eye of the spirit, the eye that does not follow the rational tyrannical epistemology that imprisons and does not want to let go.

Others critics have offered psychoanalytical Lacanian readings of the novel and have discussed how K is a figure who remains outside the symbolic discourse, someone without a father (literally and symbolically) because he refuses to be inserted into the laws of society: he remains in the Kristevan choric realm, so to speak. He is a child who refuses to learn and acknowledge the oppressive language of society. Michael's harelip would then symbolize the split (gap) between him and society, between him and the symbolical language of order, his attachment to his mother and to the land speaking to his desire to remain in the presymbolic, to remain object and subject at the same time, to remain whole. Along with this reading goes the argument that the novel becomes an endless plying of signifiers (à la Derrida), reinforcing the idea that K's identity is never captured (never truly said) through the narrative language, making him an inhabitant of the Lispectorian "between-the-lines," and remaining in the "forever unreclaimable," as Coetzee puts it above. The very fact that Michael has no real last name and is given a letter instead of a full name further suggests that he does not belong to the "societal family": his identity is undecipherable through the symbols his society operates by—he remains out of the social order (for details about a psychoanalytical reading of the novel, see Parry; Dovey; Attwell). Some critics have also pointed to the fact that Coetzee might have borrowed the letter K from Kafka's *The Trial*, whose main character is named Joseph K. (see Dovey; Merivale). As noted by Patricia Merivale, some of the themes that run through *Michael K* seem marked by Kafkan elements: "Coetzee constitutes entire episodes of *Life and Times of Michael K* by deploying the major Kafkan motifs of the 'hunger artist' and the 'burrow,' rare, though not unknown, in his earlier works . . . These motifs although interwoven and overlapping, are roughly separable into the two 'borrow' settings of the cave and (more emphatically) the farm, which segue into two 'hunger artist' camp scenes, the first of which is told in the first person, from Michael's point of view, while the second is narrated in the first person by the Medical Officer"

(160). Given Coetzee's familiarity with and interest in the works of Kafka (Merivale 152; Coetzee, *Doubling* 197-250), it is of no surprise that his fiction would reflect Kafkan elements. At the same time, some critics have pointed to the fact that the letter K does not have to have a Kafkan connection and could very well be related to an Afrikaans name. For example, Nadine Gordimer says that the K "probably stands for Kotze or Koekemoker and has no reference, nor need it to have, to Kafka" ("The Idea" 139). And Coetzee himself has stated the following: "I don't believe that Kafka has an exclusive right to the letter K. Nor is Prague the centre of the universe" (qtd. in Merivale 152). This again points to Coetzee's interest in leaving Michael K in the "unreclamable" domain.

In *The Politics of Humiliation in the Novels of J. M. Coetzee,* Hania Nashef describes several other devices used by Coetzee to maintain the "truth" about Michael K (26-36). Of interest to note here is her reference to K as a "white sheet" that refuses to be written upon. He evades the naming of the system; he escapes being imprisoned in the tentacles of a society that is ethically flawed. Here Nashef references Hardt and Negri's insightful remarks: "K's refusal to authority . . . and that very absoluteness and simplicity situate him, too, on a level on ontological purity" (203-04; Nashef 31). Indeed, K is a being that resists to be adulterated by the ethically dubious morality of his society, a society that has attempted at classifying him by using a multitude of methods pertaining to race, class, beauty, and intelligence, to name but a few.

In his insightful book, *Aesthetic Nervousness: Disability and the Crisis of Representation,* Ato Quayson maintains the hypothesis that Michael K suffers from autism and then goes on to show how this disability plays a central role on the overall narrative discourse of the novel as it affects the communication (or lack thereof) that therein takes place. The critic claims that *Michael K* generates aesthetic nervousness because the novel employs disability (autism) to show the difficulty society has in accepting and communicating with the disabled other, the different, the one who evades the accepted and normalized ways of being and communicating (see also Anna Hickey-Moody, "Un-containable Affects"). Quayson uses Bakhtin's thesis on dialogism to argue that the disability (silence) of K, affects the other characters of the novel, who upon the interface with otherness, are forced to, at least, ponder upon another way of being; they are forced to have a certain dialogue with the other, a dialogue that may be faltered (or frozen, as if at an impasse) because of the truth episteme that they may be accustomed to encounter. Quayson implies that disability creates a hermeneutical impasse, a silence that prevents full communication, full understanding of not only the character and his actions, but also the novel at large. Most importantly, he argues, Michael K both affects the narrative and is produced by it—he affects the way meaning is produced but is also affected by the way meaning has been produced in his society, because of the dialogical unfinalizability aspect of the novel, where interlocutor, addressee and social text or context are in constant conversation, always responding to utterances, meanings, or positions that are carried in language. Then, the novel can be said to be always in the process of becoming in the Bakhtinian sense, where one character learns or takes from the other while also teaching or giving to the other (See *The Dialogic Imagination*). Quayson explains it in this manner:

> In Bakhtin the "word" is always split between an addresser and an addressee, both of whom are by implication human subjects. This is so even when Bakhtin is writing about all the elements within the communication nexus (word/addresser/social context, and the overall inflections of communication) in generic terms and without specific characters in mind. But what if the addressee/interlocutor is not a human character at all but rather a structure of societal and cultural expectations not attributable to any source? What if the interlocutor within the dialogized words is not an individual but an effect generated by the specific discursive structure contained in the text itself? These questions and what they imply are directly pertinent to exploring the relation between speech, silence, autism, and dialogism. . . . In literary texts the autist's silence, though elective, is concomitantly riddled by the contradictory pressures of the dialogized novelistic discourse. This seems to go against their wish to remain undisturbed within their silence. I want to recommend that the intrinsic reading of silence as a characterological choice set against the interruptions necessarily instituted by the structures of the narrative be seen as taking place primarily from the assumed perspective of the character. My argument here is that the autist's silence must be taken as having an effect on the entire domain of the narrative discourse while also being produced and sustained by it. (Quayson 154-55)

These arguments again relate to the potential effect that the novel may have on making the reader review his or her position in the creation of meaning and truth, and thus potentially start to see (or imagine) another way. Such arguments echo some of the positions taken by Marais as noted earlier.

Breaking the mirror, breaking the "white" light

This following quotation from *Michael K* contains many messages, many capsules, which allow us to envisage Michael K—only envisage him though, not understand him, for that would be contrary to Coetzee's objective in the novel: "Because of his face K did not have women friends. He was easiest when he was by himself. Both his jobs had given him a measure of solitariness, though down in the lavatories he had been oppressed by the brilliant neon light that shone off the white tiles and created a space without shadows. The parks he preferred were those with tall pine trees and dim agapanthus walks. Sometimes on Sundays he failed to hear the boom of the noon gun and went on working by himself all through the afternoon" (*Michael K* 5). The objective is to maintain the sanctity of the other as intact as possible, so that the other might find a space from which he can start speaking, muttering unintelligible words perhaps, but real words, as if he were a newborn baby who already knows the truest language of all because it is his own, and one which we can only partially capture. K's description as illustrated here echoes Lévinas philosophy of the other: "The other is not an object that must be interpreted and illuminated by my alien light.

He shines forth with his own light, and speaks for himself . . . What we call thinking and speaking is very often only a playing with our own words and concepts or a succession of egocentric monologues. But according to Lévinas, speaking becomes serious only when we pay attention to the other and take account of him and the strange world he inhabits" (John Wild, Introduction 14-15).

Michael K's description leaves a lot unsaid, and yet it says a lot about the narrator's intention to protect Michael's integral identity, his intention to leave him outside white discourse (or discourse in general) in all its many pervasive forms. We learn (or unlearn) many things about Michael K in just one paragraph taken from the beginning of the novel. We are told, for example, that K prefers solitude to company. This solitude is preferable because it allows K to be himself: he does not have to be seen by the others who will judge him according to their standards of beauty, propriety, culture, race, and class; the others who will merely gaze and imprison him in their unethical, oppressive, and restrictive philosophy of sameness—one that forgets that there exists an other who is different and that that difference should not be seen as inferior. This philosophy is contrary to the Lévinasian concept of "face" which sees the other as an entity not totally graspable to the observing human mind, and entity that extends ad infinitum (refer back to chapter two and three for a more detailed exposition of the Lévinasian concepts of face and gaze; see also *Totality and Infinity* [50-51]). In this sense, and unlike Saramago's novel, *O ano*, where the narrator is advocating a relational ontological ethics, Coetzee's narrator seems to be advocating for what I call an individual relational ethics. Contradicting the Lévinasian interrelational ethics, K prefers to alienate himself from others: he finds his identity in isolation—at least isolation from people, for as we are told, he loves the company of plants and is happiest when he is gardening. The vegetable world does not judge him through the rational mind's eye and so he feels he can maintain his identity when around it. K prefers the parks with tall pine trees and dim agapanthus walks. This further suggests that he is at ease when in the company of nature, hiding from the eyes of people who are eager to call him names, put him into categories, people who are repelled by his looks and his hare lip, those who laugh at his difference. The tall trees and the dim agapanthus walks protect him from the eye of the others, who classify and denigrate that which does not fall into what they deem to be the norm. The vegetable world becomes the barrier that breaks the mirror of sameness: it becomes the opaque barrier that prevents the judging eye of the human observer from seeing Michael through his or her own lens. The mirror of society is intercepted (broken) and is not able to capture the image of Michael which is protected by the parks's vegetation. Nature is given supremacy over civilization: nature is gentle and protective of the individual self, whereas civilization is harsh and destructive: humans annihilate whereas nature nurtures and protects.

When working in the parks, and later on when living in the mountains and on the farm, Michael often loses the notion of time, and enters an alternate state of existence with mystical and highly liberating dimensions. At these moments, K is immersed in another world order: an order that has an uninterrupted notion of time, where there are no clocks, no civilization, and no others telling the individual what to do and when to do it. Again, civilization is undermined and nature is valued. Taking into account that the Europeans wrongly perceived the Africans as being idle, ignorant, and inferior, and tried to impose on them their own work ethic, which was often associated with the capitalist mentality of accumulation, we can then see how K is also evading that ethic. K breaks the mirror of time imposed by the consumer capitalist society that is constantly obsessed with production: he breaks it in order to reclaim his independence and humanity. In "Timeless Ecstasy of Michael K," Sarah Heider offers a good discussion of the notion of time that permeates the novel, more specifically the notion of time that Michael seems to live by when on the mountains and at the farm, when he is mostly unoccupied, just lying about:

> In these periods of idleness, his "yielding up of himself to time," K enters meditative experiences, altered states in which he is removed for an indefinite length of time from the chain of desiring-machines, coming as close as possible to death . . .but his idleness is not to be condemned, for it is part of his withdrawing from the societal machines that attempt to engage him, in the camps and hospitals, and, by making him one of their chain, to fragment him, for by being attached as a link in a chain of production he becomes a partial object in the flow of desire that fuels the machines. (85-86); Michael K experiences such an undifferentiated flow in his periods of trance or ecstasy in which time is freed from its technological harshness. No longer encumbered with days, hours, minutes, time becomes an abstract flow without beginning or end, a time flowing slowly like oil from horizon to horizon over the face of the world, washing over his body, circulating in his armpits and his groin, stirring his eyelids. (115; for a good discussion of this notion of time in Michael K and its relation to the Kafkan notion of time, see also Koetters 259-65; Coetzee, *Doubling* 197-232; this notion of time has been referred to by Coetzee as "eschatological" or as "an everlasting present" [*Doubling* 231]).

We are also told that although K enjoys his work as a guard at the public lavatories, he feels "oppressed by the brilliant neon light that shone off the white tiles and created a space without shadows" (5). Michael feels oppressed by the light shining directly on the white tiles because he feels that there is no space to hide, no space where the light cannot see, so to speak. The light becomes the symbol for the society in which K lives, a society that thinks it can understand everything and everyone through the rational mind and through the filter of its own cultural framework, which is European based. The light is Western civilization, "white writing," as Coetzee would call it. This "white writing" leaves no space for "shadows," for otherness, for respect in difference, and that is why Michael feels oppressed by it. It is an arrogant and unethical light, a light preoccupied with understanding, classifying, incorporating, and destroying—destroying the unknown and the different. And it is in the "unknown" and "different" (in the shadows) that Michael wants to remain. One can further suggest that because the light is so intense, Michael is able to see himself reflected on the tiles, which equates to him being seen (understood, captured) through the eye of the European. The tile then becomes the mirror that reflects Africa and

Africans through the eyes of Europe, and for that reason also the mirror from which Michael wants to escape. Michael eventually leaves this job to return to his work in the parks, later on hiding in the mountains and on the farm. He is therefore able to break the mirror and the blinding (disrespectful) "white" light it emits.

Being-in-the-element and entering the "real" mirror

We can easily say that Michael K lives in the Lévinasian element. For Lévinas, "to-be-in-the-element" is,

> to be within, to be inside of . . . This situation is not reducible to a representation, not even an inarticulate representation; it belongs to sensibility, which is the *mode* of enjoyment. It is when sensibility is interpreted as representation and mutilated thought that the finitude of our thought has to be invoked so as to account for these "obscure" thoughts. . . . One does not know, one lives sensible qualities: the green of these leaves, the red of this sunset. (135); Sensibility, essentially naïve, suffices to itself in a world insufficient for thought. To be separated is to be at home with oneself. But to be at home with oneself . . . is to live from . . . to enjoy the elemental. The "failure" of the constitution of the objects from which one lives is not due to irrationality or the obscurity of those objects, but to their function as nutriments. Food is not unrepresentable; it subtends its own representation, but in it the I again finds itself. (Lévinas, *Totality and Infinity* 147)

As Strode notes,

> K's delight . . . in the earth's nourishment—something that he bathes in and sustains him, to the extent that to K the earth is in general, alimentary substance is very much akin to Levinas's depiction in *Totality and Infinity* of the I's enjoyment of what he calls the "element." To the extent that K finds himself, in a sense, incarnated with extraterritorial space, he finds himself, in his physical being, affiliated with boundless space—by being abandoned space, and because K's identification with such space was as one constitutionally opposed to property, K's connection to it is other than possessive. K's condition at Prince Albert is, at the pick of his enjoyment there, one of immersion in a boundless element—such is the implication of Coetzee's language. To possess K in a disciplinary system, then, is to attempt to contain what has in its physical essence become identified with what is boundless or uncontainable. Of the elemental—what precedes or exceeds definition—K is also always already in exile, always in flight from official or centralized systems, always known in the midst of absenting himself, always knows as trace. (301-02)

When in the mountains and on the farm, K starts to hide in his burrow during the day while taking care of his crops by night. Again he evades the light, for the light is equated with the intruders who might be coming to the farm to steal his solitude and take him away to the camps, intruders telling him how to live and how to be civilized, how to enter civil law:

> he had become so much a creature of twilight and night that daylight hurt his eyes. He no longer needed to keep to paths in his movements around

Authenticity in Coetzee's *Life and Times of Michael K*   169

> the dam. A sense less of sight than of touch, the pressure of presences upon his eyeballs and the skin of his face, warned him of any obstacle. Hi eyes remained unfocused for hours on end like those of a blind person. He had learned to rely on smell, too. He breathed into his lungs the clear sweet smell of water brought up from inside the earth. It intoxicated him, he could not have enough of it. Though he knew no names he could tell one bush from another by the smell of their leaves. He could smell rain weather in the air (158).

Earlier we read: "He also ate roots. He had no fear of being poisoned, for he seemed to know the difference between a benign bitterness and a malign one, as though he had once been an animal and the knowledge of good and bad plants had not died in his soul. . . . Gradually he lost all fear of the night. Indeed, waking sometimes in the daytime and peering outdoors, he would wince at the sharpness of the light and withdraw to his bed with a strange green glow behind his eyelids" (140-42). Michael becomes so accustomed to the night and its blind darkness that the light starts to hurt his eyes. K's lifestyle in the wilderness is positive, for it allows him to get away from the light of white civilization. He becomes so much himself (so much other than white) that his eyes no longer seem to recognize the light of the day and by extension the light of civilization. The light hurts his eyes because it is a reminder of the alienation experienced while inserted in a civilization that shines excessively and does not allow the other to be other. In the wilderness, K develops (or recuperates) what we can call a prediscursive knowledge about himself and the world around him. This knowledge is not understood through the eye of what the white civilization would call reason, but instead through the eye of the body, the eye of the senses such as taste, smell and sound, the unconscious eye. K no longer needs to see with his eyes: they become unfocused as if he were a blind person, and yet his blindness equates with true vision in the sense that he no longer is inside the words, he no longer remembers the names of things, and by extension the thought and discursive system of the power structures ruling his society: in other words, he exits reason and its oppressing naming and qualification of the world. The "seeing with the eyes" is equated with distinguishing between things and giving names to them, which can be discriminatory, for one tends to base the value of things (and people) on the way they look and forgets that the way they look is only one part of their totality, their infinitum, as Lévinas would say—an infinitum which remains outside of the observer's eye. Thus the seeing with the eyes would represent entering the codes that rule Michael's society, codes about beauty, racial differences and so forth—codes which are deeply oppressive and which he wants nothing to do with.

    K needs no names for the different bushes, for he can detect their different scents. He can even smell the rain weather in the air and he knows by mere instinct which roots to eat and which ones to avoid. This knowledge is felt at the level of the body, instinct, and unconscious and is not mediated by discursive logic and language. Thus, this knowledge is pure, unoppressive and real: it is a knowledge acquired when one is truly inserted in the element, as Lévinas would say, a knowledge fundamental to us for we live "in a world insufficient for thought" (*Totality and*

Infinity 135). This knowledge represents the entrance into the real mirror, a mirror that does not reflect our thoughts but our sensations which can only be experienced in one's body, contrary to thoughts which can be abstracted from one's body, one's element, and be seen from a distance. The things around K (i.e., the plants, the roots he eats, the air he smells, and the objects he touches) become his "nutriments" and in it K finds his "I again" (*Totality and Infinity* 147). These nutriments are K's real mirror: his real ontological tool, unmediated by the logic of discourse, the discourse that would entail the annihilation of K's self by the oppressing other. Since the thought (and by extension the discourse) that rules Michael's historical reality is oppressive because it is affiliated with a cultural framework that wants to incorporate difference into sameness, then K is best listening only to the language of his senses, a language that does not speak the rules and laws of his surrounding society. This language is what I call the "real" mirror. The laws of society cease to exist, becoming incoherent systems to a being like K, who can only decipher the language of his own elements: his body, instinct, his sensual side—elements which exist by themselves without any mediating linguistic recourse. K in fact becomes very close to an animal and is associated with a variety of animals not only by the narrator, but also by other characters and even by himself: lizard, ant, parasite, insect, snail, rabbit, owl, mouse, donkey, mole, and so forth. Ironically, this association does not really carry a negative connotation, since K is not interested in living among people like (most) people. Being compared to an animal attains a positive connotation, even though we get the clear feeling that some of the characters of the novel call him those names with a derogatory intention (see also Anne Haeming, *Cultivation as Colonization,* for a discussion on the various means used by the colonialist to control and claim power over the colonized subject and his or her space and the idea of hygiene). It seems then that the narrator of the novel is having recourse to the colonialist discourse—which too often compared Africans to animals—only to invert the meaning and suggest that being animallike in this instance is far better than being humanlike, since humans have engendered the abhorrent system of apartheid. Being human for Coetzee seems to entail being evil and possessing the capacity (or is it an incapacity?) to create highly oppressive and discriminatory systems. Nature, on the other hand, appears as a nicer entity. Mike Marais has noted that initially the novel shows instances of K's need to subdue nature. He describes his act of killing the goat at the farm and even his work at the Wynberg in Cape Town as a gardener as instances where K displays a similar economy as the colonizer, in other words, as someone who wants to tame the wild, be a subject towards an object. He further indicates that this behavior changes as the novel progresses, for we note that K loses his subjectivity and becomes one with nature (Marais 37-39).

From the elemental to the cosmico-spiritual dwelling

As Lévinas notes,

> The elements do not receive man as a land of exile, humiliating and limiting his freedom . . . The solidity of the earth, the breath of the wind, the

undulation of the sea, the sparkle of the light do not cling to a substance. They come from nowhere. This coming from nowhere, from "something" that is not, appearing without there being anything that appears—and consequently *coming always*, without my being able to posses the source—delineates the future of sensibility and enjoyment . . . The future, as insecurity, is already in the pure quality which lacks the category of substance, of something . . . Quality does not withstand identification because it would represent a flux and a duration; rather its elemental character, its coming forth from nothing, constitutes its fragility, the disintegration of becoming, that time prior to representation—which is menace and destruction. . . . The future of the element as insecurity is lived concretely as the mythical divinity of the element. Faceless gods, impersonal gods to whom one does not speak, mark the nothingness that bounds the egoism of enjoyment in the midst of its familiarity with the element . . . What the side of the element that is turned toward me conceals is not a "something" susceptible of being revealed, but an ever-new depth of absence, an existence without existent, the impersonal par excellence. (*Totality and Infinity* 140-42)

From his intimate contact with the elemental on the farm, Michael K moves to another level of existence, a level of spiritual and mystical dimensions. He reaches what can be termed as a cosmico-dwelling existence, a connection with the grander and distant universe, that is,

Every stone, every bush along the way he recognized. He felt at home at the dam as he had never felt in the house. He lay down and rested with the black coat rolled under his head, watching the sky wheel above. I want to live here, he thought: I want to live here forever. It is as simple as that . . . He released the brake of the pump . . . He held his hand in the flow and felt the force beat his fingers back; he climbed into the dam and stood under the stream, turning his face up like a flower, drinking and being bathed; he could not get enough of the water . . . He slept into the open . . . Wrapped in the black coat he clenched his jaw and waited for dawn, aching after the pleasures of digging and planting he had promised himself, impatient to be through with the business of dwelling . . . I am not building a house out here by the dam to pass on to other generations. What I make ought to be careless, makeshift, a shelter to be abandoned without a tugging at the heartstrings. So if ever they find this place or its ruins, and shake their heads and say to each other: what shiftless creatures, how little pride they took in their work! It will not matter. (*Michael K* 135-58)

As the quotation above illustrates, Michael K lives completely immersed in the elemental: he is familiar with the stones and the bushes on the farm. He lays down on the earth, feeling it in his own body, he looks at the sky, feels the force of the water on his hands, drinks it and accepts it directly into his face as if he were a flower. He is so close to the elemental that he becomes elemental and organic himself: just like a flower. This closeness and intimacy with the elements give him contentment and completeness, leaving K in need of nothing else. This immediacy of life contains a mystical dimension that fulfills K's deepest needs. We are told that he "ach[es] after the pleasures of digging and planting . . . impatient to be through with the business of dwelling" (136). This aching speaks to K's immense desire to be connected to and live in the element. The fulfillment of this desire will equate to K's final immersion into the element and into the cosmico-spiritual realm, the earth becoming the place that attains a grander dimension. Relaying on a Levinasian reading and the latter's concept of the *il y a*, Mike Marais also notes that there is in the character of Michael K, especially as the novel progresses and during his last saty at the farm, "an absence of self-possession, of self subject-centered consciousness," which disallows K from feeling or perceiving the separate entities and objects around him, and also from feeling himself as a separate subject or person (Marais 42). Such a lack of cognitive differential, Marais goes on to explain, makes K enter the zone of Being in the Lévinasian sense (Marais 42-43). This engulfing in Being may also be what we feel when we read the novel thus experiencing mimesis, as Marais points out, and as noted previously—and this allows us to connect with the otherness of K, for we, pushed by the "auratic potential" and "aesthetic autonomy" of the novel, become immersed in the strangeness of K, allowing him to take residence in us, and therefore offering him our "hospitality" (see also *Writing in Crisis: Ethics and History in Gordimer, Ndebele and Coetzee,* by Stefan Helgesson, particularly the section titled "A Wrong Story, Always Wrong: Reading the Ethically Sublime in J.M. Coetzee's Life and *Times of Michael K*," where he relies on some Lévinasian concepts to explore the novel and the character of Michael K).

This spiritual dwelling is in some ways very close to the Afrikaans myth of oneness with the earth, which speaks of the deep connection the farmer has with the farm and land and even with the larger universe, and to the diffusion of individual consciousness that that entails. In his analysis of the Afrikaans *plaasroman* (farm novel) in *White Writing* Coetzee discusses how that deep connection is played out across in different Afrikaans novels:

> The final test that the bond between them [farmer and farm] is supramaterial will be passed when a mystic communion of interpenetration takes place between them, when the farmer becomes *vergroeid* (intergrown, fused) with the farm: "Never before had he felt such a bond with the earth. It was now as if the life within it were streaming up into his body . . . as if he and the earth were living in a silent understanding" [from *Groei (Growth)*]. Then there are ordinary people who, because they live close to nature, are touched on occasion with yearning and *weemoed*, drawn out of themselves by sky, sunsets, wide horizons, and other spacious perspectives . . . Then there are those who transcend *weemoed*. . . . Generally speaking, such transcendence is attained via conscious acceptance that the unit of life is the lineage, not the individual. The attainment of lineal consciousness is brought about by, and brings about, a new relation to nature which in turn sacrifices the meaning of the farm. The manifestation of the lineage in historical time is the farm, an area of nature inscribed with the signs of the lineage: with evidence of labour and bones in the earth . . . Lineal consciousness brings about a liberation from the sense of being alone in the world and doomed to die: as long as the lineage lasts the self may be though to last. (108-09)

There are, however, many differences between the Afrikaans myth of oneness with the earth and Michael K's relation with the land: while the farmer needs to possess (own) the land, demarcate his territory clearly and live a sedentary life, Michael K in fact rejects the possession of the land and he is a nomad, a wanderer. He rejects possession of any kind, for he wants to live outside historical times, unlike the farmer who through the ownership of the farm becomes inserted into history. K tries to find "forgotten corners and angles and corridors between the fences, land that belonged to no one yet" and he thinks that perhaps if "one fl[ies] high enough . . . one [is] able to see" (64). The "flying high enough" here refers to K's ability to reach beyond his immediate limits, to connect with the grander universe, without needing to possess land. This "being able to see" is not accompanied by the article "it," further pointing to the mystical dimension of K's seeing. Moreover, unlike the Afrikaans farmer, who needs to assert (and make present) his lineage at the farm "with evidence of labour and bones in the earth" (*White Writing* 108), K wants to minimize or hide the signs of his presence during his time at the farm, and not just for security reasons, as the quotation above shows (see also Head, "Gardening as Resistance," for further insights on how Michael K's relation with the land differs from that of the Afrikaner's pastoral ideal).

In *Michael K* the earth becomes the metaphor for the cosmos at large, a cosmos which extends beyond K's immediate surroundings, the faraway unknown which K only perceives spiritually or by mystical intuition as it were, just as he is able to know of any obstacle near him through "the pressure of presences upon his eyeballs and the skin of his face" (158) or just as he knows the difference between the good and the bad roots "as though he had once been an animal and the knowledge of good and bad plants had not died in his soul" (140). This last ability further reinforces the idea that K feels part of and connected to the larger order of the universe; it also suggests that life never really dies but only transforms into something else: K might have been an animal (or even another human being) in his other life and that is why he seems to "have the memory" of good and bad roots engraved in his soul. Michael K becomes similiar to Lispector's Macabéa for she also "experienced schizoid dreams in which she saw immense antediluvian animals, as if she had lived in the most remote age of this bloody land" (59-60). Both Macabéa and Michael seem to have lived other lives in the past and that might be why they have these memories. Again, and as discussed in chapter 3, these memories can be related to reincarnation (as defended in Buddhism) or to the collective unconscious in the Junganian sense. What K is today is not the only thing he is or will ever be, for he will become something else after his death, just as he seems to have been something else in his past lives. This is also contrary to the Afrikaner's philosophy of life, for the latter needs his familial lineage (reason why it is important to have many children) to be liberated from "the sense of being alone in the world and doomed to die: as long as the lineage lasts the self may be thought to last" (*White Writing* 108-09) whereas K has no desire to have children.

Thus, as in Lispector's *A hora*, we find characteristics of Zen Buddhism in *Michael K*. In her article "The Timeless Ecstasy of Michael K," Sarah Heider also discusses the existence of elements of Zen Buddhism in Michael K (85-86). For example, she tells us how meditation is a key component of K's life, how the novel emphasizes the experiencing of the elements (bareness of thought) rather than the interpreting (translating or narrativizing) of reality; and how such experiences allow K to be himself, to empty his thought, and reach a state of pure experience where time and space are felt as being inseparable. This is very similar to the sunyata and nirvana stages of Buddhism. Heider cites the following passage from the novel to support her argument: "He could lie all afternoon with his eyes open, staring at the corrugations in the roof-iron and the tracings of the rust; his mind would not wander, he would see nothing but the iron, the lines would not transform themselves into pattern or fantasy; he was himself, lying in his own house, the rust was merely rust, all that was moving was time, bearing him onward in its flow" (158-89).

In order to attain the cosmico-spiritual dwelling (the connection with the grander and distant universe), K does not need to live in or grasp any reality other than his immediate elemental reality. As he says, "I want to live here . . . I want to live here forever. It is as simple as that" (135). This "forever" speaks to his inner contentment and to the connection he feels with his surroundings, one that makes him feel part of a larger, yet unknown, unrepresentable, strange and uncertain universe. He lives in the moment and is uncertain of the future, but that does not really matter, for he only lives in the present. As he says, he is not interested in building a house that can be passed onto other generations. What he wants is carefree, uncalculating living—the type of living that does not prepare for the future or even acknowledge the past. His "time" is a time outside of the wheels of history—a time of mystical dimensions. His time has no future: it is the perpetual present, the here and the now. This conception of time is contrary to the historical temporal conception, which regulates K's society—a society that divides time in sections of past, present and future.

As Lévinas says, "The future of the element as insecurity is lived concretely as the mythical divinity of the element. Faceless gods, impersonal gods to whom one does not speak, mark the nothingness that bounds the egoism of enjoyment in the midst of its familiarity with the element" (*Totality and Infinity* 141). Through K's intimate connection and insertion into the elemental, he can envisage, feel, and perceive what Lévinas calls the "faceless gods"—that is, the beyond the here and now, in other words, the divine, the mystical. This state of existence allows K to enter the nothingness, to enter "an ever-new depth of absence, an existence without existent, the impersonal par excellence" (*Totality and Infinity* 142). Again, this nothingness is the equivalent to the Buddhist emptiness of thought. Like Macabéa, K is then a being who attains the maximum fulfillment in life. In a fashion similar to the Lispectorian heroine, K can enter the "Greater I" and become boundless; he "can fly high" and become a thinker without thoughts, a spiritual, nameless, impersonal, and atemporal entity that surpasses conventional dichotomous categories which obey a rational and dissecting logics. He can attain an "existence without existent" (142) as Lévinas calls it. In this state of existence (or being), all oppressive discourses of society are suspended and erased and distinctions between same/other, good/bad, human/ahuman,

human/divine, superior/inferior and so on become unimportant, for life in all forms is an equally valuable part of the greater whole. This Greater Whole (or I) rejects discriminations of all sorts.

K's concept of the origins of his own mother seems to also reflect a mystical (Buddhistlike) apprehension of reality: "When my mother was dying in hospital, he thought, when she knew her end was coming, it was not me she looked to but someone who stood behind me: her mother or the ghost of her mother. To me she was a woman but to herself she was still a child calling her mother to hold her hand and help her. And her own mother, in the secret life we do not see, was a child too. I come from a line of children without end. He tried to imagine a figure standing at the head of a line, a woman in a shapeless grey dress who came from no mother; but when he had to think of the silence in which she lived, the silence of time before beginning, his mind baulked" (160-01). This description tells us that K sees all people ultimately not as being descendents of or connected to a single mother and father, but rather another large entity (force). Again, this would seem to echo the lineal consciousness of the Afrikaans myth as referred above. And yet, we know that Michael has lost his mother and will most likely not have children himself, for not only is he what most women would consider physically repellent, but he also does not even yearn for sexual love, and therefore his familial lineage is broken. As already noted, K has no intention of building a house at the farm to pass onto other generations. What K has, then, is his connection with the element and consequently with the larger universe, without the "bodily" familial connection present in the Afrikaans myth of oneness with the land. Moreover, K does not seem to have a father, or at least he is unknown—the patriarchal figure who occupies a central position in the Afrikaans myth since he is the one who, through his name, keeps the lineage alive.

In *Michael K* people (and things) then become all equal children (parts) of the "Greater I," an "I" that even though we cannot intellectually and rationally perceive, exists. This is why K's mind baulks when he tries to "think of the silence of time before beginning" (161). This silence refers to an ahistorical (and a-storical) apprehension of reality where things are not divided or seen in discriminatory ways, where there is no discourse (and language) classifying and organizing reality and deciding the value of things and people. This silence cannot be thought, it is true emptiness; it is a silence that is not silence because calling it "silence" is already adulterating what it truly means. This silence goes even beyond the collective unconscious in the Jungian sense according to the Zen monk Hogen: "We can actually penetrate beyond the depths of the collective unconscious of human nature and there come to the bottomless sea of the Buddha-nature. If we go beyond the collective unconscious layers, thereby breaking through the final barrier of the unconscious layers, we experience true birth completely anew in the ocean of true emptiness. This is infinite freedom of no-self, no-mind, no idea; this is self completely unconditioned. Here in the infinite no-mind we find flowers, the moon, our friends and families, and all the things just as they are" (qtd. in Brazier 81). As Brazier notes: "Zen . . . is not seeking the construction of an over-arching story. It seeks, rather, a pre-story identity: the face we had before we or anyone else ever conceived of us. If we can return to the root this way, then we can appreciate all the stories without being enslaved by any of them" (230). K himself is described by the medical officer as being "a human soul above and beneath classification, a soul blessedly untouched by doctrine, untouched by history, a soul stirring its wings within that stiff sarcophagus, murmuring behind that clownish mask," a "precious . . . creature left over from an earlier age, like the coelacanth or the past man to speak Yanqui" (207). Once again K becomes very close to Macabéa. They are both described as old souls, entities who have been living for a very long time and possess a deep knowledge, perhaps because they have experienced various life cycles and thus have had the opportunity to accumulate many memories. This might also mean that they are near the end of the cycle of birth and death (*samsara*) and close to "being blown out of existence" (entering the ultimate nirvana).

Unlike the makers of South African history, who have lost their soul by hierarchizing people according to discriminatory categories, K is able to recognize the sanctity of all life and to perceive another dimension of existence, a type of life that is unmanned, unnameable and lies outside historical categories. He is empty of discourse, he is nirvanic, a hero like Macabéa, who has reached a higher dimension of existence. He is a model whom the South African society must emulate so that it can exit its highly discriminatory system of classification of life and people. K's insertion into the mystical becomes more intense as he spends more time on the farm alone. His entering into the mystical realm is accompanied by his eating of things from the earth: ants, roots, flowers, birds, and other things, and especially by eating the fruits of his own labor—the pumpkins and the melons. The more he eats of these items, the less hungry he feels, even though he seems to be aware of the fact that he needs to eat more nutritious food if his body is to survive. As his body is fed with the bounty of the earth, he becomes more like a star, an entity whose boundaries are not bound to terrestrial spheres, an entity capable of rising above:

> As he tended the seeds and watched and waited for the earth to bear food, his own need for food grew slighter and slighter. Hunger was a sensation he did not feel and barely remembered. If he ate, eating what he could find, it was because he had not shaken off the belief that bodies that do not eat die. What food he ate meant nothing to him. It had no taste, or tasted like dust. When food comes out of this earth, he told himself, I will recover my appetite, for it will have savour. After the hardships of the mountains and the camp there was nothing but bone and muscle on his body. His clothes, tattered already, hung on him without shape. Yet as he moved about his field he felt a deep joy in his physical being. His step was so light that he barely touched the earth. It seemed possible to fly; it seemed possible to be both body and spirit. He returned to eating insects. Since time poured upon him in such an unending stream, there were whole mornings he could spend lying on his belly over an ant-nest picking out the larvae one by one with a grass-stalk and putting them in his mouth. (139)

His eating from the bounty of the earth has a cleansing effect, suggesting again that civilization is presented in the novel as corrupt, inhumane, and unjust, and nature is the opposite of that. Unlike the food given to him at the camps Kenilworth and Jakkalsdrif and at the reformatory Huis Norenius, which K associates with oppression, suffering, and the erasure of his difference, the food that comes from the earth—and especially the pumpkins and melons that he grows himself—have a therapeutic effect on Michael's soul, so therapeutic in fact that he experiences a moment of true spiritual ecstasy when eating it:

> He lifted the first strip to his mouth. Beneath the crispy charred skin the flesh was soft and juicy. He chewed with tears of joy in his eyes. The best, he thought, the very best pumpkin I have tasted. For the first time since he had arrived in the country he found pleasure in eating. The aftertaste of the first slice left his mouth aching with sensual delight. He moved the grid off the coals and took a second slice. His teeth bit through the crust into the soft hot pulp. Such pumpkin, he thought I could eat every day of my life and never want anything else. And what perfection it would be with a pinch of salt, and a dab of butter, and a sprinkling of sugar, and a little cinnamon scattered over the top! Eating the third slice, and fourth and fifth, till half the pumpkin was gone and his belly was full, K wallowed in the recollection of the flavours of salt, butter, sugar, cinnamon, one by one. (156)

The eating of his fruits becomes equated with the entering into the cosmic realm again, and this time perhaps even in a more intense way. These fruits came from the earth, which he had been aching to cultivate so that he could "be through with the business of dwelling" (136), as he says. There is in K's planting activity a more direct and fierce attempt to connect with the elemental. K's cultivation represents his entering into the earth literally in the sense that he has to touch (dig) the earth, but also because the earth then enters (nourishes) his fruits and by extension him, since he will eat these fruits. Such direct interrelation (interchange) between K and the earth is equivalent to the ultimate merging of K's "I" into the "Greater I": the distinction between himself and the earth is overthrown and he finally feels at home, his "business of dwelling" (136), having finally been accomplished. When eating the fruits he cultivates, K does not thank God (the sky) but rather the earth where they came from: "The fragrance of the burning flesh rose into the sky. Speaking the words he had been taught, directing them no longer upward but to the earth on which he knelt, he prayed: 'For what I am about to receive make us truly thankful'" (155). Such a gesture further suggests that K's immediate surroundings are seen as the route to attain the connection with the larger divine element. As in Saramago's novel, *O ano* and also in *A hora*, the divine or mystical element is not to be found or discovered in the heavens, in the absent, in the faraway, but rather in the immediate connection with the elemental. This living in and of the earth is the ultimate cosmico-dwelling. This has an even more specific meaning in Coetzee's novel, if we take into account the fact that Michael K is not allowed to possess land (the most elemental element) in South Africa, a country where a small elite of whites has taken away land from people like him.

In her article "Eating (Dis)Order: From Metaphoric Cannibalism to Cannibalistic Metaphors," Kyoko Yoshida also argues, among other things, that Michael K in fact suffers from aphasia. He cannot process and understand language and thus replaces language with food but only the good or real food; in sum, he commits what she calls symbolic or metaphoric cannibalism, further evidencing K's oneness with the mother, earth, greater self. As illustaretd above, he experiences this oneness when he eats the pumpkins that he cultivated in the patch of land where he spread his mother's ashes, and so the food becomes the mother and he becomes the mother because he eats the food. Furthermore, because K only wants this food from the land and rejects the food from the camps, we can then suggest that he rejects anything that is not real, not literal; he rejects what I will call the intermediaries of life, the things that make us socially functioning beings, namely, the language system, a system that is full of absences in the sense explained by Kristeva and Cixous (taking after Lacan) (see *Three Steps on the Ladder of Writing, Pouvoirs de l'horreur: essai sur l'abjection,* and Felluga, "Modules on Lacan," respectively) and already discussed in previous chapters. This symbolical world order that we enter when we replace language with things forever separates us from the Real Order, from the physicality or reality unmediated by language, the realm where one had oneness with the mother thus creating a void and a yearning for the lost wholeness. Michael K tries to recapture this Real Order by entering the physicality of things and refusing to speak and understand the language around him, the Symbolical Order that names, separates and imprisons him in reductive categories of self and other. Michael K tries to be antimetaphorical and regain literalness of being. As Yoshida writes,

> To K who refuses to explain, the narrator vented his fumed irritation: "We don't want you to be clever with words or stupid with words, man, we just want you to tell the truth!" (190). The narrator speaks from the world where the bread of life differs from actual bread. For Michael K, there is only one: the real bread, so he cannot either choose one or the two. K suffers a type of aphasia that estranges symbol from sustenance, metaphors from objects, language from things, words in mouth from words in mouth. The difficulty here is that his limited intelligence allows him to speak only in literal terms and his euphoric communion with the Mother (Earth) further alienates him from verbal communication. (226)

> Metaphor is "a basically dualistic trope that depends upon a difference between its inside and outside, its literal and figurative meaning; 'antimetaphorical' positions dream of abolishing this duality in order to return to a proper and literal meaning" (Kilbour 12). In reality, words are not foods. But for K, the only food (or word) worthy of eating (or speaking) is the food (or the word) that is word (food). After the words or foods ate "eaten up," nothing remains but a complete self, or, to the narrator's eye, "a black whirlwind of roaring utter silence." (142)

The promise of life in a saner society and "imagining the unimaginable"

The taste of Michael K's own fruits is so wonderful that he thinks he could spend the rest of his life eating that type of food. And yet, he cannot help imagining the taste the pumpkin would have with added salt, sugar, cinnamon, and butter. With these elements, the taste of the pumpkin would attain perfection, as K says above. K's desire for the taste of these ingredients can be taken as his desire to be among people, in a society, that is, a society that would share its goods equally among its people, while at the same time respecting difference—in sum, a society that can allow for otherness to exist without wanting to incorporate it into sameness. K's solitude on the farm is positive, for it allows him to be himself and get rid of the "poison" that rules his society. And yet, the yearning to mingle and taste the savor of community and civilization is still present in Michael, and this is the reason why "the recollection of the flavours of salt, butter, sugar, cinnamon" (156) comes to him. This recollection speaks of Michael K's capacity to "imagine the unimaginable," as Coetzee says himself, pointing again to the intertwinement between the writer and the written and the impossibility of writing in a totally neutral way or telling the other accurately, just like in Lispector's novella, *A hora*. It speaks of K's capacity to go beyond the atrocious historical reality of the present and have a glimpse of a society that is respectful to and treats all of its people with dignity. The very fact that K thinks of all the ingredients that exist to make the pumpkin taste better can also suggest that K believes in the idea that difference should not only be accepted and respected, but that it also makes for a better world: a more complete and tasty world, as it were, where all (everything and everyone) is valued, appreciated and has a role to play in his or her community. Alone on the farm, and alone with his "bare" pumpkin, K would eventually die, for he in fact needs more food (in the literal and symbolical sense) to grow and survive as a person. As the Buddhists would put it: "one is all" and "all is one" and thus "one needs all" and "all needs one."

In the end, the society that imprisons Michael takes him from the farm (the element) and back to itself, back to all its camps, all its laws, all its discriminatory policies, at least for a while, since he eventually escapes from Kenilworth and the people who want to give things to him (i.e., the group of nomads made up of the pimp and the two prostitutes), to end up at this mother's former residence in Sea Point, Cape Town. Although Michael is now back among society, his evasion from the Kenilworth camp and from the people who pity him, and his refuge into his mother's old residence, does have a positive tone, especially in light of the metaphor of the ending. By imagining the possibility of a voyage back to the farm one day, with an old man, whom he will drive in a wheelbarrow; and by envisaging the extraction of water from the earth—after the destruction of the dam by the soldiers—K shows again the capacity to imagine the unimaginable: a society free of war and racism, where nourishment (and land) can be found and given to all people so that they might finally be able to live with the dignity all human beings deserve: "And if the old man climbed out of the cart and stretched himself (things were gathering pace now) and looked at where the pump had been that the soldiers had blown up so that nothing should be left standing, and complained, saying 'What are we going to do about water?', he, Michael K, would produce a teaspoon from his pocket, a teaspoon and a long roll of string. He would clear the rubble from the mouth of the shaft, he would bend the handle of the teaspoon in a loop and tie the string to it, he would lower it down the shaft deep into the earth, and when he brought it up there would be water in the bowl of the teaspoon; and in that way, he would say, one can live" (250). This positive ending of *Michael K* goes hand in hand with the idea of what Coetzee's sees as an "awareness of an idea of justice":

> community has its basis in an awareness and acceptance of common justice. You use the word *faith*. Let me be more cautious and stay with *awareness*: awareness of an idea of justice, somewhere, that transcends laws and lawmaking. Such awareness is not absent from our lives. But where I see it, I see it mainly as flickering or dimmed—the kind of awareness you would have if you were a prisoner in a cave, say, watching the shadows of ideas flickering on the walls. To be a herald you would have to have slipped your chains for a while and wandered about in the real world. I am not a herald of community of anything else, as you correctly recognize. I am someone who has intimations of freedom (as every chained prisoner has)—of people slipping their chains and turning their faces to the light. I do not imagine freedom, freedom *an sich*; I do not represent it. Freedom is another name for the unimaginable, says Kant, and he is right. (*Doubling* 340-01)

Although Coetzee does not see himself as the "herald of community," he believes in the possibility of justice beyond laws and lawmaking. It is that belief that makes him write as he does; it makes him write books where antiheroes become heroes precisely because they can envisage the unimaginable, the justice that lies beyond laws and lawmaking, just like Michael K does in the metaphor of the ending. Behind this belief lies the idea that the exiting of highly oppressive historical realities is possible when one is in touch with one's soul, for in the soul all becomes equal, all becomes one. In the soul there is no discrimination of any sort, as Michael K has shown us throughout the novel. To be able to attain this awareness, this view of existence, is to be able to attain a state of grace, of enlightenment, the nirvanic, as the Buddhists would put it. Most importantly, behind this belief also lies the idea that human beings have the capacity to be aware of such an existence, even if only in a very slight (or barely conscious) way: an existence where discriminations are erased. And more importantly yet, this awareness constitutes the first step to working towards making a better world, right here on earth, right there in South Africa, right there in Rio de Janeiro if we think about *A hora*. This is "imaging the unimaginable": glimpsing the light, not saying it or representing it in the narrative arena, for as Coetzee notes, "freedom" is "unimaginable." His narrative then is a glimpse at the soul, at the light that lies beyond all lawmaking and laws—the Law before the law. His narrative is a voyage from the historical to the spiritual. It is the Capsule with all the capsules inside—a capsule that we cannot really encapsulate in our rhetorical and discursive analysis. Like *A hora*, *Michael K* can also be seen as a koan: "a formulation, in baffling language, pointing to the ultimate truth," that which "cannot be solved by recourse to logical reasoning but only by awakening a deeper level of the mind beyond the discursive intellect" (Kapleau 335-36).

It is again appropriate to bring up the arguments made by Mike Marais in *The Secretary of the Invisible*. One of the central implications made throughout this book is that Coetzee's intention in *Michael K*, and many of his other novels of the apartheid era, is to present the life, being, and ways of K or other characters respectively—their alterity—as something that must run parallel to the actual historical reality and materiality of South Africa, and not as something that has lesser value. As he puts it, "These utopian settings in Coetzee's fiction of the late-apartheid period cannot but be related to the . . . desire of this writer to write fiction that 'rivals' rather than 'supplements' the conflictual relations out of which South Africa's history has 'erected itself'" (Marais 37). This stance again reinforces the idea that Coetzee wants to imagine the unimaginable. Coetzee becomes the "secretary of the invisible," the vehicle that gives voice (and house and sight) to the unseen, the stranger, the otherly, even if, as we know, this voice, is forever illusive evading the totalizing capturability of history and story. He is practicing the "ethic of hospitality." As the commentary on the back cover of Marais's book aptly states, "It is shown that the form of ethical action staged in Coetzee's writing is grounded not in the individual's willed and rational achievement but in his or her invasion or possession by the strangeness of the stranger." This ethic of hospitality, Marais argues, has a strong aesthetic dimension: for Coetzee, the writer is inspired to write by being acted upon by a force that is beyond the phenomenal world. The writer is a secretary of the invisible. She or he is responsible to and for the invisible. Marais maintains that this understanding of writing as an involuntary response to that which exceeds history is evident from the first in Coetzee's fiction. Also noted by Dominic Head, even in its seemingly apoliticality and textual illusiveness à la Derrida, the novel still reminds us that we are indeed in the realm of the ugly political, where mechanisms of repression are constantly at work. It is perhaps this reminder that makes us imagine another way, a kinder way:

> The novel makes the problem of interpretation central, and gives the issue of ilusiveness a material political edge even though it retains its poststructuralist connotations. There is clearly an obvious parallel with Derridan notions of textuality in the elusiveness of Michael K; yet the way in the novel is rooted in its context ensures that its treatments of textuality are more than mere abstractions. For example, the absence of any overt reference to Michael K's racial identity or appearance is a denial of apartheid's obsessive system of classification. (*The Cambridge Companion* 56)

As pointed out by Carrol Clarkson when referring to the ethos of Coetzee work, "it is surely when the medium of the artwork is at the breaking-point of what it can convey, when the artist is forced to articulate that there is perhaps 'too much truth for art to hold' (Coetzee, *Doubling the Point* 99), that the work exposes and plays a creative part in shifting the limit of what can be said, and what can be imagined. That act of saying and imagining rests on the responsiveness—or shall we say charity—of we, the readers: the ageing guardians of what is written" (Clarkson 393).

Conclusion

Contos do nascer da terra illustrates the importance of rescuing traditions and values that have been overshadowed by the culture of the colonialists and postcolonialists: they speak of the importance of the birth (or rebirth) of the land. The stories analyzed point to the fact that language is more than a communication tool: it is in fact a way of being, of finding oneself, and also a way of understanding the world. Couto's stories speak to the need to listen to oral traditions, its myths and wisdoms, so that Mozambicans can regain the epistemologies of the past. The reconnection with this past and its ways will allow the country to regain its language in the true sense. Only then can Mozambique emerge as a more egalitarian nation, a nation that brings the old, the suppressed into the present and makes it live (and alive) again (even though the old will also be changed by the new, by the foreign, by that which was brought in by colonialism, since history cannot be obliterated). Through Couto's stories the histories and cultures of the many different Mozambican peoples pass: they can speak and say their ontology, their epistemology. Couto's language is not an exact mirror of how people speak in Mozambique. However, there is no doubt that his language does indeed represent the Mozambican cultures at a much deeper level than does the standard Portuguese language. By breaking up the colonial language, Couto is able to get closer to the soul of Mozambique, to its philosophy of life and epistemology: he is able to bring the word closer to the thing it is describing, so that we are able to regain some of what might have been lost in the process of transposing African values and realities into European languages and realities.

The Mozambican government has acknowledged the importance of Bantu languages for the preservation of African cultures in Mozambique and has taken some measures to develop, preserve, and maintain those same languages. However, it has not yet given those languages official status, a decision which can only serve to dismiss the real importance of those languages and create an ambiguous feeling about their crucial significance among Mozambicans. As Armando Lopes puts it,

> Today, when compared to the inherited and reinforced prestigious status enjoyed by the Portuguese language in Mozambique, we see that the status of Bantu languages and the present efforts to develop and promote them in society still have a long way to go. It is a fact, though, that the post-

> independence years, unlike the years of colonial control have witnessed several attempts by authorities and language planning agencies to redress this imbalance. But, true language maintenance ultimately lies with official status recognition of the Bantu languages and the concurrent implementation of shelter programmes. The present maintenance-oriented permission reflected by Article 5.2 of the Constitution is necessary, but not sufficient for powerless Bantu languages to be maintained and developed. What they need is maintenance-oriented promotion, which necessarily implicates allocation of economic resources to support these languages. The existing pronouncements tend to be vague, and the economic prerequisites for promoting Bantu languages have been deficient. The argument that a bilingual (Bantu/Portuguese) Mozambican can use the official language (Portuguese) in official situations is flawed by the following arguments: If languages cannot be used in official situations, they will not be adequately learned and developed; and if they are not properly learned, how can people fully and consciously identify with languages which are poorly known, and in some instances (still a tiny minority) not known at all? . . . To afford Bantu languages official right is, in my opinion, the proper way to revitalize and explicitly promote them . . . Efforts to treat every language equally and give each equal respect would augur well for the future of the country. (120)

Of course Mozambique has many other more immediate problems to deal with, such as hunger, the reconstruction of the country's infrastructure after many years of civil bloody war, and recent devastating floods. For now, though, at least we have Mia Couto who, through his "creative wordplay" ("brincriação vocabular"), as his writing is often referred to, is able to better tell of the many Mozambican identities. As Idílio Rocha puts it, Couto's idiolect "is the linguistic paradigm of what that country by the Indian Ocean should be, politically and socially, were it a nation, or were to become one" ("é o paradigma linguístico do que deveria ser política e socialmente aquele país do Índico se pátria fosse ou se o viesse a ser" [qtd. in Ornelas 37]). In the last story analyzed the father does indeed relearn the old ways; he gets in touch with his little girl, and consequently, with his nation. Let us hope that, like the father, the postcolonial state will also be open enough to allow non-Western epistemologies to be nurtured in Mozambique. Only then can both the state and the Mozambican people truly benefit from each other: the Western influence cannot be dismissed, but the African "self" has to find room to blossom and emerge from the shadows where it has been kept. It has to be seen; it has to be properly understood and cultivated.

Couto's figurative baby is thus born and it is certainly beautiful, both in how it dresses itself and in how it goes beyond the surface to uncover the richness and the depth of what lies beyond a language trying to find (read, understand) another language, or better yet, a language trying to find many other languages, many other cultures, many other ways of seeing the flower, the bird, the human being, God, and the universe. The "real" baby is still awaiting to be born. We hope (and pray) that it will find the warmth it needs to leave its womb, so that Couto's stories will become history, or better yet, histories, and then, the much expected and longed-for beautiful baby will finally be delivered.

O ano da morte de Ricardo Reis is a very complex novel that touches upon multiple epistemological and ontological aspects of human existence and the power of art, language, and rhetoric—the power that the latter have to be used in unproductive ways by society and by oppressive political regimes. Saramago's ultimate message, then, might be that as long as the artist and the human being are imprisoned solely in their own mind, a mind which has been fed all kinds of "bad and insufficient food," they are condemned to live only partially and in fact contribute to the perpetuation of old myths—myths which have negative consequences for all human beings and prevent them from living a fuller life. The fact that Pessoa tells Reis that once dead, one loses the capacity to read can be seen as suggestion that Reis has always been a dead poet (and a dead human being), for he is unable to write poetry that "reads" and "drinks" in phenomenological reality. In this sense, and contrary to what he proclaimed, Reis does not "content [himself] with the spectacle of the world" and looks for happiness and fulfillment outside his immediate surroundings: outside his body, his neighbourhood, and his country. The novel strongly argues for the need to have engaged and grounded artists, and by extension human beings, who work from and within reality, with and within their community and not aloof ones, who "content [themselves] with the spectacle of the world," a spectacle which often becomes quite destructive and oppressive through the very work of human hands.

The literal physical death of Ricardo Reis in Saramago's novel could therefore be seen as a positive augury, a passage into an era where artists and humans can all contribute to the demolition of some old myths—myths which have been at the root of much human suffering, alienation, oppression, and unequal opportunities—and create a more grounded world, one that will reflect the truest "colors" of who we are, why we are what we are, and what we should be striving for. What we need is to appreciate the "saints" that we can see, touch, hear, smell, and taste and which can do the same to us, as Saramago, Lévinas, and Irigaray would put it—and the rest, the true spiritual and intellectual ecstasy, will follow. Lídia's baby boy symbolizes that desacralized and yet sacred ferment of the genuine artist and human being, who can write, love and live with all his (her) "tongues": the ear, the eye, the heart, the finger, the soul, and the intellect. In other words, the finally reformed Ricardo Reis who would be rightly and rightfully suited to be the "successful governor of a real republic." As Saramago says, "the ferment is nothing in this world yet, yet already it has some influence in governing it" (309) ("ainda não somos nada neste mundo e já temos parte no governo do mundo" [357])—suggesting thus that whatever love Reis was able and willing to offer Lídia, it was enough to generate real, beating life. Thus it might just be appropriate to call *The Year of the Death of Ricardo Reis*, *The Year of the Death of the Un-engaged Art*ist, or perhaps even, *The Year of the Death of the Un-Engaged Human Being*.

While it might be true that art does not have to be an exact reflection of reality, it is also true that humans often model themselves in, and through art, and often look for archetypes (role models) in different artistic media, be it films, theater, paintings, poetry, or novels. This is why art must in some ways be held accountable and faithful to the real. Otherwise, we are just engaging in vicious cycles and creating or recreating unrealistic paradigms—being bad parrots, as Saramago might say, parrots that imitate and repeat what people say but fail to find their truest and individual language, a language that corrects, deconstructs, and searches. And this will bring much unhappiness and discontent to an already very complicated human condition. We are, after all, very much what we read, watch on TV, and see on film screens and theater stages. And if those stages only show Greco-Latin Lídias, how are the real Lídias going to feel about themselves? That they are not real, not worthy of loving, not good enough, not complete? In this sense then, Ricardo Reis is wrong when he affirms that "a stage performance should never be natural, what is presented on stage is theater, {not life, it is not life,} life cannot be reproduced, even the most faithful of reflections, that of a mirror, transforms right into left and left into right" (103) ("a representação nunca deve ser natural, o que se passa num palco é teatro, não é a vida, não é vida, a vida não é representável, até o que parece ser o mais fiel reflexo, o espelho, torna o direito esquerdo e o esquerdo direito" [126]). To pick up on Reis's own expressions, what must really be avoided is for "the left of the stage" to become "the right of life."

In *A hora da estrela,* Lispector is pointing to the fact that in the name of advancement, success, happiness, and knowledge, society has alienated itself from its "most real truth" by inventing a complex language system which claims a superior understanding of the world when in fact it often robs us of many freedoms and the authenticity of being. And she is telling us that it is necessary for us to reclaim the lost language so that our authentic self can be restored and we can then live and exist in a more authentic way. The author is advocating for the need to cleanse our minds of all the damage created by modern life and so-called high civilization so that we can start afresh, or at least reach a point where we can reevaluate our ideals and belief systems. She is advocating for the need for silence: for a return to the authentic, to the world before the word, when words were facts not acts, when "facts [were] words told by the world" (68) ("factos [eram] palavras ditas pelo mundo" [71]). As Lispector suggests in *The Stream of Life*, language is like the addictive "zerbino" (29-30) drink, without which humans do not know how to live anymore. Does that mean, however, that we have to be always dependent on the same boring zerbino drink? Can we not diminish our dependence on this drink by inventing or rediscovering another drink? Can we taste or at least envisage the drink before the drink, the language before or beyond language, the language of all languages? Indeed we can, for as I have demonstrated, Lispector does try to represent (and with a certain degree of success) the language of all languages, the languages of nonaddiction, so that we can see life afresh again—and exist in a more authentic way. By allowing Macabéa to speak through poetry and nonlinguistic modes, Lispector shows us the truest and nonaddicted Macabéa. Moreover, Lispector also shows that Macabéa might indeed be superior to many of us, for she is a being who, despite the extreme material poverty continuously regulating her life, is capable of experiencing the ultimate and highest state of life, of being, of consciousness, of enlightenment. She is not dumb after all, but rather lives according to another order or dimension of existence. As Cixous puts it,

> The "person" whom Clarice has chosen, that apishness of a woman, is almost a woman. But she is so much that apishness of a woman, that she might perhaps be more of a woman than anyone else, more immediately woman. She is so minimal, so low, that she is at the base of being, as if she were immersed in an intimate relationship with the first manifestation of life on earth; she is crabgrass; and she ends in the crabgrass, like crabgrass. While crabgrass, while woman-thread she is in fact physically and affectively below genesis, in the beginning and in the end. Thus, more immediately than us, who are white and heavy, she shows the subtlest elements of what we can call "to-be-woman," for like people who are extremely poor, she is aware and makes us aware of the insignificances that constitute our essential riches, and which we, with our common riches forget and repress . . . Pity is deforming, it is either paternalistic or maternal. It lubricates and hides, and what Clarice Lispector wants to do here is to leave this being naked and show it in its miniscule greatness.

> A "pessoa" que Clarice escolheu, esse arremedo de mulher, é uma quase mulher. Mas ela é de tal modo quase mulher, que talvez seja mais mulher do que qualquer outra, mais imediatamente mulher. Ela é de tal modo mínima, tão infima, que está no rés-do-chão do ser, como se estivesse numa espécie de relação íntima com a primeira manifestação de vida na terra; ela é capim; e ela acaba no capim, como capim. Enquanto capim, enquanto fiapo de mulher, ela se situa fisicamente, afetivamente, de fato abaixo da génese, no começo e no fim. Portanto, mais imediatamente do que nós, que somos brancos e pesados, ela mostra os elementos mais sutis do que se pode chamar "ser-mulher," porque, como as pessoas extremamente pobres, está atenta e nos faz atentar para as insignificâncias que constituem as nossas riquezas essênciais e que nós, com nossas riquezas comuns, esquecemos e reprimimos . . . A piedade é deformante, é ou paternalista ou maternal. Lubrifica, encobre, e o que Clarice Lispector quer fazer aqui é deixar nu esse ser em sua grandeza minúscula. (*A Hora de Clarice* 135-41)

Macabéa is the being shown in her "miniscule greatness," the being that can rise above all social roles and regulations so that she can feel the world inside her without the restrictions and barriers that society imposes. She is someone who can feel the world and herself in a grander and more encompassing way and outside the rational restricting lens. Macabéa can experience Zen precisely because she can void her mind of the many sociocultural concepts that often serve as inhibitors for human beings, impeding them from achieving true fulfillment. In that sense, then, we could say that Macabéa is the perfect human being—the being our society needs to emulate so that it can also reach this enlightened stage of consciousness.

Why would we feel pity for Macabéa then? As Cixous indicates above, pity is "deforming," it is either "paternalist" or "maternal," it "lubricates" and it "hides." But why hide a being that is perfect in its own way, a being who is above many of us, who continuously and stubbornly claim the higher quality of our lives only because we "eat lobster" (*The Hour* 1), as Lispector would say? Rather than feeling sorry for

Macabéa then, Lispector is telling us that we ought to feel sorry for ourselves, for we have become blind to the most fundamental aspect of being alive: experiencing the world and ourselves in a more authentic way. This would certainly explain the title of the novel. "The hour of the star" is the perfect title for a book discussing a character who is a star (a model) that ought to be emulated. The death of the star at the end is an indication that the society in which Macabéa lives is too far from its mystical consciousness (its nirvana) or from its authentic nature: and this is why it failed to understand the value of a human being who inhabits that superior realm. The death of our star means that contemporary Brazilian society is far from reaching its human, social, and cosmic potential. In that sense, Lispector's book becomes a plea to the world—and more specifically to Brazilian society—a plea for humans to move towards such a state, a state where they will find their ultimate and truest fulfillment.

This "thing," as Lispector calls her narrative, is not a narrative, or better yet, it is a narrative trying to be a nonnarrative, a word fishing for the "nonword" (14), as Lispector puts it in *The Stream of Life*. Did this "thing" capture the "thing"? In some ways it did, but as Lispector says, "What was the truth about my Maca? As soon as we discover the truth, it no longer exists: the moment has passed. {I ask myself: 'what is it?' Reply: 'it is not.'} (84) ("Qual foi a verdade da minha Maca? Basta descobrir a verdade que ela logo já não é mais: passou o momento. Pergunto: o que é? Resposta: não é" [85]). Thus, the truth of Macabéa is not captured in her narrative. Macabéa remains that which has not been told "in-the-lines" of the narrative, for the mere act of telling that truth in Lispector's language kills Macabéa: it freezes and adulterates her identity in the pages of the narrative and in the words used. Therefore, Macabéa ultimately remains unknown to and untold by the author and us the readers too. The author becomes an author without characters, except herself, or not even herself, since writing also functions as a meditative and enlightening exercise for the author and the encounter with her "Great" and more authentic "I," as already discussed.

The author becomes a thinker without thoughts, and the novella becomes a thought without a thinker, to use Epstein's title. And the characters are still in search for the right author, or maybe not, for the right author is no author at all; the right author is formless, like air. As Lispector reminds us in *The Stream of Life*, "The true thought seems to have no author" (82). But that is also sunyata—the ultimate stage of being. For as Lispector further adds, "beatitude has that same characteristic" (82). And since this ultimate stage of being rejects discrimination and undermines intellectual rhetoric, then Lispector's writing has also written about the truest self of Macabéa. In other words, even though Lispector's writing may initially be motivated by her individual needs and desire to attain sunyata, her novella ends up working for the benefit of the poor other, if nothing else, at least because of the very nature of the sunyata attained by Lispector. On the other hand, given the fact that Lispector is in some ways very much like Macabéa—that is, they both often experience the bliss of sunyata even though Macabéa might not always consciously know it, they both love music and nonverbal ways of communicating; they both like to be alone and they both have an attraction for the choric "impropre" or "immonde" (*Pouvoirs* 10) of the Kristevan abject and for the uncanny—we can again suggest that Lispector is intensely reflecting her own self in her protagonist. She is transposing several of her own characteristics onto her character and making her very much a look-alike of herself. And so the cycle, or the circle, or the intertwinement of I and you, of writer and written continues. But that is also part of Buddhism, for Buddhism is highly interrelational and ultimately rejects divisions of object/subject, I/you, same/other, I/it, small I/great I, and so forth. And the dedication of *A hora* speaks precisely to interrelationality:

> I dedicate this {thing to dear old Schumann and his beloved Clara who are now bones, alas, alas. I dedicate it to the deep scarlet crimson, like the color of my blood, the blood of a man in his prime and so I dedicate it to my own blood}. I dedicate it, above all, to those gnomes, dwarfs, sylphs, and nymphs who inhabit my life. I dedicate it to the memory of my years of hardship when everything was more austere and honorable, and I had never eaten lobster. I dedicate it to the tempest of Beethoven. To the vibrations of Bach's neutral colors. To Chopin who leaves me weak. To Stravinsky who {astounds} me and makes me soar in flames. To *Death and Transfiguration*, in which Richard Strauss predicts my fate. Most of all, I dedicate it to {today's vigil and to today itself, to the transparent veil} of Debussy, to Marlos Nobre, to Prokofiev . . . to all those {prophets of the present} who have touched within me the most alarming and unsuspected regions; to all those prophets of our age who have revealed me to myself and made me explode into: me. This me that is you, for I cannot bear to simply be me, I need others in order to stand up, {so giddy that I am, and awkward}, for what can one do except meditate in order to plunge into that total void which can only be attained through meditation . . . I am aware of the existence of many things I have never seen. And you too. (The Author's Dedication [alias Clarice Lispector] 1)

> Pois que dedico esta coisa aí ao antigo Schumann e sua doce Clara que são hoje ossos, ai de nós, ai de nós. Dedico-me à cor rubra muito escarlate como o meu sangue de homem em plena idade e portanto dedico-me a meu sangue. Dedico-me sobretudo aos gnomos, anões, sílfides e ninfas que me habitam a vida. Dedico-me à saudade da minha antiga pobreza, quando tudo era mais sóbrio e digno e eu nunca havia comido lagosta. Dedico-me à tempestade de Beethoven. À vibração das cores neutras de Bach. A Chopin que me amolece os ossos. A Stranvisnky que me espantou e com quem voei em fogo. À "Morte e Transfiguração," em que Richard Strauss me revela o destino? Sobretudo dedico-me às vésperas de hoje e a hoje, ao transparente véu de Debussy, a Marlos Nobre . . . a todos esses profetas do presente e que a mim me vaticinaram a mim mesmo a ponto de eu neste instante explodir em: eu. Esse eu que é vós pois não agüento ser apenas mim, preciso dos outros para me manter em pé, tão tonto que sou, eu enviesado, enfim que é que se há de fazer senão meditar para cair naquele vazio pleno que só se atinge com a meditação. . . . Sei de muita coisa que não vi. E vós também. ("Dedicatória do Autor [Na verdade Clarice Lispector]" 1)

Can we then say that literature, poetry, and language make something happen? Yes, I want to say. And so after all, the Lispectorian "yes" of the beginning of *A hora* might just mean what it says: yes, but the big YES.

Coetzee does not go as far as Lispector, for he does not kill Michael K at the end of the novel, even though, as illustrated, Macabéa's death functioned as her ultimate liberation from the "stories" of her society (including the very Lispectorian narrative), and by extension from the prison of history. The final metaphor of *Michael K* is more positive in the sense that there remains the possibility of envisaging a South Africa that will give to all its people equally, a society that will find a way to resolve its historical nightmares, so that all its citizens might one day be able to truly speak their identity and live in truer community. Like Lispector, Coetzee distrusts his own narrative and his capacity to tell the oppressed South African other of color but he still seems to believe that narrative can find a way to approach the unknown other by using certain narrative mechanisms that are less historical or storical. Coetzee is able to have a glimpse of the other, a glimpse only, not the true image of the other, for that would be to fall into unethical "white writing," to commit extreme discursive hubris, as Marta Peixoto has put it in relation to Lispector's writing. Throughout my analysis, I myself, have also committed discursive hubris. My attempt to explore the meaning behind the capsules or metaphors of Michael K is also an attempt to frame him, to insert him in the discursive realm, to pin down who he might be, or what he might want or need or expect from the future. Thus, it is at this point wise to remind my reader and myself that my analysis of K's identity must also remain, to use Coetzee's own words, in the "forever unreclaimable" (*Doubling* 206). For, as Lispector wisely tells us, "Writing is the way followed by someone who uses words like bait: a word fishing for what is not a word. When the non-word—the whatever's between the lines—bites the bait, something has been written. Once the between the lines has been hooked, you can throw the word away with relief. But there ends the analogy: the non-word, in biting the bait, incorporates it. What saves you, then, is to write absentmindedly" (*The Stream* 14) ("Escrever é o modo de quem tem a palavra como isca: a palavra pescando o que não é palavra. Quando essa não-palavra—a entrelinha—morde a isca, alguma coisa se escreveu. Uma vez que se pescou a entrelinha, poder-se-ia com alívio jogar a palavra fora. Mais aí cessa a analogia: a não-palavra, ao morder a isca, incorporou-a. O que salva então é escrever distraidamente" [*Água viva* 20]). Have I, then, also written "absentmindedly" about Michel K? Hopefully yes, and yet in a sufficiently present-minded fashion so that my reader may be able to understand me.

In other words: hopefully I have been a gentle trickster and yet tricking enough to trick you into my trick. The following Flathead Myth is illustrative of the difficulty of thinking outside language and discursive rhetoric, the difficulty of starting clean: "Coyote said, 'I am going to choke the Giant with this tamarack tree.' The woman said, 'You might as well throw that stick away. Don't you know you are already in the Giant's belly'" (qtd. in Friedrich 441).

Despite the fact that the deeper politics of agency (of writing) described in this work, and followed by Lispector and Coetzee, might be more positive in the sense that they go deeper into the historical, linguistic, and structural fabric of society and show the phalacies and oppressions engendered by it, it would be naïve to assume that this deeper political agency, is implementable in societies still based on specific, inflexible, and deeply entrenched laws, societies where language and rhetoric are seen as the real and ultimate truth, societies where the Lispectorian big YES and the Coetzian "unimaginable" are still not envisaged or imagined—at least not in a manner sufficient to provoke change. It would be disingenuous simply to state that a more obscure, meta-narrative and meta-linguistic way of writing about the political can bring about manifest political change, that it can reach a wide audience and be understood as a call to action. Perhaps, then, the first step is to point to and clearly paint the oppressive laws in a Luckácsian manner; to scream at them in the pages of books until enough people hear them, until enough ears get hurt by the sad sound of the writer's song; to aim at "choking the Giant with the tamarack tree," as the Coyote says above. But then someone might ask: are we not inside the Giant's belly already and eating the Giant's food, even while trying to choke that very same Giant and the food that it gives us? We are indeed, some of us will say. And surely some stubborn person will strike right back with her or his stick: yes, but if we choke the beast that feeds us long enough and with a long, strong, and sharp enough stick, we could very well be able to create a gentler beast, a beast that is less of a zerbino drink, as Lispector would say. And so the quandary (and the cycle) continues: to be deeper or to be bolder? Who has the most reason (or unreason): the Coyote or the Woman?

As a final and brief afterthought, I would like to say that writing on two writers who are less overtly political (Lispector and Coetzee) and a writer who is as innovative with language as Couto is, has allowed me to satisfy some of my most personal and profound needs: the need for novelty and beauty in language and literature; the need to go beyond the here and now (beyond history); the need to experience a certain mystical or spiritual fulfillment through highly poetic and subjective writing—to experience what Derek Attridge as called "the singularity of literature," its otherness or ethicality (32-64). For, like Lispector herself, I also feel that "ever since I have come to know myself, the social problem has been more important to me than any other issue: in Recife the black shanty towns were the first truth that I encountered. Long before I felt 'art,' I felt the profound beauty of human conflict . . . The problem of justice for me is such an obvious and basic feeling {that it does not bring me any surprise} . . . Also because for me, to write is a quest. I have never considered any feeling of justice as a quest or as a discovery, what worries me is that this feeling {for} justice should not be so obvious to everyone else" (*The Foreign Legion* 124-45) ("Desde que me conheço o fato social teve em mim importância maior do que qualquer outro: em Recife os mocambos foram a primeira verdade para mim. Muito antes de sentir "arte," senti a beleza profunda da luta . . . O problema de justiça é em mim um sentimento tão óbvio e tão básico que não consigo me surpreender com ele . . . E também porque para mim escrever é procurar. O sentimento de justiça nunca foi procura em mim, nunca chegou a ser descoberta e o que me espanta é que ele não seja igualmente óbvio em todos" [*A Legião Estrangeira* 149]).

Works Cited

Abrahamsson, Hans, and Anders Nilsson. *Mozambique: The Troubled Transition: From Socialist Construction to Free Market Capitalism.* Trans. Mary Daly. New Jersey: Zed Books, 1995.

Althusser, Louis. *Lenin and Philosophy and Other Essays.* Trans. Ben Brewster. New York: Monthly Review, 2001.

Amorim, Silvia. *José Saramago. Art, théorie et éthique du roman.* Paris: Harmattan, 2010.

Anderson, Benedict. *Imagined Communities: Reflections on the Origin and Spread of Nationalism.* London: Verso, 1991.

Anthony, Elizabeth. "Temporal Convergence: Poiesis and the Arts of Dwelling in Time." *Convergence: Creative Arts Therapies* (2011): <http://art-therapy.concordia.ca/co_anthony.htm>.

Arnaut, Ana Paula, and Carlos Reis, eds. J*osé Saramago.* Lisboa: Edições 70, 2008.

Attridge, Derek. *J.M. Coetzee and the Ethics of Reading: Literature in the Event.* Chicago: U of Chicago P, 2004.

Attwell, David. *J.M. Coetzee and the Politics of Writing.* Berkeley: U of California P, 1993.

Auden, Later. "In Memory of W.B. Yeats." *The Broadview Anthology of Poetry.* Ed. Herbert Rosengarten and Amanda Goldrick-Jones. Peterborough: Broadview, 1993. 553-56.

Avram, Wes. "On the Priority of 'Ethics' in the Work of Emmanuel Lévinas." *Journal of Religious Studies* 24.2 (1996): 261-84. <http://www3.baylor.edu/American_Jewish/resources/jphil_articles/levinas-ethics.pdf >.

Bâ, Amadou Hampâté. *Aspects de la civilisation africaine (personne, culture, religion).* Paris: Présance Africaine, 2000.

Baden, Sally. *Post-conflict Mozambique: Women's Special Situation, Issues and Gender Perspectives to Be Integrated into Skills Training and Employment Promotion.* Bridge Development-Gender Report (1997): < http://www.bridge.ids.ac.uk/reports/re44c.pdf>.

Baptista-Bastos. *José Saramago: aproximação a um retrato.* Lisboa: Sociedade Portuguesa de Autores: Publicações Dom Quixote, 1996.

Barfield, Owen. *Poetic Diction: A Study in Meaning.* New York: McGraw-Hill, 1964.

Barrientos, Alberto, and José Vicente Rodríguez, ed. *Lira mística, Santa Teresa de Jesús, San Juan de la Cruz.* Madrid: Espiritualidad, 1977.

Works Cited

Beauvoir, Simone de. "Introduction to *The Second Sex*." *The Second Wave: A Reader in Feminist Theory*. Ed. Linda J. Nicholson. New York: Routledge, 1997. 11-16.

Beauvoir, Simone de. *The Second Sex*. Ed. and Trans. H.M. Parshley. London: Vintage 1997.

Beitner, Marvin. "Multiple Personality." *psycologydoc.com* (2003): <http://psychologydoc.com/multiple_personality.htm >.

Benson, Carol. "Bridging the Experimentation-Implementation in Bilingual Schooling: The Role of the Researcher." *Development, Education and Language in Central Asia and Beyond*. Ed. Hywel Coleman, Jamylja Gulyamova, and Andrew Thomas. Tashkent: British Council, 2005. 64-77.

Bhabha, Homi. *The Location of Culture*. London: Routledge, 1994.

Blum, Roland Paul. "Emmanuel Lévinas's Theory of Commitment." *Philosophy and Phenomenological Research* 44.2 (1983): 145-68.

Boas, Franz. *Race, Language and Culture*. New York: Free Press, 1966.

Borges, António José. *José Saramago: da cegueira à lucidez*. Sintra: Zéfiro, 2010.

Boxer, Charles. *Mary and Misogyny: Women in Iberian Expansion Overseas, 1415-1815, Some Facts, Fancies, and Personalities*. London: Duckworth, 1975.

Brazier, David. *Zen Therapy: Transcending the Sorrows of the Human Mind*. New York: John Wiley and Sons, 1996.

Camus, Albert. *L'Etranger*. Paris: Gallimard, 2005.

Carvalho, António. "O exílio de António Lobo Antunes." *Noticiário Cultural: Diário de Notícias* (22 March 1998): <http://www.instituto-camoes.pt/arquivos/literatura/exilantuns.htm>.

Cassirer, Ernst. *An Essay on Man: An Introduction to a Philosophy of Human Culture*. New Haven: Yale UP, 1962.

Chamberlin, Edward J. *If This Is Your Land, Where Are Your Stories?: Finding Common Ground*. Toronto: Knopf Canada, 2003.

Chevalier, Jean, and Alain Gheerbrant. *A Dictionary of Symbols*. Trans. John Buchanan-Brown. London: Penguin, 1996.

Chiziane, Paulina. *Niketche: Uma História de Poligamia*. Lisboa: Caminho 2002.

Cixous, Hélène. *A hora de Clarice Lispector / L'Heure de Clarice Lispector*. Trans. Rachel Gutiérrez. Rio de Janeiro: Exodus Editora, 1999.

Cixous, Hélène. *Reading with Clarice Lispector*. Ed. Verena Conly. Minneapolis: U of Minnesota P,1990.

Cixous, Hélène. *Three Steps on the Ladder of Writing*. Trans. Sarah Cornell and Susan Sellers. New York: Columbia UP, 1993.

Cixous, Hélène, and Chaterine Clément. *The Newly Born Woman*. Trans. Betsy Wing. Minneapolis: U of Minnesota P, 1986.

Clarkson, Carrol. *J.M. Coetzee: Countervoices*. New York: Palgrave Macmillan, 2009.

Coetzee, J.M. *Doubling the Point: Essays and Interviews*. Ed. David Attwell. Cambridge: Harvard UP, 1992.

Coetzee, J.M. *Foe*. Toronto: Stoddart, 1986.

Coetzee, J.M. *Life and Times of Michael K*. London: Secker & Warburg, 1983.

Coetzee, J.M. *Waiting for the Barbarians*. New York: Penguin, 1982.

Works Cited

Coetzee, J.M. *White Writing: On the Culture of Letters in South Africa*. New Haven: Yale UP, 1988.

Coleridge, Samuel Taylor. *Biographia Literaria*. Ed. J. Shawcross. Oxford: Oxford UP, 1962.

Couto, Mia. *Contos to nascer da terra*. Lisboa: Editorial Caminho, 1997.

Couto, Mia. *O último voo do flamingo*. Lisboa: Editorial Caminho, 2000.

Couto, Mia. *The Last Flight of the Flamingo*. Trans. David Brookshaw. London: Serpent's Tail, 2004.

Da Silva, Raul Calane. *Gotas do sol*. Maputo: Associação dos Escritores Moçambicanos, 2006.

De Oliveira, Isaura. "Lisboa Segundo Saramago: A História, os Mitos e a Ficção." *Colóquio / Letras 151-152* (1999): 357-78.

De Souza, Ana Aparecida Arguelho. *O humanismo em Clarice Lispector: um estudo do ser social em A hora da estrela*. São Paulo: Musa Editora, 2006.

Derrida, Jacques. *Of Grammatology*. Trans. Gayatri Chakravorty Spivak. Baltimore: The Johns Hopkins UP, 1998.

Devonish. Hubert. *Language and Liberation: Creole Language Politics in the Caribbean*. London: Karia, 1986.

Dijkstra, Bram. *Idols of Perversity: Fantasies of Feminine Evil in Fin-de-Siècle Culture*. Oxford: Oxford UP, 1986.

Doodley, Gillian. *J.M. Coetzee and the Power of Narrative*. Amherst: Cambria, 2010.

Dovey, Teresa. "J.M. Coetzee: Writing in the Middle Voice." *Essays on African Writing: A Re-evaluation*. Ed. Abdulrazak Gurna. Oxford: Heinemann, 1993. 46-57.

Dovey, Teresa. *The Novels of J.M. Coetzee: Lacanian Allegories*. Craighall: Donker, 1988.

Dupré, Louise. "La Poésie en prose au féminin. Jeux et enjeux énonciatifs." *Recherches sémiotiques / Semiotic Inquiry* 5.3 (1995): 9-24.

Eagleton, Terry, and Drew Milne, ed. *Marxist Literary Theory: A Reader*. Oxford: Blackwell, 1996.

Epstein, Mark. *Thoughts without a Thinker: Psychotherapy from a Buddhist Perspective*. New York: Basic Books, 1995.

Fanon, Frantz. *Black Skin, White Masks*. London: Paladin, 1970.

Fanon, Frantz. *The Wretched of the Earth*. New York: Grove, 1968.

Felluga, Dino Franco. "The Abject, abjection (Kristeva)." *Introductory Guide to Critical Theory*. Purdue University (2011): <http://www.cla.purdue.edu/english/theory/psychoanalysis/definitions/abject.html>.

Felluga, Dino Franco. "The Modules on Lacan." Introductory Guide to Critical Theory. *Purdue University* (2011): <http://www.cla.purdue.edu/english/theory/psychoanalysis/lacanstructure.html>.

Felluga, Dino Franco. "Modules on Kristeva I: On Psychosexual Development." Introductory Guide to Critical Theory. *Purdue University* (2011): <http://www.cla.purdue.edu/english/theory/psychoanalysis/psychintroframes.html>.

Feracho, Lesley. "Textual Cross-Gendering of the Self and the Other in Lispector's A hora da estrela." *Linking the Americas: Race, Hybrid Discourses and the Reformulation of Feminine Identity*. Albany: State U of New York P, 2005. 85-108.

Fernandes, Ceres Costa. *O Narrador Plural na Obra de José Saramago*. São Luís: U Federal do Maranhão, 1990.

Ferreira, António. "As vozes de Lídia." *Ágora. Estudos Clássicos em Debate* 3 (2001): 247-68. <http://www2.dlc.ua.pt/classicos/Lídia.pdf>

Firmino, Gregório. *Revisiting the "Language Question" in Post-Colonial Africa: The Case of Portuguese and Indigenous Languages in Mozambique*. Ph.D. Diss. Berkeley: U of California, 1995.

Fishman, Joshua. "Nationality-Nationalism and Nation-Nationism." *Language Problems of Developing Nations.* Ed. J. Fishman, C. Ferguson, and J. Das Gupta. New York: Wiley, 1968.

Fox, Richard G., ed. *Nationalist Ideologies and the Production of National Cultures*. Washington: American Anthropological Association, 1990.

Friedrich, Paul. *Language, Context and the Imagination: Essays*. Stanford: Stanford UP, 1979.

Frier, David Gibson. *The Novels of José Saramago: Echoes from the Past, Pathways into the Future*. Cardiff: U of Wales P, 2007.

Gómez Aguilera, Fernando, ed. *José Saramago nas suas palavras*. Trans. Cristina Rodrigues and Artur Guerra. Lisboa: Caminho, 2010.

Gordimer, Nadine. "The Idea of Gardening: *Life and Times of Michael K* by J.M. Coetzee." *Critical Essays on J.M. Coetzee*. Ed. Sue Kossew. New York: Prentice Hall International, 1998. 139-44.

Governo de Moçambique. Instituto Nacional de Estatística. *Educação 2000-2001*. (2000-2001): <http://www.ine.gov.mz/>.

Governo de Moçambique. Instituto Nacional de Estatística. *II Recenseamento Geral Da População E Habitação 1997: Resultados Definitivos-País Total*." (1997): <http://www.ine.gov.mz/censo2/Recens.htm>.

Governo de Moçambique. Instituto Nacional de Estatística. *Quadros do 3° Censo Geral da População e Habitação* (2007): <http://www.ine.gov.mz/censo2007>.

Gowans, Christopher W. *Philosophy of the Buddha*. London: Routledge, 2003.

Grob-Lima, Bernadete. *O percurso das personagens de Clarice Lispector*. Rio de Janeiro: Garamond, 2009.

Guidin, Marcia Ligia. *A hora da estrela, Clarice Lispector*. São Paulo: Editora Atica, 1994.

Gutierrez, Rachel. "Clarice Lispector." Trans Carla Sherman. *vidaslusofonas.pt* (2011): <http://www.vidaslusofonas.pt/clarice_lispector2.htm>.

Haeming, Anne. *Cultivation as Colonization: The Spatial Basis of Human Creation in the Works of Timothy Findley and J.M. Coetzee*. Norderstedt: Books on Demand, 2006.

Hay, J. Margaret, and Sharon Stichter, ed. *African Women South of the Sahara*. Harlow: Longman, 1995.

Head, Dominic. "Gardening as Resistance: *Life and Times of Michael K*." *J.M. Coetzee*. Cambridge: Cambridge UP, 1997. 93-111.

Head, Dominic. *J.M. Coetzee*. Cambridge: Cambridge UP, 1997.

Head, Dominic. *The Cambridge Introduction to J.M. Coetzee*. Cambridge: Cambridge UP, 2009.

Heidegger, Martin. *Poetry, Language, Thought*. Trans. Albert Hofstadter. New York: Harper and Row, 1975.

Heider, D. Sarah. "The Timeless Ecstasy of Michael K." *Black/White Writing: Essays on South African Literature*. Lewisburg: Bucknell UP, 1993. 83-98.

Helgesson, Stefan. *Writing in Crisis: Ethics and History in Gordimer, Ndebele and Coetzee*. Scottsville: U of Kwazulu-Natal P, 2004.

Hewson, Kelly. "'Making the '"Revolutionary Gesture': Nadine Gordimer, J.M. Coetzee and Some Variations on the Writer's Responsibility." *Critical Essays on J.M. Coetzee*. Ed. Sue Kossew. New York: Prentice Hall International, 1998. 145-56.

Hickey-Moody, Anna. "Un-containable Affects: Disability and the Edge of Aesthetics." *Cultural Studies Review* 15.2 (2009): 204-08.

Humboldt, Alexander von. *Cosmos. Essai d'une description physique du monde*. Trad. H. Faye. Milano: C. Turati, 1846-51.

Humboldt, Alexander von. *Essays on Language*. Trans. John Wieczorek and Ian Roe. Ed. T. Harden and D. Farrely. Bern: Peter Lang, 1997.

Hyde, Lewis. *Trickster Makes This World: Mischief, Myth, And Art*. New York: Farrar, Straus and Giroux, 1998.

Iddiols, Kathy. "Disrupting Inauthentic Readings: Coetzee's Strategies." *J.M. Coetzee in Context and Theory*. Ed. Boehmer, Elleke, Kathy Iddiols, and Robert Eaglestone. London: Continuum, 2009. 185-97.

Iisuka, Takeshi. *The Quest for the Self: Zen in Business and Life*. New York: New York UP, 1995.

Irigaray, Luce. *An Ethics of Sexual Difference*. Trans. Carolyn Burke and Gillian C. Gill. Ithaca: Cornell UP, 1993.

Irigaray, Luce. "The Fecundity of the Caress." *Feminist Interpretations of Emmanuel Levinas*. Ed. Tina Chanter. University Park: Pennsylvania State UP, 2001. 119-44.

Jacobs, Joseph, and M. Seligsohn. "The Maccabees." *jewishencyclopedia.com* (2002): <http://www.jewishencyclopedia.com/view.jsp?artid=17&letter=M>.

Jameson, Fredrick. "Third World Literature in the Era of Multinational Capitalism." *Social Text* 15 (1986): 65-88.

Jamisse, Frederico. "Mia Couto e pai cúmplices na escrita." *Domingo* (1 September 2001): <http://www.instituto-camoes.pt/icnoticias/noticias01/miacoutopai.htm>.

Jeremias, Luísa. "O meu segredo é transportar a meninice." *A Capital* (2000): <http://www.instituto-camoes.pt/arquivos/literatura/mcoutoentrv.htm>.

Jeremias, Luísa. "Sou um contrabandista entre dois mundos." *A Capital* (2000): <http://www.institutocamoes.pt/arquivos/literatura/miacontrabandista.htm>.

Joyce, James. *Ulysses*. London: Bodley Head, 1955.

Jung, Carl G. *The Essential Jung*. Ed. Joseph Campbell. Trans R.F.C. Hull. New York: Penguin, 1976.

Jung, Carl G. *The Integration of the Personality*. Trans. Stanley M. Dell. London: Routledge and Kegan Paul, 1940.

Kafka, Franz. *Collected Stories*. Ed. Gabriel Josipovici. London: Everyman's Library, 1993.

Kaphagawani, N. Didier, and Jeanette G. Malherbe. "Epistemology and the Tradition in Africa." *The African Philosophy Reader*. Ed. Coetzee. New York: Routledge, 2003. 219-29.

Kapleau, Philip, ed. *The Three Pillars of Zen: Teaching, Practice, and Enlightenment.* Trans. Notes Philip Kapleau. Boston: Beacon, 1967.

Ki-Zerbo, Joseph, ed. *Methodology and African Prehistory.* London: Heinemann, 1989.

Koetters, T. Joseph. *Authors Going Alien: Textual Production in the Novels of J.M. Coetzee.* Ph.D. Diss. Berkeley: U of California, 1998.

Kossew, Sue, ed. *Critical Essays on J.M. Coetzee.* New York: G.K. Hall, 1998.

Kristeva, Julia. *Pouvoirs de l'horreur: essai sur l'abjection.* Paris: Seuil, 1980.

Kristeva, Julia. *The Kristeva Reader.* Ed. Moi Toril. New York: Columbia UP, 1986.

Labin, Michel, ed. *Moçambique: Encontro Com Escritores.* Porto: Fundação Eng. António De Almeida, 1998.

"Languages of Mozambique." *ethnologue.com* (2004): <http://www.ethnologue.com/show_country.asp?name=Mozambique>.

Lévinas, Emmanuel. *Difficult Freedom: Essays on Judaism; Freedom on Tablets of Stone.* Trans. Séan Hand. London: Athlone, 1990.

Lévinas, Emmanuel. *Proper Names.* Trans Michael B. Smith. Stanford: Stanford UP, 1996.

Lévinas, Emmanuel. *The Lévinas Reader.* Ed. Séan Hand. Oxford: Blackwell, 1989.

Lévinas, Emmanuel. *Time and the Other.* Trans. Richard A. Choen. Pittsburgh: Duquesne UP, 1987.

Lévinas, Emmanuel. *Totality and Infinity: An Essay on Exteriority.* Trans. Alphonso Lingis. Pittsburgh: Duquesne UP, 1969.

Lispector, Clarice. *A descoberta do mundo.* Rio de Janeiro: Editora Nova Fronteira, 1984.

Lispector, Clarice. *A hora da estrela.* Rio de Janeiro: Rocco, 1999.

Lispector, Clarice. *A legião estrangeira: contos e crónicas.* Rio de Janeiro: Editora do Autor, 1964.

Lispector, Clarice. *A paixão segundo G.H.: Romance.* Rio de Janeiro: Sabiá, 1968.

Lispector, Clarice. *Águav viva.* Rio de Janeiro: Rocco, 1998.

Lispector, Clarice. *Correspondências.* Rio de Janeiro: Rocco, 2002.

Lispector, Clarice. *Discovering the World.* Trans. Giovanni Pontiero. Manchester: Carcanet, 1992.

Lispector, Clarice. *Near to the Wild Heart.* Trans. Giovanni Pontiero. New York: New Directions, 1990.

Lispector, Clarice. *Perto do coração selvagem.* Rio de Janeiro: Sabiá, 1969.

Lispector, Clarice. *The Foreign Legion: Stories and Chronicles.* Trans. Giovanni Pontiero. Manchester: Carcanet, 1986.

Lispector, Clarice. *The Hour of the Star.* Trans. Giovanni Pontiero. Manchester: Carcanet, 1986.

Lispector, Clarice. *The Stream of Life.* Trans Elizabeth Lowe and Earl Fitz. Minneapolis: U of Minnesota P, 1989.

Lobo Antunes, António. *O Manual dos Inquisidores.* Lisboa: Publicações Dom Quixote, 1996.

Lopes, Armando. "The Language Situation in Mozambique." *Language Planning in Malawi, Mozambique and the Philippines.* Ed. Robert B. Kaplan and Richard B. Baldauf Jr. Philadelphia: Multilingual Matters, 1999. 86-132.

Lucas, Fábio. *O Caráter Social da Literatura Brasileira*. Rio de Janeiro: Editora Paz e Terra, 1970.

Lukács, George. *Studies in European Realism*. New York: Grosset & Dunlap, 1964.

Macherey, Pierre. *A Theory of Literary Production*. New York: Routledge, 1988.

Macri, Anthony. "The Otherness of Selfhood: Levinas and Existential Inquiry." *Loyola College* (2011): < http://www.anthonymacri.com/Otherness-Selfhood.pdf>.

Madureira, Luís. *Imaginary Geographies in Portuguese and Lusophone-African Literature: Narratives of Discovery and Empire*. Lewiston: Edwin Mellen, 2006.

Makaryk, R. Irena, ed. *Encyclopedia of Contemporary Literary Theory: Approaches, Scholars, Terms*. Toronto: U of Toronto P, 1993.

Manuel, Christopher. "Marian Apparitions in Fátima as Political Reality: Religion and Politics in Twentieth-Century Portugal." *Harvard University Center for European Studies* (2011): <http://www.ces.fas.harvard.edu/publications/docs/pdfs/manuel.pdf>.

Marais, Michael. *Secretary of the Invisible: The Idea of Hospitality in the Fiction of J.M. Coetzee*. Amsterdam: Rodopi, 2009.

Marques, Irene. "Confused Slaves of Many Traditions: The Search for the Freedom Dance in Chiziane's *Niketche: A Tale of Polygamy*." *Research in African Literatures* 41.2 (2010): 133-59.

Martins Rodrigues de Moraes, Anita. *O inconsciente teórico: investigando estratégias interpretativas de Terra sonâmbula, de Mia Couto*. São Paulo: Annablume, 2009.

Martins, Celina. *O entrelaçar das vozes mestiças: análise das poéticas da alteridade na ficção de Édouard Glissant e Mia Couto*. Estoril: Principia, 2006.

Maylam, Paul. *South Africa's Racial Past: The History and Historiography of Racism, Segregation, and Apartheid*. Aldershot: Ashgate, 2001.

Mbiti, John. *African Religions and Philosophy*. London: Heinemann, 1969.

Merivale, Patricia. "Audible Palimpsests: Coetzee's Kafka." *Critical Perspectives on J.M. Coetzee*. Ed. Graham Huggan and Stephen Watson. New York: St. Martin's, 1996. 152-67.

Mikhail, Bakhtin. *The Dialogic Imagination: Four Essays*. Ed. Michael Holquist, Trans. Caryl Emerson and Michael Holquist. Austin: U of Texas P, 1981.

Miranda, Jorge. *As Constituições Portuguesas: 1822-1826-1838-1911-1933-1976*. Lisboa: Livraria Petrony, 1976.

Montaigne, Michel de. *The Essays of Montaigne*. Trans E.J. Treichmann. Oxford: Oxford UP, 1953.

Morphet, Tony. "Reading Coetzee in South Africa." *World Literature Today* 78.1 (2004): 14-16.

"Mozambique: Government Plans to Reduce Illiteracy." *allafrica.com* (2011): <http://allafrica.com/stories/201102240112.html>.

Nashef, Hania. *The Politics of Humiliation in the Novels of J.M. Coetzee*. New York: Routledge, 2009.

Newitt, Malyn. *A History of Mozambique*. London: C. Hurst, 1995.

Ngũgĩ wa Thiong'o. *Decolonizing the Mind: The Politics of Language in African Literature*. London: J. Currey, 1986.

Nicholson, Linda J., ed. *Feminism/Postmodernism*. New York: Routledge, 1990.

Okolo, Chukwudum B. "Self as a Problem in African Philosophy." *The African Philosophy Reader*. Ed. P.H. Coetzee and A.P.J. Roux. New York: Routledge, 2003. 209-16.

Oliveira, Catarina. "Contador de estórias abensonhadas." *Lusitano: Noticiário Cultural*. Lisboa, (10 June 2000): <http://www.instituto-camoes.pt/arquivos/literatura/abensonhado.htm>.

Omine, Akira. "Religion and Language: The Soteriological Significance of Religious Language." *California: Center for Contemporary Shin Buddhist Studies On-Line Publication Series* (2000): <http://www.shin-ibs.edu/pdfs/OmineOne.pdf>.

Ornelas, José. "Mia Couto no Contexto da Literatura Pós-colonial de Moçambique." *Luso-Brazilian Review* 33.2 (1996): 37-52.

Parry, Benita. "Speech and Silence in the Fictions of J.M. Coetzee." *Critical Perspectives on J.M. Coetze*. Ed. Graham Huggan and Stephen Watson. Madison: U of Wisconsin P, 1996. 23-45.

Paulo, Ferreira Leonídio. "Vaticano não perdoa blasfémia do ateu." *Diário de Notícias* (10 September 1998): < http://www.instituto-camoes.pt/escritores/saramago/vaticannaoperd.htm>.

Peixoto, Marta. *Passionate Fictions: Gender, Narrative, and Violence in Clarice Lispector*. Minneapolis: U of Minnesota P, 1994.

Penner, Richard A. *Countries of the Mind: The Fiction of J.M. Coetzee*. Westport: Greenwood P, 1989.

Pessoa, Fernando. *Fernando Pessoa & Co.: Selected Poems*. Ed. and Trans. Richard Zenith. New York: Grove, 1998.

Pessoa, Fernando. *Fernando Pessoa: Sixty Portuguese Poems*. Trans. F.E.G. Quintanilha. Cardiff: U of Wales P, 1971.

Pessoa, Fernando. *Odes de Ricardo Rei*s. Rio de Janeiro: Nova Aguilar, 1976.

Pessoa, Fernando. *Os melhores poemas*. Selecção de Rita Lopes. São Paulo: Global, 1985.

Pessoa, Fernando. *Poemas de Ricardo Reis*. Ed. Luiz Fagundes Duarte. Lisboa: Imprensa Nacional Casa da Moeda, 1994.

Petrarca, Francesco. *Francis Petrarch: Songs and Sonnets from Laura's Lifetime*. Trans. Nicholas Kilmer. London: Anvil, 1980.

Plato. *Plato's Republic*. Ed. and Trans A. Richards. Cambridge: Cambridge UP, 1966.

Plato. *Timaeus and Critias*. Trans. Desmond Lee. London: Penguin, 1977.

Pratt, Marie Louise. *Imperial Eyes: Travel Writing and Transculturation*. London: Routledge, 1992.

"Proposal of Mozambique." *Action Research Projects: Curriculum Change and Social Cohesion in Conflict-Affected Societies* (2002-2003): <http://www.ibe.unesco.org/Regional/social_cohesion/sc_mozam.htm>.

Quayson, Ato. *Aesthetic Nervousness: Disability and the Crisis of Representation*. New York: Columbia UP, 2007.

Quayson, Ato. *Postcolonialism: Theory, Practice or Process?* Oxford: Blackwell, 2000.

Reis, Carlos. *Diálogos com José Saramago*. Lisboa: Caminho, 1998.

Roberts, Maureen. "Depression: Soul's Quest for Depth, Meaning & Wholeness" and "Soul in Exile: Schizophrenia, Jung & a Psychiatric Evaluation of Psychiatry." *jungcircle.com* (2011): <http://www.jungcircle.com/Schizophrenia.html>.

Rosa, João Guimarães. *Ficção completa*. Rio de Janeiro: Editora Nova Aguilar, 1994.

Rossoni, Igor. *Zen e a poética auto-reflexiva de Clarice Lispector: uma literatura de vida e como vida*. São Paulo: Editora Unesp, 2002.

Rothwell, Phillip. *A Postmodern Nationalist: Truth, Orality, and Gender in the Work of Mia Couto*. Lewisburg: Bucknell UP, 2004.

Roy, Louis. *Mystical Consciousness: Western Perspectives and Dialogue with Japanese Thinkers*. New York: State U of New York P, 2003.

Saramago, José. *A jangada de pedra: romance*. Lisboa: Editorial Caminho, 1988.

Saramago, José. *Blindness*. Trans. Giovanni Pontiero. London: The Harvill Press, 1997.

Saramago, José. *Ensaio sobre a cegueira: romance*. Lisboa: Caminho, 1995.

Saramago, José. *Ensaio sobre a lucidez*. Lisboa: Editorial Caminho, 2004.

Saramago, José. *Memorial do convento: romance*. Lisboa: Caminho, 1995.

Saramago, José. *O ano da morte de Ricardo Reis*. Lisboa: Editorial Caminho, 1984.

Saramago, José. *O evangelho segundo Jesus Cristo: Romance*. Lisboa: Caminho, 1991.

Saramago, José. *The Gospel According to Jesus Christ*. Trans. Giovanni Pontiero. San Diego: Harcourt Brace, 1994.

Saramago, José. *The Year of the Death of Ricardo Reis*. Trans. Giovanni Pontiero. San Diego: Harcourt Brace Jovanovich, 1991.

Saramago, José. *Uma voz contra o silêncio*. Ed. Francisco José Viegas. Lisboa: ICEP, 1998.

Sartre, Jean-Paul. *Being and Nothingness: A Phenomenological Essay on Ontology*. Trans. Hazem E. Barnes. New York: Washington Square, 1992.

Scott-Buccleuch, Robert, and Mário Teles de Oliveira. *An Anthology of Brazilian Prose (from the Beginnings to the Present day)*. São Paulo: Editôra Ática, 1971.

Sharples, R.W. *Stoics, Epicureans and Sceptics: An Introduction to Hellenistic Philosophy*. New York: Routledge, 1996.

Sikka, Sonia. "The Delightful Other: Portraits of the Feminine in Kierkegaard, Nietzsche, and Lévinas." *Feminist Interpretations of Emmanuel Levinas*. Ed. Tina Chanter. University Park: Pennsylvania State UP, 2001. 96-118.

Skidmore, Thomas E. *Black into White: Race and Nationality in Brazilian Thought: With a Preface to the 1993 Edition and Bibliography*. Durham: Duke UP, 1993.

Skjon, Lee. "The Pragmatics of Language and Violence in Mozambique's Postcolonial War, 1975-1992." Paper presented at *Semiotics: Culture in Context*. Conference, University of Chicago (19 April 2001).

Skjon, Lee. "The Vanguardist Imperative, Statement of Nation, and the Language Question in Mozambique's *Sociedade Nova*, 1975-85." Paper presented at *Semiotics: Culture in Context* conference, University of Chicago (10 January 2002).

Soares Fonseca, Maria Nazareth, and Maria Zilda Ferreira Cury. *Mia Couto: espaços ficcionais*. Belo Horizonte: Autêntica Editora, 2008.

Soyinka, Wole. *Death and the King's Horseman*. London: Mathuen Drama, 1998.

Strode, Timothy F. *The Ethics of Exile: Lévinas, Colonialism and the Fictional Forms of Charles Brockden Brown and J.M. Coetzee*. Ph.D. Diss. New Brunswick: Rutgers U, 2003.

Stroud, Christopher. "Portuguese as Ideology and Politics in Mozambique: Semiotic (Re)construction of a Postcolony." *Language Ideological Debates*. Ed. Jan Blommaert. Berlin: Mouton de Gruyter, 1999. 443-80.

Suzuki, Daisetz Teitaro. *The Essentials of Zen Buddhism: Selected from the Writings of Daisetz T. Suzuki*. Ed. Bernard Phillips. Westport: Greenwood, 1973.

Teffo, J. Lebisa, and Abraham P.J. Roux. "Metaphysical Thinking in Africa Themes in African Metaphysics." *The African Philosophy Reader*. Ed. P.H. Coetzee and A.P.J. Roux. New York: Routledge, 2003. 161-74.

Théoret, France. *Entre raison et déraison. Essais*. Montréal: Herbes rouges, 1987.

Thera, Narada. "Rebirth." *Buddhism in a Nutshell. buddha.net* (1992-2004): Buddha Dharma Education Association <http://www.buddhanet.net/pdf_file/nutshell.pdf>.

Thomaz, Omar, and Rita Chaves. "Escrita desarrumada." *Folha de S. Paulo* (18 November 1998): <http://www.instituto-camoes.pt/arquivos/literatura/escrtdesarrumd.htm>.

Vaz de Camões, Luís. *Os Lusíadas*. Guimarães: Guimarães Editores, 2001.

Vaz de Camões, Luís. *Os melhores poemas de Luís de Camões*. São Paulo: Global Editora, 1984.

Viegas, José Francisco, ed. *José Saramago: Uma voz contra o silêncio*. Lisboa: Editorial Caminho, 1998.

Viegas, José Francisco. "As reacções, Saramago e o Nobel." *Diário de Notícias* (1998): <http://www.instituto-camoes.pt/escritores/saramago/asreaccoes.htm>.

Vieira, Luandino. *Luuanda: estórias*. Lisboa: Edições, 1972.

Vines, Alex. *Renamo: Terrorism in Mozambique*. London: Centre for Southern African Studies, University of York, 1991.

Walcott, Derek. *Collected Poems, 1948-1984*. New York: Farrar, Straus, and Giroux, 1986.

Walker, Cherryl. "Women and Gender in Southern Africa to 1945: An Overview." *Women and Gender in Southern Africa to 1945*. Ed. Cherryl Walker. Cape Town: David Philip, 1990. 1-31.

Wild, John. Introduction. *Totality and Infinity: An Essay on Exteriority*. By Emmanuel Lévinas. Trans. Alphonso Lingis. Pittsburgh: Duquesne UP, 1969.

Wilde, Oscar. *The Artist as Critic: Critical Writings of Oscar Wilde*. Ed. Richard Ellmann. New York: Random House, 1969.

Whorf, Benjamin. *Language, Thought, and Reality: Selected Writings*. Cambridge: MIT P, 1964.

"Women." *lupinfo* (1993): <http://www.1upinfo.com/country-guide-study/portugal/portugal63.html>.

Wordsworth, William. *Lyrical Ballads*. London: Longman, 1992.

Yoshida, Kyoko. "Eating (Dis)Order: From Metaphoric Cannibalism to Cannibalistic Metaphors." *J.M. Coetzee in Context and Theory*. Ed. Boehmer, Elleke, Kathy Iddiols, and Robert Eaglestone. London: Continuum, 2009. 135-46.

Zeller, Eduard. *The Stoic, Epicureans and Sceptics*. Trans. Oswald J. Reichel. London: Longmans Green, 1880.

Zorzanelli, Rafaela Teixeira. *"Esboços não acabados e vacilantes": despersonalização e experiência subjetiva na obra de Clarice Lispector."* São Paulo: Annablume, 2006.

Index

abject, 143
Abrahamsson and Nilsson, 16, 23, 38
absence of self-possession, 172
Adorno, 115, 158
aesthetic autonomy, 158, 172
aestheticizing impulse, 115
aesthetic nervousness, 164
African, 183
African animistic principles, 32
African epistemologies, 8, 36, 122
African holistic conception, 53
Africanness, 20
African traditional epistemology, 28
African values, 20
Afrikaans, 175
Afro-Brazilians, 109
Afrocentric episteme, 3, 4, 27, 54
Afrocentric values, 3
ahistorical, 175
ahuman other, 1, 8
alterity, 62
Althusser, 119
Amado, 105, 130, 138, 156
ambivalent metaphor, 2, 7, 123, 131, 160, 162
Amorim, 65, 101
Anderson, 15
animistic and holistic, 18
Anthony, 120, 122
antimetaphorical, 178
apartheid, 161, 163, 170
aphasia, 178
Appollonian, 131
Arguelho de Sousa, 117
Aristotle, 57
Arnaut, 65
art for art's sake, 9
art for political's sake, 9
artificial reality, 61
assimilado, 16
assimilation, 18
a-storical, 175
Attridge, 158, 190

Attwell, 2, 155, 163
Auden, 115
aura, 158
auratic potential, 158, 172
authenticity, 135
authenticity of being, 155
authentic self, 136
authorial hubris, 138
autism, 164
autobiographical, 120
Avram, 64

Bâ, 27, 33, 37, 52, 53
Baden, 27
Bakhtin, 164
Bakhtinian, 54
Bantu, 25, 48
Bantu languages, 17
barbarians, 30
bareness of thought, 153
Barfield, 131
Beauvoir, 57
Being, 172
Benjamin, 158
Bhabha, 31, 32
bilingualism, 14, 16
Blanchot, 158
Blum, 64
Boas, 25
bolder politics, 9
bold political posture, 1
Borges, 65
Boxer, 58
braiding, 54
Brathwaite, 31
Brazier, 121, 151
Brazil, 55, 117
Buddhism, 7, 126, 140, 152, 188
Buddhist Mantra, 132

Cabral, 31
Calane da Silva, 53
Camões, 58, 59

203

Camus, 77
cannibalism, 95
Caruso, 144
Carvalho, 90
Cassirer, 144
Catholic Church, 97
Césaire, 31
Chamberlin, 7, 19, 30, 44
Chiziane, 27
chora, 41, 44, 49, 123, 124, 150, 151
choric realm, 42, 125, 163
choric self, 48, 49, 50, 54
Christianity, 65
Cixous, 7, 41, 61, 121, 122, 123, 125, 131, 138, 178, 186
Clarkson, 181
classism, 78
Coetzee, 1, 7, 9, 24, 31, 123, 154, 155, 156, 157, 158, 159, 160, 161, 162, 163, 165, 166, 167, 172, 177, 179, 180, 181, 189, 190
Coetzian unimaginable, 190
cogito, 84, 112
cognitive differential, 172
Coleridge, 101
collective archetypes, 145
collective consciousness, 152
collective memory, 36
collective unconscious, 145, 175
collectivization of land, 22
colonial gaze, 31
colonial independence, 19
colonialism, 1, 3, 9, 27
colonialist discourse, 170
colonialist masters, 19
colonial language, 20, 28
colonial/postcolonial, 8
colonization and postcolonization, 18
colonized subject, 170
common ground, 7
Communal Villages, 22
comparative cultural analysis, 8
compartmentalization, 20
Conley, 130, 136
cosmogonic, 54
cosmogonies, 18
counter-ideology, 117
Couto, 1, 3, 9, 17, 18, 20, 22, 23, 25, 27, 29, 32, 33, 35, 36, 39, 40, 41, 44, 48, 49, 50, 52, 54, 101, 123, 132, 135, 144, 160, 182, 183, 190
cultural agency, 26
cultural colonization, 3
cultural dilemmas, 18
cultural hegemony, 15

cultural identity discourses, 1
cultural imperialism, 3, 4

deeper politics, 9
Democritian language, 145
Democritus, 144
de Oliveira, 95
depersonalization, 143
de Queiroz, 105
Derrida, 163, 181
Descartes, 83
Devonish, 16
dialogical, 54
dialogical unfinalizability, 164
dialogism, 164
différance, 132
Dijkstra, 58, 68
Dionysian, 131
discursive logic, 169
Dis-peasant, 21, 22, 23
dissecting logics, 174
distended ego, 8
divinity, 1
Doodley, 160
Dovey, 160, 161, 163
Dupré, 61
dwelling, 122

Eastern, 36
Eastern Zen philosophy, 35
economic imperialism, 1, 3
écriture au féminin, 61
écriture féminine, 7, 61, 123, 131
elementality, 1
emptiness of thought, 142
endogenic, 18
endogenization, 18
epistemological and ontological splits, 44
epistemology, 4, 18, 20, 60, 163
epistemology of holism, 20
Epstein, 71, 124, 126, 140, 146, 187
ethic of hospitality, 181
ethics, 5, 6
Ethiopia, 56
Eurocentric model, 24
Eurocentrism, 161
Europeanize, 13
European languages, 20
European Portuguese, 14
exogenic values, 3

face, 139
fado music, 144
Fanon, 31
feminist, 1, 7

Feracho, 112
Fernandes, 70
Ferreira, 63
Ferreira Cury, 18
Firmino, 4, 13, 14, 15, 18, 22
Flathead Myth, 189
Fox, 15
Frelimo, 16, 22, 23
Frier, 78

Gaza and Tete, 13
gaze, 69, 89, 166
genital mutilation, 27
Gilman, 110
Gipsy, 70
Glissant, 54
gods, 36
Gómez Aguilera, 57, 65, 79
Gordimer, 156, 157, 164
Great Mother, 40
Greco-Latin, 185
Greece, 70
Grob-Lima, 106
Guimarães Rosa, 17
Gutierrez, 123

Haeming, 170
Hand, 78
Hardt and Negri, 164
Hay and Stichter, 27
Head, 160, 162, 173, 181
Hegelsson, 172
hegemonic, 113
hegemonic discourse, 109
Heidegger, 120, 122, 131
Heideggerian philosophy, 7
Heider, 163, 167, 173
Hellenism, 138
hermeneutical impasse, 164
heteroglossic, 54
historical discourse, 2
holistic identity, 8
Horace, 59, 62, 64, 70
hospitality, 172
house of spirits, 23
Humboldt, 25
Husserl, 5
Hyde, 44

Iddiols, 158
idealist conceptions of love, 72
ideality, 4
ideological state apparatuses, 119
Iisuka, 142
il y a, 172

imagined community, 15
individual self, 166
inflamingos, 27
institutionalized racism, 156
intermediaries of life, 178
interweaving technique, 54
in-the-element, 77
Irigaraian, 7
Irigaray, 1, 7, 58, 87, 88, 97, 127, 130, 148, 184
Iser, 158

Jameson, 3
Jewish, 70, 138
jouissance, 123
Joyce, 105, 155
Jung, 1, 35, 122, 145
Jungian psychology, 7

Kafka, 163
Kapleau, 126, 133, 134, 180
Koan, 133
Kristeva, 41, 124, 125, 143, 178
Kristevan abject, 187

Labin, 17, 21, 23
Lacan, 178
Lady of Fátima, 96
language of national identity, 16
language question, 13
Lévinas, 1, 5, 7, 57, 61, 63, 64, 87, 99, 102, 127, 130, 138, 154, 160, 165, 168, 169, 174, 184
Lévinasian, 7
life as a cycle, 35
língua de unidade nacional, 14
linguistic negation, 7
linguistic regeneration, 7
Lins, 105
Lispector, 1, 6, 7, 9, 35, 61, 105, 106, 107, 108, 112, 114, 119, 121, 122, 123, 124, 125, 126, 127, 128, 129, 130, 132, 133, 134, 137, 138, 139, 143, 145, 146, 148, 151, 152, 154, 155, 156, 173, 179, 185, 187, 189
literalness of being, 178
Lobo Antunes, 68, 90
logocentric, 129
Lopes, 13, 182
Lukács, 157, 159
Lusophone Africa, 31
Lusophone writers, 17

mabeco, 30, 31
Maccabees, 138

Macherey, 106
Macri, 91
Madureira, 18
Makonde, 15
Makua, 15
Malherbe, 33
mandala, 134
Mandela, 156
Mantras, 126
Manuel, 96
Marais, 158, 165, 170, 172, 181
Marian incarnations, 86
Martins, 18, 54
Martins Rodrigues de Moraes, 18
Marxist, 7, 23, 118
Marxist material model, 18
Maylam, 156
Mbiti, 28, 32, 35
Merivale, 163
Merleau-Ponty, 5
metaphor, 142, 151, 173, 179, 180, 189
metaphoric cannibalism, 177
metaphoric language, 116
Michelet, 57
Millet, 105
mimesis, 158
Mimic dog, 32
Mimic person, 32
mise en abyme, 39, 40, 47, 54, 132, 160, 163
Mondlane, 31
Montaigne, 30
Morphet, 157
mother/earth/greater self, 178
Mozambican consciousnes, 20
Mozambican cultures, 20
Mozambican epistemologies, 3, 20
Mozambicanization, 18
Mozambique, 3, 13, 14, 15, 16, 17, 18, 20, 22, 23, 25, 27, 37, 39, 44, 47, 54, 182, 183
Mudras, 126
multicultural and multilingual, 13
multilingualism, 16
mystical consciousness, 1, 154

Naipaul, 31
narcissism, 123
narrative strategy, 2, 7
Nashef, 164
nation, 1, 4
national consciousness, 15
national identity, 3, 14
nationalism, 15, 16
national language, 15
national/Mozambican languages, 13
nationhood, 3, 15
nation-state, 15, 16
nativization, 18
Neto, 31
Newitt, 22
Ngũgi, 14, 25
nirvana, 126, 146, 152, 153, 174, 176, 187
non-intelligent, 125
nostalgia, 19, 144

official language, 13, 14
Okolo, 33
Olympian God, 119
oneness, 178
ontological purity, 164
oppressive structures, 2
oral knowledge, 20
orature, 18
Ornelas, 183
other, 31, 64, 89, 99, 109, 111, 131, 137, 138, 143, 157, 158, 161, 165, 169, 179
othering, 3, 4
otherness, 8, 62, 88, 151, 158, 160, 164, 172
overstanding, 30, 144

Palestine, 138
Parry, 163
patriarchal discourse, 61
patriarchal society, 148
patriarchal system, 5
Peixoto, 2, 107, 109, 112
Penner, 161
performative, 134
Pessoa, 55, 56, 78, 80, 184
Petrarca, 58, 59
phallocentrism, 78
phenomenological reality, 77, 184
phenomenology, 1, 5
PIDE, 93
Pirandello, 126
Plato, 41, 49, 60, 151
poetic language, 131, 132, 133
poetics of delayed revelation, 54
polygamy, 27
polyphonic, 57
poor other, 1, 78, 113
poor subject, 1
Portugal, 55, 68, 91, 92
Portuguese colonial cultural legacy, 17
postcolonial, 3, 7, 15, 18
postcolonial African societies, 13
postcolonial condition, 19
postcolonialism, 1, 3, 9

Index

postcolonial nation, 3
postcolonial state, 20, 183
postcolonial subject, 1, 3
Pratt, 24, 29, 31
precolonial, 27
precolonial African, 18
precolonial epistemes, 3
presymbolic reality, 131
presymbolic world, 143
primary language, 153
process of becoming, 164
provisional language, 157
psychoanalysis, 123
psychoanalytical, 7
Puritan theology, 58

Quayson, 3, 164, 165
Québécois Canadian feminists, 61

racialization, 3
Rastafarian, 29, 144
realist tradition, 157
reality, 4
Real Order, 178
regionalist novel, 6
reincarnation, 146, 152
Reis, 4, 5, 8
Renaissance, 60
RENAMO, 22
represent, misrepresent, 1
Republic, 60
rhetorical, 9
rhetorical discourse, 135
Rhodesia, 23
Roberts, 122
Rocha, 183
Rossini, 122
Rothwell, 17, 50
Roy, 153
Russian doll, 40, 46

Salazar, 55, 91, 96, 97, 137
same, 137
sameness, 99, 160, 166
Saramago, 1, 4, 5, 8, 9, 55, 56, 59, 65, 67, 69, 70, 72, 73, 75, 77, 89, 90, 92, 96, 98, 100, 101, 102, 130, 132, 137, 148, 153, 154, 166, 177, 184, 185
Sartre, 78
satori, 123, 142
saudade, 140, 144
schizophrenia, 122
Scott-Buccleuch, 105
secretary of the invisible, 181
self-erasure, 77

self/other, 178
Shangaan, 15
Shona, 15
signified, 132
signifier, 131, 132
singularity of literature, the, 190
Skjon, 4, 16, 22, 23
Soares Fonseca, 18
socially committed literature, 105
social symbolic values, 120
Sonia Sikka, 87
Sontag, 158
sorceresses, 27
South Africa, 23, 177, 180, 181, 189
Soyinka, 36
space of magic, 21
Spain, 56
spatio-temporal reality, 82
spiritual enlightenment, 28
spiritual nirvana, 125
Stanner, 19
statement, 16
Statement of Nation, 16
state-nations, 16
storical, 189
storyteller, 20
Strode, 163, 168
Stroud, 22, 23
St. Thomas of Aquinas, 57
subaltern subjects, 1
subjective experience, 143
subjectivity, 170
sublimation, 123
sunyata, 126, 132, 151, 152, 187
Suzuki, 133, 142, 146, 153
symbolical language, 128
Symbolical Order, 178
symbolical world, 138
symbolical world order, 178
symbolic language, 145
Syrian, 138

tantric Buddhism, 126, 134
Teffo and Roux, 36
Teixeira Zorzanelli, 143
Teles de Oliveira, 105
Teresa of Avila, 58
the bolder, 9
Théoret, 61
transcultural, 9
transnational, 8
trickster, 39, 44, 48, 102, 189

Ugolina, 92, 93, 94, 95, 100, 138
unconscious, 123, 142

unconscious self, 135
universality, 8
unnameable, 176

vaster and grander self, 8
Venerable Thera, 146
Vieira, 17
Vines, 22
Virgin Mary, 74

Walcott, 31, 41, 47
Walker, 27
Western, 27, 36
Western epistemologies, 183
western hegemonies, 3
Western hierarchical classification, 25
western paradigms, 4
Western philosophies, 7, 35
Western (Portuguese) hegemony, 3
Western psychoanalysis, 7
West Indies, 29
white hegemony, 4
white sheet, 164
white writing, 7, 167, 189
Whorf, 25
Wild, 166
Wilde, 61
Woolf, 105
Wordsworth, 121
world of the living and the world of the dead, 18
Wright, 160

Yeats, 115
Yoshida, 177

Zen, 7, 121, 175
Zen Buddhism, 1, 5, 123, 125, 133, 142, 146, 173
Zen Buddhist, 142, 151
Zen concepts, 4
Zenith, 59
Zen philosophy, 35